DOC

The University of Alabama Press   Tuscaloosa

DOC

THE STORY OF A BIRMINGHAM

JAZZ MAN

FRANK "DOC" ADAMS AND **BURGIN MATHEWS**

The University of Alabama Press
Tuscaloosa, Alabama 35487-0380
uapress.ua.edu

Hardcover edition published 2012.
Paperback edition published 2019.
eBook edition published 2012.

Inquiries about reproducing material from this work should be
addressed to the University of Alabama Press.

Typeface: Minion Pro and Impact

Cover image: "Doc" Adams, Alabama Jazz Hall of Fame, 2011;
courtesy of Garrison Lee
Cover design: Michele Myatt Quinn

Paperback ISBN: 978-0-8173-5959-1

A previous edition of this book has been catalogued by the Library
of Congress as follows:
Library of Congress Cataloging-in-Publication Data
Adams, Frank, 1928–
Doc : the story of a Birmingham jazz man / Frank Adams and
Burgin Mathews.
p. cm.
Includes index.
ISBN 978-0-8173-1780-5 (cloth : alk. paper) — ISBN 978-0-8173-
8646-7 (e book)
1. Adams, Frank, 1928– 2. Jazz musicians—Alabama—
Birmingham—Biography. 3. Clarinetists—United States—
Biography. 4. African-Americans—Alabama—Birmingham—
Biography. I. Mathews, Burgin. II. Title.
ML419.A24A3 2012
781.65092—dc23
[B]   2012006704

"In my intergalactic music, every person is a key to something."

—Sun Ra

Contents

List of Illustrations ix

Acknowledgments xi

Introduction xv

1 **Family** 1

2 **The Church** 18

3 **Schoolboy** 32

4 **"Fess"** 50

5 **Outer Space** 68

6 **First Gigs and Birmingham Clubs** 86

7 **Summers on the Road** 99

8 **Howard** 114

9 **Bounce, Bebop, Blues, and Swing** 136

10 **Teacher** 150

11 **Bandleader** 173

12 **Friends and Mentors** 190

13 **Building a Family, Making Ends Meet** 202

14 **The Movement** 215

15 **Keeping the Spirit** 236

16 **"Doc"** 246

Index 261

Illustrations

Charter inductees to the Alabama Jazz Hall of Fame, 1978   xvii

Frank Adams   xviii

Family, ca. 1929   4

Missionary Society members   22

Lincoln Elementary band, ca. 1938   45

William Wise Handy, ca. 1940s   48

Fess Whatley and Cadillac   52

Birmingham's first jazz band, the Jazz Demons, 1920s   54

Industrial High School debate team, ca. 1939   128

Lincoln Elementary students outside band room, 1965   155

Jimmy Chapell, Clarence Curry, Frank Adams, Martin Barnett, and
   Robert McCoy, 1950s   174

Frank Adams, saxophone, backing a female impersonator, 2728 Club,
   late 1950s   176

Ivory "Pops" Williams, Selena Mealings, Frank Adams, and Martin
   Barnett, 2728 Club, mid-1960s   177

Doris Adams, 1953   184

Frank "Mr. Sax" Adams promotional card, 1960s   187

Ivory "Pops" Williams, 1970s   191

Joe Guy, trumpet, with Charles Clarke, Mary Alice Clarke Stollenwerk,
   and Jesse Evans, 1950s   196

Frank Adams, receiving award for work with the Boy Scouts, and Doris
   Adams, early 1970s   203

Ella Eaton Adams, mother of Oscar and Frank, with Doris
   Adams, 1964   205

Family portrait, 1975   211

Justice Oscar Adams   228

Saxophone section, Birmingham Heritage Band   241

Alabama Jazz Hall of Fame inaugural induction ceremony, 1978   242

"Doc" Adams, Alabama Jazz Hall of Fame, 2011   247

Acknowledgments

Though it is Frank Adams's voice you hear throughout this book, several individuals have contributed, behind the scenes, in valuable ways—confirming or clarifying historical details, offering photographs and clippings from their own collections, suggesting new areas for discussion, and offering various other forms of support and encouragement. First, I am grateful to composer Benny Golson for sharing his thoughtful, eloquent reminiscences of his early days with the Howard Swingmasters. Dr. Tolton Rosser, director of the Birmingham Heritage Band, has also shared his own valuable perspective on the city's jazz legacy. For me, one of the most profound experiences in this process has been an afternoon spent with Dr. Adams and Mrs. Anne-Marie Adams, widow of Oscar Adams Jr. To hear these two great souls swap stories about the late Justice Adams was a gift, at some moments hilarious and at others deeply moving, that I will not forget.

Early on, Dr. Adams encouraged me to contact Tommy Stewart, a trumpeter, arranger, and longtime friend of Adams, whose interest in jazz history—particularly local jazz history—is inexhaustible. My trips to Stewart's home revealed a wealth of information on Birmingham jazz, compiled in scrapbook after scrapbook. Similarly, the home of Mrs. Roberta Lowe—wife of the late J. L. Lowe, founder of the Alabama Jazz Hall of Fame—is in itself something of a jazz museum. As Adams emphasizes in the pages of this book, jazz in Birmingham would not be what it is without J. L. Lowe's passionate dedication to the preservation of the city's musical heritage. Mrs. Lowe sparks with her own passion and has maintained her husband's archive of jazz-related materials, which she has so graciously shared.

Deepest thanks are due to Patrick Cather, to whose firsthand recollection and enthusiastic support I have often turned in this project. Sifting with Patrick through old records, files, photos, and memories has been an unforgettable experience and an invaluable ingredient in the making of this book. I have been entertained heartily by his late-night boogie-woogie piano and spellbound by his own stories of Pops Williams, Fess Whatley, and the Woodland Club; I am truly grateful for his generosity and for the friendship that has resulted from these conversations.

Thanks are also due here to Garrison Lee, for his outstanding photography; Carol Ealons, for her own work in documenting Birmingham jazz, and for her assistance with archival prints; Jerry Whitworth, for the portrait of Oscar Adams Sr.; and Dr. Leah Tucker, for her important, ongoing leadership at the Alabama Jazz Hall of Fame. We are also grateful to the editors and staff at The University of Alabama Press, including Dan Waterman and Jon Berry, and to copyeditor Joan Matthews, for their assistance, input, and encouragement.

A constant theme in this book is the power of family. For their many forms of support, friendship, and inspiration, I would like to recognize my own family, with gratitude and love: George and Betty Mathews; Jud Mathews and Kim Mowery; and, of course, Henry and Elliott, who are already great lovers of music.

In so many ways, this book is tribute to the many individuals who have helped shape the life of Frank Adams; regrettably, it would be impossible to name in the pages of any book all those who have contributed in some way to that life. However, Dr. Adams would like to acknowledge a handful of individuals who deserve particular mention. First and foremost, family: Dr. Adams's wife, Doris; son, Frank Eaton Adams Jr.; daughter-in-law, Patrice Adams; and grandson, William. Dr. Adams expresses gratitude to and for the family of his brother, Oscar Adams Jr., including the late Willa Ingersoll Adams and her three children with Oscar: Frank Theodore Adams Jr., Oscar W. Adams III, and Gail Adams Harding.

Thank you, also, to the many teachers and administrators at Lincoln Elementary School, Parker High School, and Howard University, and to those professors who contributed to Dr. Adams's ongoing education since Howard: to Raymond King at Samford University; Nathan Essex at The University of Alabama; Donald Henderson at UAB; and Hugh Thomas at Birmingham-Southern College. Thank you to Dr. G. Ray Coleman, Reverend Joshua U. Johnson, and the entire Metropolitan A.M.E. Zion family, past and present. Thanks go also to friends and colleagues John Cottrell, John Springer, George Pruitt, John McAphee, Cathy Crenshaw, Jesse Lewis, Peggy Sparks, Joel Boykins, "Lucky" Leon Davis, Sherri Nielson, John M. Long, and the late Thomas Lyle, whose passing during the making of this book was deeply felt. Dr. Adams acknowledges with gratitude, too, several organizations in which he has participated for many rewarding years: the Southside Baptist Church jazz band, directed by Cheryl Simonetti; the 313th Army Band; the Birmingham Heritage Band; Local 256-733 Musicians Union; the Norton Board of Advisors at Birmingham-Southern College; and the Shades Valley Rotary Club. He would also like to thank, for their support, dedication, and enthusiasm, the "Jazzy Parents": Pamela Ansari, Wysteria Huffman, Leslie Belser, Jane B. Lee, Vanessa Guyton, Reverend Howard Lee III, Kenya Gibson, Patricia Jackson, Matilda Merriweather, Reginald Crummie, Gary Malone, Helen Williams, Alethea Liptrot, and Debora Phillips.

Students often impact and inspire their teachers in ways those students never know. Though, of course, we cannot name them all here, Dr. Adams would like to mention a few of his outstanding students, and their families: Jeronne and Isaac Ansari, Easter Barfield, the family of Reverend Luke Beard, Matthew Belser, Nell Carter, Charles Daniels, Willie Florence, Terry Gardner, Dwight and Dwayne Houston, Rudell Houston, Colenzo Hubbard, Timothy and Wesley Huffman, Rudy Jackson, Gina Killin, Oscar Lee, Barbara Johnson Powell, Ricky Powell, Harold Price, Alvin Smith, Dede and Fletcher "Sputnik" Shepherd, Charles Stevens, Ruben Studdard, L. Truman, Ansel and Suman Uswatte, Walter Wallace, Frank Walton, George Washington, Mose Whit, and Charles and Le'Charles Sigler. Special acknowledgment goes to Dathia and Arthur Means, and to Debora Carter Mayes. We also recognize here five students who have joined Dr. Adams as inductees, themselves, to the Alabama Jazz Hall of Fame: James "Guitar" Allen, Sherman Carson (aka Foxxy Fatts), Frank Davis, Nathan Miller, and Ona Watson.

When we began the interviews that would evolve into this book, one source of common ground Dr. Adams and I quickly found was our shared profession and mutual passion as teachers. We would like to join together here in dedicating this book—with absolute affection and deepest regard—to all those remarkable individuals we have been lucky to call our students.

Finally, and most importantly, Dr. Adams dedicates this book, with his unending love, to his wife of more than fifty years: Doris Adams, whom he calls Dot—his tweety-bird.

BURGIN MATHEWS
January 2012

Introduction

BURGIN MATHEWS

FRANK ADAMS PICKED UP A PHRASE FROM SONNY Blount, the intergalactic bandleader who later became Sun Ra, eccentric legend of avant-garde jazz: "What's in you," Blount used to say, "will come out."

Adams was only a teenager when he joined Blount's band. He had studied music in the segregated school system of Birmingham, Alabama—studied and played enough to read music fluently, to perform marches and church songs, and to have earned for himself a small local reputation as a promising instrumentalist. He was still a newcomer to all-out *jazz*, though, and his eyes were opened by his strange new mentor's vision, his drive, his music, and his talk. "That was an experience," Adams says of his tenure with Blount, "that changed my life."

The band rehearsed in Blount's dilapidated old tenement, a different world altogether from the elegant home in which Adams was raised. It was a far cry, too, from the sophisticated "society" venues Adams had become accustomed to playing under Birmingham's preeminent bandleader, John T. "Fess" Whatley. But walking through Blount's door meant a kind of musical immersion Adams had never experienced—and an immersion, too, into the weird philosophical and spiritual teachings of the bandleader who, even then, claimed to have come from outer space.

In that house Frank Adams learned lessons that would stick with him for the rest of his life.

Blount might put on a new record, or point his young followers to an innovative musician who was passing through town. "Listen to *him*," Blount would say; "listen to what he's *saying*." For Blount, technical virtuosity wasn't enough: what mattered was the unique message that each musician had to deliver. Sonny Blount pushed his own players to listen for those messages—and to search also, inside themselves, for their own, characteristic modes of expression: "What's in you," he said, and said again, "will come out."

What's important, Blount preached, is that thing in you that *is* you: that voice, that spirit, that message, that *sound* that forces its way out from within, that is wholly individual and altogether necessary and that has, inevitably, to come out. What matters is what you have to say that you alone can say.

Frank Adams graduated from Parker High School in 1945 and spent the next four years at Howard University, where he helped found the school's first jazz band, the Howard Swingmasters, at the same time pursuing his education under some of the era's leading academic heavyweights. He teamed up with Duke Ellington saxophonist Jimmy Hamilton and got work as a sub with the Ellington Orchestra, performing often over the next two years with one of American music's most towering figures; in the meantime, he also found work sitting in with a range of bandleaders, both celebrated and obscure, including Louis Jordan, Lucky Millinder, and Tiny Bradshaw. In 1950, he came back to Birmingham, where he started his own band and launched a career in public education that would last over four decades. When a call from the Count Basie Orchestra offered him a permanent gig, he turned the offer down to stay at home, encouraging his young students, building a family, and rooting himself deep in the local music scene. All the while he pursued his own unending education, earning degrees from the University of Chicago and Birmingham's Samford University; in 1988 he was awarded his doctorate in education from The University of Alabama. Today Adams is a legendary figure in Birmingham, where he is known under the affectionate nickname "Doc."

For many years, Adams has been the face and the voice of the Alabama Jazz Hall of Fame, a community institution headquartered in downtown Birmingham's historic Carver Theatre. Founded by local musician and educator J. L. Lowe, the Hall of Fame was born in 1978, with an induction ceremony to honor the city's most outstanding and most influential musicians; operating for years out of a cramped two-room facility, the Hall of Fame expanded in 1993 into a full museum and performance stage. Adams—in 1978, the youngest of the first group of inductees—has been a part of the Hall of Fame from its beginnings. From 1997 to 2001, he served as its executive director, and since 2002, he has been its Director of Education, Emeritus. He teaches free music lessons to children and adults, orchestrates an annual student jazz band festival, and is the resident tour guide at the Hall of

Charter inductees to the Alabama Jazz Hall of Fame, 1978: Sammy Lowe, Erskine Hawkins, Frank Adams, Amos Gordon, and Haywood Henry. Also inducted that year, posthumously: Fess Whatley. Courtesy of Frank Adams.

Fame's museum. He is an active performer in the Birmingham Heritage Band, a group dedicated to preserving and furthering the local music tradition, and is a frequent speaker to groups of all ages. In Doc Adams, the history of Birmingham jazz walks, talks, breathes, and blows.

One of Adams's early coconspirators in music was the celebrated saxophonist and composer Benny Golson, a fellow alum of the Howard Swingmasters. Adams, Golson recalls today, "had the best, sweetest, [most] captivating and arresting sound around. Everyone thought for sure that he would be . . . the lead alto with some world-famous band, standing out as the great saxophonist he was." Instead, Adams "slipped off" and returned home to Birmingham—where to this day "he generously pours himself out as a gift offering." If Adams walked away early from the major leagues of the big-name bands, he remained active in music and in education, where the generosity of his giving and the inspiration of his example have been indeed profound. "His candle," Golson says, "is as bright as the brightest candle in life's darkness."[1]

This kind of esteem for Adams is common; indeed, the walls of Adams's home are covered with several decades' worth of awards,

Frank Adams. Courtesy of
Frank Adams, with thanks
to Carol Ealons.

plaques, and thank-yous from a great range of schools, civic organizations, churches, and music programs. According to Tommy Stewart—a local trumpeter and arranger and a frequent collaborator, over the years, with Adams—there are a few things that anyone will quickly discover about the man. "First of all," Stewart explains, "he's going to be a great teacher. Dr. Adams can *teach*. He knows how to get the students, and when they come out of his class, they're going to be *playing* something. Second of all, you're going to get a guy who's real particular about things. He's real careful, he does a good job, he's meticulous—even though he seems real unassuming to most people. And the third thing you're going to find out about him: he's a humanitarian. He's going to figure out a way to ask you how he can help *you*—'What can I do for you, what do you need to know? Sit down, let me tell you this.'—and pass his knowledge on." Stewart continues: "He's a great lead saxophone player, and you can get his personality through the way he plays his horn. He plays with feeling. *Feeling* is the most important thing."[2]

As local bandleader Tolton Rosser adds: "What's in his heart comes out in his horn."[3]

For Adams, the practice, learned under Sonny Blount, of hearing and unraveling what others have to say transcends the musical: to this day, Adams approaches every personal interaction as a possible avenue into a fuller understanding of the human condition. Experience and insight have labeled him "Doc," but he is, besides master teacher, the eternal student, a perpetual awestruck searcher even in his eighties. Ever listening to and learning from others, he has sought along the way the expression of his own unique voice. It is a voice that has become well known across Birmingham, and it is a voice that something to say.

This book should serve two principal aims: First, and most obviously, it offers the spoken autobiography of a remarkable man and a gifted storyteller. A second, corollary aim of the book is to tell the story, largely so far untold, of Birmingham jazz. Though histories of jazz have been dominated by a handful of key cities—among them New Orleans, New York, Kansas City, and Chicago—Birmingham's unique musical culture also proved significant in shaping the course of American jazz. If the city's roster of musicians includes only a handful of big names, it is the legion of Birmingham sidemen, arrangers, and teachers who really constitute the core of the city's contributions, exerting from the sidelines their impact on the music.[4]

In large part, the local jazz heritage developed from the institutional structures built, in the early years of the twentieth century, by the city's black middle class. In an era of strict segregation, Birmingham's African-American community developed important social institutions—including banks, schools, small businesses, and fraternal orders—through which they could exert a certain amount of autonomy, and from which they developed a sense of community strength and racial pride. A rich musical tradition was one of the outgrowths of this foundation. Birmingham's black business district, rooted along 4th Avenue North, was home to a number of theatres, fraternal lodges, and night clubs, where jazz could be heard and performed. In particular, the black fraternal societies—the Masons, the Knights of Pythias, and others—actively supported the development of jazz by offering active society venues for local and national performers. Downtown churches, meanwhile, provided musicians like Frank Adams some of their first opportunities for musical training and public performance. The greatest nurturer of the music community, though, was undoubtedly the schools, where music was taught as a professional avocation. It is fitting that Adams himself, like so many local players, has spent his career as both a working musician and as an educator: in Birmingham, to a degree that is unusual among jazz places, jazz and education are inextricably, fundamentally linked. Indeed, the unique character of Birmingham's jazz legacy derives from the music's roots in the city's black schools.

The most fertile training ground for Birmingham's black musicians was for many years Industrial High School. Founded in 1900, Birmingham's only high school for blacks was an institution rooted squarely in Booker T. Washington's philosophy of "practical" education, promoting manual training in industrial and mechanical trades. If the school sought to prepare its students for the kind of menial jobs most available, then, to blacks, it prided itself also on its academic underpinnings, its cultural offerings, and its emphasis on community values. Boasting its reputation as the world's largest high school for blacks—by the time Frank Adams enrolled in the 1940s, the student population was well over three thousand—Industrial became a source of community pride. Though the school was renamed A. H. Parker High School, for its first principal, in 1937, the oldest generation of black Birminghamians still remember it as "Industrial"; throughout his own reminiscences, Frank Adams uses the two names more or less interchangeably.

Ironically, the industrial emphasis of the school created for some students an intensive musical training that would have otherwise been impossible. Alongside such fields as shoe repair, printing, and carpentry, music entered the curriculum as an "industrial" discipline: a practical, manual skill from which students could expect to derive a sustainable living. The figure at the center of this training was John T. Whatley—nicknamed "Fess" for "Professor"—whose career as the school's printing teacher and unofficial bandmaster lasted from 1917 to 1964. In many ways, today's Alabama Jazz Hall of Fame stands as a shrine to Whatley: the legendary "maker of musicians" whose rigid instruction produced, for more than half a century, so many of Birmingham's top jazz players. Whatley was celebrated by blacks and whites alike as the city's leading bandleader, and if his own reign as performer did not extend far beyond the state, his influence as a teacher sent wide ripples into the pool of American jazz. In the heyday of the swing era, all the major big bands in the country—those of Count Basie, Duke Ellington, Cab Calloway, Benny Goodman, and others—included one or more Birmingham players, most of whom cited Whatley as their teacher. Whatley students shared a common culture and heritage that they carried with them into whatever bands they joined: they were strictly disciplined; they could read music—a skill that would become increasingly significant with the rise of the big bands—and they were versatile, in many cases doubling capably on a second instrument. Their strict professionalism, formal training, and instrumental flexibility often made them indispensable members of the bands they joined.

As a teenager, Frank Adams studied under Whatley, taking a lead position in the high school marching band and performing also in Whatley's professional dance band, the Vibraphone Cathedral Orchestra. Whatley's band specialized in elite functions, performing at the upscale dances and balls of the black social clubs and also, often, "over the mountain": in the affluent white communities just on the other side of Birmingham's Red Mountain. For a period, Adams played simultaneously in Whatley's band and in that of the experimental, idiosyncratic Sonny Blount. The contrasting experiences would define Adams as a musician and as an educator for the rest of his life. In many ways, Whatley and Blount represent competing, if codependent, impulses of Birmingham jazz—and, indeed, of the jazz idiom in general. If Blount embodied freedom from rules and restriction—a break from strict rigidity and an immersion instead into experiment, improvisation, and self-exploration—Whatley embodied discipline and structure to the extreme. Together, the two approaches dramatize the very essence of jazz, with its fundamental tradition of improvisation and innovation within an established form. Despite their differences, Whatley and Blount shared essential qualities, which may be found today in the playing and philosophy of Frank Adams: the carefully stylized spectacle of pure showmanship, and an absolute, single-minded devotion to craft.

Other musicians proved significant to the development of a local jazz culture. One of the critical figures of this tradition was multi-instrumentalist Ivory "Pops" Williams. A sort of grandfather to Birmingham jazz, Williams was responsible for first bringing the young John Whatley from Tuscaloosa, Alabama, to Birmingham, and giving him some of his earliest musical experience. With Whatley, he organized the city's first musicians union for blacks, membership to which would become a prerequisite for Birmingham jazz players. Born in 1879, Williams lived to be 102, and for decades his presence exerted an important influence on the Birmingham scene. When Frank Adams started his own band in the 1950s, he persuaded Williams to join him as bassist and the two men enjoyed a long and fruitful collaborative friendship. When Adams became the music director of Birmingham City Schools, Williams challenged him to expand the schools' musical culture beyond brass, reeds, and drums, to include formal education in strings. With Pops's encouragement and under Adams's leadership, a hugely successful strings program was born in the schools of Birmingham, one that continues to benefit Birmingham students today.[5]

For many listeners, both locally and nationally, the city's greatest star was trumpeter and bandleader Erskine Hawkins. During the 1930s and '40s, young, black Birmingham musicians did not need to look far to find inspiration and encouragement: in local-born Hawkins—and, indeed, in every member of his celebrated orchestra—aspiring musicians could witness the hometown embodiment of national success, cultural sophistication, sartorial style, and instrumental virtuosity. For young Birmingham players, Hawkins and his band represented the most visible, viable link to a world beyond; meanwhile, the Hawkins orchestra gave listeners up north and across the country a glimpse into the world back home. Throughout its history, the band remained always an ensemble of Birmingham-bred musicians—among them, Sammy Lowe, Paul and Dud Bascomb, Haywood Henry, and Avery Parrish—most of whom were products first of Fess Whatley and of Alabama State, the Montgomery college where, as the 'Bama State Collegians, they got their start. The group's roots were best memorialized in their most famous tune, "Tuxedo Junction," which borrowed its name from a popular dancehall just outside Birmingham, in the community of Ensley.

In their mastery of their craft, in their confident and cool stage presence, in their impeccable dress, and in their professional success, big band musicians like Hawkins crafted a model of authority and class that appealed to many young black men in pre–civil rights Birmingham. The jazz band changed the rules of the game. In later years, Sun Ra himself described the impact of those performances: "The black people were very oppressed and were made to feel like they weren't anything, so the only thing they had was the big bands. Unity showed that the black man could join together and dress nicely, do something nice, and that was all they had. . . . So it was important for us to hear big bands."[6]

If the bands provided a means of black achievement, community, and pride, in some ways they also offered a model of community that at its best could transcend race altogether. Frank Adams notes that, even in the days of Birmingham's deepest, most pervasive segregation, jazz could give performers in and beyond Birmingham a language that operated outside of the racial divisions of the day. Even in 1950s Birmingham there was an attitude among musicians, says Adams, that, "Hey, man, we play for different clubs and things, but when it comes to jamming and playing this music, this soul music, we get together on it; and we're brothers in this." He continues: "We go our separate ways—but at *night*, when you're asleep, then we get together and work on this *jazz* music. We respect each other. We can't show this kind of love out in the open, because we've got so many that feel that this is crossing the line, that it shouldn't be that way. But the musicians: we're brothers. We don't show it, but we're just like each other."

This is a story of Birmingham, Alabama, through the twentieth century, and as such, it is a narrative that registers that city's complex history of black and white relations. Certainly Frank Adams has been witness to the forms of discrimination and injustice that, for many observers, have long been synonymous with the name "Birmingham": a city whose fire hose and police dog images will always loom large in our nation's collective memory. But Adams speaks also of the ways in which that story resists easy classification and generalization: of whites who forged relationships with blacks, despite the pressures of the day, and of blacks who, in the deepest heart of segregation, transcended all restrictions to create a vibrant and empowering society of their own making.

In her study of Birmingham's black middle class, historian Lynne Feldman describes the processes through which black businesses, social organizations, and families built a thriving community rooted in "their own separate economy," "an infrastructure of organizations designed to serve their needs and desires," and "an increasing race consciousness and solidarity."[7] No neighborhood better embodied these themes than Birmingham's Smithfield community; and—as a local civic leader, a spokesperson for the rights of African-Americans, and editor and owner of *The Birmingham Reporter*, one of the Southeast's leading black newspapers—Frank Adams's father, Oscar, stood at the very heart of this community.

As a prominent newspaper publisher, and as a leader, locally and nationally, in the A.M.E. Zion Church and the Knights of Pythias, Oscar Adams Sr. was active in working for the social and political betterment of African-Americans throughout and beyond Alabama. From 1918 to 1934, he adopted in the pages of his newspaper a powerful editorial voice that rallied for the advancement of the black community, championing in particular the developments of its social and fraternal organizations. Adams's paper enthusiastically reported and supported the successes of the black community, relaying the activities of its religious and economic leaders, applauding the cultural contributions of Industrial High School, and reprinting political speeches made by Adams himself in his appearances throughout the state. If the paper's social reports delighted in showing off the galas and soirees of an elite community with carefully refined middle-class values, the paper also confronted the most serious issues of the day, exposing episodes of racial violence and discrimination without equivocation. Adams also contributed a column, "What Negroes Are Doing," to the *Birmingham News* from 1918 to 1946 (after his death, his secretary and assistant, Mattie B. Rowe, continued the column). For most of those years, he served as the only African-American on the paper's staff; in this role, he wielded significant influence as the black community's most prominent voice to white Birmingham.

In a variety of other capacities, Adams continually addressed issues of importance to blacks. He advocated for civil rights and social advancement as president of the Colored Citizens' League, which would become Birmingham's first, albeit short-lived, chapter of the NAACP. In 1919, he served on a committee of African-Americans from across the state, mostly members of the middle class, who presented to the governor and state legislators a list of grievances, decrying a culture of lynching, segregation, and educational inequalities, among other problems facing Alabama's blacks. The committee found an unreceptive audience, but Adams and others remained persistent in advocating for social justice. Always—often in the absence of greater justice—Adams emphasized the role of black fraternal organizations in providing a framework of mutual support within the black community. His own Knights of Pythias emphasized "the principles of Friendship, Charity, and Benevolence," qualities, he said, on which the advancement of the race depended: "If ever," Adams insisted, "any people in all the world needed a conscientious friendship institution, one that really practices the brotherhood of man and the fatherhood of God, it is the American Negro; and he never needed an institution of such nature and kind more than he needs it today."[8]

Adams's outspokenness brought him support from many, while making him the target of criticism and even threats from his detractors: while some blacks labeled him an accommodationist for his willingness to work with whites, white extremists railed against his vocal stance on racial matters. Frank Adams recalls death threats sent to his father from the Ku Klux Klan, and indeed, on several occasions the Klan attempted, without success, to bully the elder Adams. "Well," begins an undated note from Mattie Rowe, Adams's secretary: "I had a call this afternoon from the Knights of the Ku Klux Klan—couldn't get the name of the distinguished gentleman, but anyway he represented the Klux who said 'Is Adams there?' to which I answered, 'No, he is out of the city.'"

The caller asked who was in charge while Adams was away.

"The secretary."

"Who is he?"

Ms. Rowe—remembered today by Frank Adams as "a woman of dignity"—answered back, "This is *she* speaking."

"Well, tell Adams we don't like his issue of August 4th at all and we are not going to have him sending out such stuff for you niggers to read, and tell him he better not say anything else about us."

"So," Ms. Rowe's memo to Adams concludes, "this was my first conversation with the Kluxers."[9]

Oscar Adams Jr., older brother to Frank, recalled that on another occasion a group of Klansmen visited his father's office in person: "They weren't going to have a Black man saying those things about the Klan," Adams remembered. The newspaperman responded by shoving the Klansmen down a staircase.[10]

In time, the younger Oscar Adams would pick up and expand on the political legacy of his father. In 1947, this Oscar Adams became the second African-American lawyer, after attorney Arthur Shores, to practice in Birmingham, and he was the first admitted to the Birmingham Bar Association. Indeed, Adams's career would be marked by a series of notable firsts: In 1967, with white partner Harvey Burg, he opened the state's first integrated law firm; two years later, with James Baker, he formed the first African-American firm in the state, Adams and Baker (later Adams, Baker, and Clemon, with the addition of partner U. W. Clemon). Adams developed a reputation for his handling of discrimination cases, including school desegregation and voting rights cases, and his firm became active in the legal battles of the civil rights era. During the arrests that made Birmingham famous in the 1960s, Adams represented literally thousands of jailed demonstrators and counted among his clients Martin Luther King, the Southern Christian Leadership Conference, and the NAACP. In 1980, Adams was appointed the first African-American Supreme Court justice in Alabama. He ran for and won a full term in 1982—the first black elected to any statewide political office—serving in that position until his retirement in 1993.

While his brother pursued a landmark career in politics, Frank Adams took a different path. Operating from separate spheres—Oscar in politics and law, Frank in music and education—both Adams brothers became esteemed and influential community leaders. Working through the school system and the jazz community, Frank Adams refined a voice and exerted a presence that would leave a lasting impact.

This book is a work of oral history: of memory, observation, impression, and storytelling. Adams recalls episodes from his earliest years in the most vivid detail and shapes those details into engaging, funny, and powerful stories; his ability to riff on a familiar theme is as evident in his speech as it is in his instrumental solos. The narrative that follows, then, is Adams's story, in his own words, drawn from over two years of interviews, conducted more or less weekly from July 2009 to October 2011. My role has been that of interviewer and editor, transcribing and synthesizing for the printed page material from close to one hundred cassette tapes. An essential goal in the project has been to keep intact the rhythm, style, energy, and impact of Adams's speech, remaining true to both the content and the tenor of his storytelling. In the process I have relied on the editorial conventions common to this sort of oral history. I have removed some of the interruptions and repetitions that are natural to the spoken word, but that translate less effectively to the printed page, and have rearranged passages from multiple interviews into chronological or thematic sequences. Where more than one version of the same story were recorded, I have combined pieces from separate tellings to get the fullest account of the events. The words all belong to Adams. When a phrase from our transcripts has been changed for the sake of clarity or accuracy, the decision has been made together: "Doc" and I have collaborated at all stages and in nearly every draft of this process.

A master musician and seasoned public speaker, Adams is sometimes asked to describe the source of his inspiration. Interestingly, his answer may say little, on the surface, about music: instead, he will launch into a story about his grandmother, Mrs. Eaton; about his brother, Oscar; about a character from the old neighborhood, now long gone. His inspiration and influence stem from people, both everyday and extraordinary, musicians and nonmusicians alike. If Adams's autobiography holds interest for its glimpses of such legendary figures as Duke Ellington and Sun Ra, Satchel Paige and Thurgood Marshall, the greatest gift here is the litany of names otherwise unknown, the procession of characters most of the world has forgotten. In Adams's memory, these saints and sinners walk larger than life.

There is Arthur "Finktum" Prowell, who died standing up and singing; Bishop Benjamin Garland Shaw, who jumped from behind his pulpit pointing fingers and threatening Hell; neighborhood bullies George and Blue, who came into the world as fully formed terrors, springing from trees with bricks in their hands. There is Wallace Rayfield, the pioneering black architect, and Henry Derricot, his blind carpenter; itinerant pianist Godpa Taylor, and Tanglefoot Carson, the peach-gang general. There is Prof Green, the self-proclaimed "Little Giant of Song," a Howard intellectual and eccentric, perpetually striving to "get heavy" and "win some note"; and there is the unforgettable "Dr. Hamburger." Here, too, are forgotten and nearly forgotten shadows from jazz and vaudeville history: comedians Mantan Moreland, Ironjaw Wilson, Sweetie Walker and Snake; Reverend George Wilson Becton, flamboyant Harlem evangelist; and George from Georgetown, unknown to most, but proclaimed by the jazz elite the greatest trumpeter in the world. Of particular significance is the roster of Birmingham jazz musicians, from Fess Whatley and Pops Williams to J. L. and Sammy Lowe. Woven throughout this narrative, too, is the tragic story of bebop sax innovator Joe Guy, who spent his final years playing alongside Adams in Birmingham clubs, ultimately succumbing to his long addiction to heroin.

A few personalities loom especially large—most notably, perhaps, those of the two Oscar Adamses. Retelling stories of his father, Adams speaks the man's words deep from his chest, heavy with an authority Adams still actively admires. Adams reserves a similar reverence for his brother; "I think about my brother, Oscar, every day," he said, more than once over the course of our interviews. Certainly, both Oscar Adamses—father and son, newspaperman and judge—deserve further profiles and study of their own. Hopefully this book will be only the first to begin documenting their important legacies.

Recalling his friend and mentor, Pops Williams, Adams muses: "The thing about it was, he was a living history, because he was *there*." He played alongside W. C. Handy and Bessie Smith; he played for the silent movies and for P. G. Lowery's celebrated Ringling Brothers Circus Band; he fostered the genesis and witnessed the fruition of the Birmingham jazz community, in which he remained a creative force until his death. In many ways, Adams today, with his own wealth of experience and perspective, has inherited the position once held by Williams: as living link to the past and as elder keeper of the local jazz tradition. Like Pops, he was *there*. And, as he says in these pages, he's "still here": looking constantly forward, creatively envisioning the road ahead even as he honors the past.

If Adams relishes the remembrance of the men and women who have helped shape his life, he processes that life, also, in terms of "defining experiences": those moments that leave an everlasting impact on each of us. For Adams, even the seemingly smallest, quietest moments can prove, in retrospect, definitive. Other events are immediately recognizable as life-altering, opening up the world to us in new ways and shattering our preconceived interpretations. Great or small, he says, these moments enter one's fabric and remain forever inside. Always the teacher, Adams encourages young people to look for those defining moments in their own lives. We do not ask for those moments, he says; but good or bad, they shape us. By becoming conscious of these life-shaping, definitive experiences—by acknowledging them, reflecting on them, and sharing them with others—we can better understand ourselves, and each other.

Notes

1. Benny Golson, e-mail to Ray Reach, August 11, 2011. Thanks to Benny Golson and Ray Reach for permission to reprint.

2. Tommy Stewart, interview with the author, June 25, 2010.

3. Tolton Rosser, interview with the author, 2011.

4. Scholarship and reminiscence on the subject of Birmingham jazz are scattered throughout a variety of sources. Certainly the first, best resource for this history is the Alabama Jazz Hall of Fame itself, whose museum offers two stories of photographs, artifacts, and information pertaining to the local culture. *Jazz in the Magic City*, a 1985 documentary film by Sandy Jaffe, provides an informative overview of Birmingham's jazz legacy, featuring interviews with and performance footage of several key local musicians. John Szwed's definitive 1997 biography of Sun Ra, *Space Is the Place* (New York: DaCapo Press, 1998)—besides offering a fascinating, exhaustive look at Sun Ra and his music—describes at some length the Birmingham scene from which the young Sonny Blount first emerged. Two unpublished works are particularly helpful in fleshing out the story of Birmingham jazz. One is the memoir of Sammy Lowe, *A Man from Tuxedo Junction (From Jazz to Swing to Rock to Soul): Diary of a Black Musician,* which contains numerous reminiscences of the musician's Birmingham years. The other, *The Birmingham Jazz Community: The Role and Contributions of Afro-Americans (up to 1940),* is a dissertation by local musician Jothan McKinley Callins, completed in 1982 for the University of Pittsburgh. Two Birmingham authors, Carolyn Marzette-Bolivar and Carol Ealons, have more recently contributed to the preservation of the city's jazz story with their own research and writing. Marzette-Bolivar's *Swing Lowe: A Family's Dedication to Preserving Music in the Magic City* (New York: Vantage Press, 2001) features reminiscences from both J. L. and Sammy Lowe. Ealons's *Tuxedo Junction: Right Back Where I Belong* (Birmingham: self-published, 2012) contains archival photographs and biographical profiles culled from years of exhaustive and devoted research. The present author, meanwhile, is at work on a full narrative history of Birmingham jazz, to complement the personal reminiscences offered here by Frank Adams.

5. For a fuller examination of Williams's biography and significance, see Callins, 42–52.

6. Phil Schaap, "An Interview with Sun Ra," *WKCR* 5, no. 6 (March 1989): 28. Quoted in Szwed, 17.

7. Lynne Feldman, *A Sense of Place: Birmingham's Black Middle-Class Community, 1890–1930* (Tuscaloosa: University of Alabama Press, 1999), 3. Feldman's work provides a useful, detailed history of the development of Birmingham's black middle class, with particular emphasis on the ways in which

a range of social institutions created and sustained the community. Her studies of the black fraternal societies and of Industrial High School are particularly relevant here.

8. "Annual Address and Report of Oscar W. Adams, Grand Chancellor," 50th Grand Lodge, Knights of Pythias of North America, South America, Europe, Asia, Africa and Australia, August 3, 1937, Oscar W. Adams papers, Manuscript, Archives, and Rare Book Library, Emory University. For Oscar Adams's biography, see Mattie B. Rowe, "What Negroes Are Doing," *Birmingham News*, May 19, 1946; Richard Bailey, *They Too Call Alabama Home: African American Profiles, 1800–1998* (Montgomery, AL: Pyramid Publishing, 1999), 9–11; Feldman, 17, 107–8, 158–59.

9. Mattie Rowe, undated correspondence, Oscar W. Adams papers, Manuscript, Archives, and Rare Book Library, Emory University. Some punctuation has been standardized for publication here.

10. Bailey, 7.

DOC

1
Family

I was born on Groundhog's Day, February the second, 1928—I think that makes me eighty-three. I was fortunate enough to be born into a family where my dad, Oscar W. Adams, owned his own newspaper, *The Birmingham Reporter,* and wrote for the *Birmingham News*—it's hard to believe—and at one time he was part-owner of the Birmingham Black Barons, when Satchel Paige was pitching. He'd carry me everywhere he would go. And he'd say, "When you go to the bank"—that was unheard of then, a little fellow going to the bank—"when you go in, you tip your hat. And when you ride the elevator, if a lady's on there, you take your hat off." Said that "if you're walking with a lady"—see, I *remember* these things—"if you're walking with a lady, you always walk on the *outside,* and that's to protect her." He was teaching me all kinds of lessons.

He said one day: "Because you are small, going to the post office, someone may stop you. And if they do that, you walk up to them." He said, "I don't care what color they are: they could be black, white, or blue." Said, "*Grab* their hand, and shake their hand, and say, '*I'm Frank Adams!*' Look them in the face and don't blink." He'd say, "*Squeeze* their hand. They'll tell you who they are. If not, they'll let you go, and they'll go about their business—they're not *worth* knowing." I always think about that.

Both of my parents had college degrees; that was something unusual at that time, in the black community. My mother finished Talladega College, and Dad finished Alabama A&M College in Huntsville. As far as music was concerned, my brother, Oscar, and I were just beginning to play, and my dad would say: "I *know* music. I know all *about* music." He said, "I played music with W. C. Handy, the Father of the Blues, at A&M College." But the thing that got us, he said: "I played the slide *trambone*." My brother and I said, "*Tram*-bone?" And Daddy knows music?"

The first thing I really remember is picking up my brother's clarinet. He was already in the elementary school band. My brother, Oscar, later became a Supreme Court justice—the first black Supreme Court justice in Alabama. I picked his horn up off the bed one day and puffed up my jaws and made a *terrible* sound. He snatched that horn away from me and said, "*Roll* your lip back! Don't puff out your jaws like that—and blow easy!"

That was my first music lesson. The first note I made was a G—a little, soft note. And that started me on my career in playing. When I got to the elementary school, I could already play everything the band played, because I lived about a block away from the school and I could hear them practice. I'd pick up the instrument and try to find the note.

One Easter—I always think about this when Easter comes around— Dad said, "You boys are going to play 'The Old Rugged Cross' in Sunday school." It was just about three weeks away, and my mother panicked because she knew that we didn't even know, hardly, how to put the horns together; we'd just started. She said, "They can't do that— that's going to be so *humiliating*. Why would you let those boys go up there and embarrass themselves like that, Oscar?"

He said, "They're going to do it. So don't worry." Said, "I want it as a duet."

"How could they play it? They don't even know the *melody* of 'The Old Rugged Cross'!"

"*They'll do it.*"

So we packed up and went to the church, the Metropolitan A.M.E. Zion Church, and went down to the basement. There was a lady by the name of Elmonia B. Nix, I never will forget it. The piano was one of those pianos that, if you struck it hard, you'd think a rat would jump out of it. It was awful. It was out of tune and all of it; the keys were tarnished where someone had been pounding on them and knocked the ivory off—I know you've seen pianos like that, too. Our instruments had all kinds of rubber bands around them to hold them together. We went down there and worked for about forty-five minutes. She'd say, "Put your finger down there; put your finger up here . . ." And she wouldn't know a *note* if it had an overcoat on—and walked up and said, "*I'm a note!*" But there we were, and we didn't know any better.

We came out of there, and believe it or not, we could play "The Old Rugged Cross" as a duet.

That Sunday, Easter morning, our dad announced—because he was the superintendent of Sunday school for twenty-some-odd years, twenty-seven years—he said: "Oscar and Frank are going to play 'The Old Rugged Cross.'" Man, we stood up there. We looked at each other. My mother was just cringing. But Miss Elmonia Nix played a few chords, and we struck into "Old Rugged Cross"—we played it so well, the church stood up and gave us a *standing* ovation. And that sort of hooked me on music.

My brother, Oscar, was the one that was always so smart. The whole family, cousins and all, realized that at an early age: they realized that Oscar was just different. He got a couple of double promotions—you could double-promote, for instance, from the third grade to the fifth, if your grades were that good—and he got double-promoted twice. That made him finish elementary school very early. Of course, I didn't get *any* double promotions.

One day they were talking about it in the living room. They were saying, "Oscar is doing so well in school, he just catches on." They came up to me—I wasn't doing *bad,* but I was average. And they said, "We're concerned about Frank. He seems to not be getting things as quickly as he should." My grandmother was listening. And *I* was listening.

My grandmother—Mrs. Linette Eaton—was a magnificent person; I loved her so much. I loved Mother, too, but Grandma . . . if you've got a good grandmother, man, you've got the best thing in the world going for you. Because Grandmother will forgive, when nobody else will forgive.

My grandmother said, "You know, Frank's all right. But," she said, "everybody can't be a lawyer, or a teacher, or a doctor. We've *always* got to have people to clean the streets."

I heard that—man, I went back to school and improved my grades. I could *see* myself cleaning the streets. So it made a difference: I started

Family, ca. 1929. Left to right: Family friend Annie Colga, Oscar Adams Jr., grandmother Linette Eaton, Frank Adams, and Oscar Adams Sr. Courtesy of Frank Adams.

trying to study, trying to do a little better. I think it really changed my way of thinking about things.

Grandmother was probably the wisest person in our family, because of her age and experiences. She didn't have the formal education that my mom had or my dad had. She was less educated, but she had a way of doing things that was different. She insisted that I *memorize* everything. I can still remember poems that I was taught back there: Grandma would have you recite the words to get the diction and the pronunciation right, but it wasn't *yours* until you remembered it. I'd stand and recite it, and at the end of it I'd bow.

My grandmother—who came up not too long after slavery—when I would do something good, she would say, "No ladder child could do better." That was a compliment. That was Grandma. When I got to Howard University, I started thinking, what does she *mean*, "no ladder child"? And I found out, that meant no *mulatto* child. No mulatto! That meant, in her mind, in her experiences, that the mulatto children always had more educational advantages than the black ones—but *I* had done so well, they couldn't have done any better! So in her mind was always the superiority of the mulatto: that was her measuring stick. Now, I couldn't argue with Grandma. She had lived longer; she had been through all of this; and she was of a complexion, really, that could classify *her* as a mulatto. There was no way in the world that you could talk to her or explain, "Mrs. Eaton, there's no difference." Her experiences were that, when she came up, the mulatto child just caught on to things better.

Really, my grandma was my best buddy. I think if I had gone to prison, Grandma would be the only one that would sit with me or get me out; the rest of them would say, "Too bad." Grandmother was the one who, when you were starving in college, would send you a basket of chicken. By the time it got to you, some of it would be rotten, but the guys would see that package from Birmingham in the post office—they'd come to your room and eat it all up. I remember the first time I saw these little M&Ms with the peanuts in them—when they first came out, Grandma sent me a little tray of them.

My grandmother worked for the Levys. They were people that owned lots of property, and she would work parties for them. My mama would go with her sometimes. On cold nights, say, two o'clock in the morning, when they would finish the job, they would wake us up—and you talk about the biggest shrimp in the *world* that they brought back, shrimp as big as your hand, and the oysters, and the caviar. There was no refrigeration, so they had to eat it then or it would spoil. You wouldn't know what you were waking up for, but your little tummy would be *full* when you went back to sleep.

I have a happy remembrance of that.

Another thing that changed my life: we had a big library. This was where Daddy kept all the books that *he* studied. He was always reading. He said—he would tell older people, and everybody—"If you hang around me, you'll get a college education." He would buy these encyclopedias, and he had all the Harvard Classics. One Christmas we were thinking we were getting some toys—other guys were getting skates—and here comes the express wagon that delivers the packages. This big box was sitting in the middle of the floor—we *knew* it was some goodies. But when he opened it up, it was *The Life of Abraham Lincoln*—in about twenty volumes! He had them all around the wall.

At that time, we had what we called the *Blue Back Speller*. And the *Blue Back Speller* didn't use all the phonics and techniques that we use now. You would spell a word like *baker*: B-A-K-E-R, *baker*. M-A-K-E-R, *maker*. F-A-K-E-R, *faker*. All those words would rhyme, and I'd read that *Blue Back Speller*—until they got to the word *chrysanthemum*, and the rhyming scheme was all over! I kept trying to spell it. Dad would come home, and he'd be in the library. He had a fireplace, and the fire would be crackling, and he'd sit down. I was struggling.

He'd say, "Listen, Frank." He'd point at me. "If you don't spell those words by next Wednesday, I'm going to whip you until your *nose* bleeds." Good God almighty. He wouldn't do it, but I didn't know that. I'd take the book to *bed;* to the *restroom*. And when I got ready to spell, I was in such an excited situation—I was so afraid—that water just started running out of my eyes. I started spelling the whole book.

"*Boy!*" he said, "*Hush! About face! And get out of here!*"

The only whipping I ever got was when I was much smaller—and it was a defining experience, which I remember today. My mom was holding me, and I *bit* my mother. God, I bit my mother. He snatched me off of her and took me, BAM, across that floor—*little* fellow! I can remember now the way the tile on the floor looked; it was a black and white tile. He took a strap and said, BAM, "Don't you ever do that!" No matter how much he cared for me, that was his *wife*. I was his child, but he whooped me like I was another man. It was *brutal:* he didn't try to kill me, but he swung me around and around and around. I learned then that you don't bite a woman—especially a man's wife.

He put some things in my head that, the way he put them, are still there.

One time, they were talking about dope: that some entertainer, somebody, was using "dope." That was real popular during the Harlem Renaissance—morphine and heroin, all that kind of stuff. Cab Calloway was coming through Birmingham, and somebody said he would keep cocaine in this handkerchief he had. And my daddy said—I remember, we had just seen a Dracula movie—"You don't want to be a *dope fiend*." That meant that you would grow these *fangs*, the way he said it—like Dracula.

"*Dope fiend*."

When I got to college, and the guys started passing around a reefer . . . my daddy came out from somewhere: "*Dope fiend!*" I could see that vision! I'd start screaming: "Get that stuff away from me!" And they'd accept that—they'd say, "He's a nice player, man, but don't mention dope to him—he goes crazy."

The thing about my daddy was: early on, he established a whole culture for us. He really worked tirelessly as a student when he got to A&M, and when he finished there, he came to Birmingham and organized his paper. He got involved in things like the Black Barons and the Pythian Lodge—he was the Grand Chancellor, for a long time, of the Knights of Pythias. And he didn't mind spending money on worthwhile things—in fact, my mother said that two months before he died, he retired the mortgage on our home. He'd borrow it, he'd pay it back, he'd borrow it—but before he died, it was mortgage-free. He had paid it off and had enough insurance left for my brother to get his books for law school.

My dad was such a strong superintendent in the church that he became the endowment secretary for the A.M.E. Zion Church nationally. The endowment secretary would go and buy property to start new churches. One time we celebrated the fact that he had bought a spa in Hot Springs, Arkansas. That was a big investment for the church. They made money off that, and he built other churches. In the meantime he was writing this newspaper, *The Birmingham Reporter*—and for many years he also wrote the only article in the *Birmingham News* by a black. It was called "What Negroes Are Doing," and he would tell about the different meetings that the blacks were having: lodge meetings and church funerals and all that kind of thing. A lot of people bought that newspaper just for that one column.

I remember going out to see the Black Barons, out at Rickwood Field. By him writing about it and having some interest in it, we had a seat right behind the pitcher's mound. That's when Satchel Paige was at his height of glory; he would call the whole infield in, and strike out the team. It was monotonous, really—he'd come in and take out the Kansas City Monarchs or anybody else, one by one. He had that ball jumping up and down.

I watched it real carefully. Satchel's ball would go out here and come back in, and it was just impossible to hit it. I watched him throw a ball at Rickwood Field, on a projectile—a *straight* line, not going up and down, but straight across the field—and *drop,* right at the plate.

All that magic was going on when I was coming up.

My family came from, I guess, pretty good stock, because my great-grandfather served during Reconstruction: Frank Threatt was one of the congressmen in Alabama during Reconstruction.

One of the earliest experiences I had was going to Demopolis, Alabama—I must have been no more than about six or seven—for the funeral of Frank Threatt. He was buried in the Catholic cemetery, the first black buried in there, so I guess that was the beginning of integration. In later years my brother had in his law office a picture of Frank Threatt, and my daddy would always talk about him, because he was on my mother's side and that was like royalty.

I have a picture of my mother's father, Charles Browning Eaton. He was a bartender at a place called the Funkenstein in Demopolis. I have his watch here; it still runs. Look at the date on the inscription: 1892. This was probably about all he had. I've got it now, and I'll pass it down.

He died before he was thirty—some of these skeletons are beautiful— he died at the Funkenstein bar at twenty-one years old. A young guy, he just drank himself to death. So when you go through these family histories, you're going to find all sorts of things. You've got the legislator on one hand, and then you've got these others. But they all have their significance.

My dad grew up in a little town called Gulf Crest. When I was touring with the army band, years later, I went down there and I couldn't find Gulf Crest; it's not on the map now. They worked in the turpentine fields, where you tapped the trees for turpentine. When he got ready to go to A&M College—he often told me this—he said that he went to his stepfather to tell him he was going. My daddy had seven stepfathers. His stepfather climbed down from this tree, and all he said was, "Good luck, son." When Daddy got to the Terminal Station, he had a valise—the only thing he had in it was maybe a change of clothes, he was so poor—and he went to buy some fruit. When he got back, somebody had stolen his bag. So when he got to A&M College, he had nowhere to go. They told him that he could work in the mess hall, and he said he slept on the floor. The next year, they made him the bursar: he was the one to purchase the food for the lunchroom. That's how he worked his way through A&M.

My mother, Ms. Ella Eaton, before she got married to my dad, was an elementary school teacher. At that time, if a woman got married, she had to give up her teaching. It was prohibited: no married women could teach school. That wasn't right, but that was the way it was. She always said, the first check she got from teaching school, she bought a piano with. Even though she wasn't a musician, she just wanted to have a piano in the house.

When I was coming up, that was one of the only pianos in the community—and there was a fellow, we called him "Godpa" Taylor. I don't know who he was the godfather of, but everybody called him "Godpa." He came from Sipsey. And every year, if you had a piano, Godpa Taylor was a master pianist, and he would come to the home. The neighbors would know by word of mouth that Mr. Taylor was coming, and he would play. He didn't charge anything.

Godpa Taylor was a *finished* musician, and he was smart. He played Liszt and Brahms and everything. During the holiday, if you had a piano, you'd hear, *knock, knock, knock*—Professor Taylor at the door. He'd come in and concertize, then go up to another place. Some people bought pianos just so Professor Taylor would come. The little children would sit there: he would take you and put your hand on the key, say, "This is C." And he'd play not only the classics—he'd play a little rag-time music, too, and everybody'd listen; then he'd go into some ferocious house-party piano.

We always had somebody at the house. By his newspaper and his connections, our dad knew just about all the superstars at that time: Satchel Paige, and everybody. He had been friends with Booker T. Washington. And when anybody was of some note, regardless of what their race was, he would get them by the house to meet you.

He brought W. C. Handy there one night. It was cold, and my brother and I were back in the sleeping porch and in our pajamas. He called us to the front room, and this man was standing there with this homburg hat on, and all of this big chinchilla coat on, and Dad said, "I want you all to meet a great man. This is the *Father of the Blues,* W. C. Handy. He was my teacher. Shake his hand." We squeezed Mr. Handy's hand and we went back to the bed, and Oscar said: "Man, have you ever seen a hat like that? That guy sure was sharp, wasn't he?"

We jumped back in the bed. We didn't know anything about W. C. Handy. But Daddy would introduce you to the president of the United States if he could.

I remember one day he brought a man in by the name of Mr. Huckabee, who was a member of the Knights of Pythias. The fraternities would always have their dues set—but in hard times, if you didn't have the money, you could bring some vegetables or something to pay your dues.

Daddy said, "I want you to meet this man. This is Mr. Huckabee." Said, "Shake his hand." But he said, "Watch *out* for Mr. Huck's hand!" This man's hands had so many calluses that he couldn't close them. He couldn't make a fist because of all the calluses. Dad said, "He's a hard worker, Mr. Huckabee."

Something else I remember: when the bishops would come to our home, they had a room that they stayed in, and we had a huge leather chair. We had two of them—great big chairs—and they would rare back in them. The next day, when they would leave, we'd go over there and look in the cushions, and we'd find little knives and coins that had gone out of their pockets—they'd relax themselves, and we'd find little tidbits of things. We enjoyed that.

Our home was a significant thing in the community. It was an outstanding corner-lot house, and people in that neighborhood really *looked* to our house. My dad said, "Always try to get you a house on the corner." That was just in my upbringing. "Brick house. Wood is good, but get you a brick house on the corner. So you anchor the block."

We had the only radio in the whole community. So part of my education was that when Joe Louis would fight, they would all gather in our house and root for Joe Louis to knock the guy out in one round. I remember the time when they had Orson Welles's "The War of the Worlds," where the Martians had invaded, and they were coming down the Hudson River. When my daddy got home, in our front room, we had pastors, we had ministers, and we had all the people in the community sitting on the floor, listening to this Orson Welles thing—that the Hudson River is flowing over, these Martians are coming in—and people at that time were jumping out of their windows over this. They thought it was true if they didn't catch the first act.

My dad was coming home to get his evening nap. "O. W.," they called him, "what are we going to do?" He said, "I see three or four ministers there. Why don't you just *pray?*"—and walked on and got his nap.

After a while you could hear him snoring.

Another time, it was a hot day; there was a church across the street, and this man was having a revival. You could hear him exhorting, with a loud voice. Daddy came home to get his dinner; he came walking down the hall and said, "Man, my God. Does he think the Lord is hard of hearing?"

My grandmother was *strictly* religious. She said, "Blasphemy! You devil!"

Daddy said that Grandma was his best friend. She really didn't like him—she *never* liked Daddy—but he would take her to the church conferences whenever he had to be reelected as extension secretary. She would tell the people what a terrible person he was, a rabble-rouser and all. And he would pay her way up there; he'd say, "I take Mama Eaton, because I know she's going to talk against me—and that's going to make people vote *for* me. She's my best weapon."

Sure enough, when the vote would come out, it would be ten to nothing in his favor.

One time growing up, we had a church convention, a Sunday school convention, going to Cincinnati, Ohio. There was a place in Atlanta that had fried chicken, and the train would stop there—you could get, maybe for a dollar, a big dinner of fried chicken to take back to the train. Atlanta was famous for its fried chicken. But before we left the church, my daddy said, "Listen. We're going to Cincinnati, and we're not going to bring all those old bags of greasy food on the train. We're going to the diner." Wow, man: the *diner*. To get to the dining car, you had to go all the way through the segregated section, the white section, all through those coaches back there: the train is jostling and you're going to be stumbling, and you don't want to fall and hit anybody— you hit some white person that was halfway asleep, they wake up and look at you, there's no telling what would happen—but he insisted that we go to the diner.

So that morning, Daddy got ready: he's going to the dining car. We walked and walked—you had to go through, maybe, ten coaches. In the diner, they had the partition between the whites and blacks, but very few blacks would go back there. And the experience when we did get there was one that changed my life. I had had some food before, but we were sitting there, and we saw things on the menu that I had never heard of. A *honeydew melon*? I had had a cantaloupe, but this *green* thing—and oysters on the shell, and the lamb chops—I had never seen anything like that.

What we were doing: we were being educated to the finer things.

Daddy said, "Order up. Order up. Order up. What do you want, Frank? Do you want this? Do you want *this*? Order up."

But here's what happened: those waiters, boy, that you've seen spinning their plates—well, you *talk* about spinning! Listen, listen, listen— you talk about putting on a *show*. Because we were like *them,* and they never saw people like us back in that dining car. Some of them we even knew, because they were in the church; we had four or five in the church that were Pullman porters. They had the platters they could turn with their hands, and all kinds of things—they didn't just *serve* your food.

Dad said, "You got to leave a tip." Everybody put down their tip. We put more money up than anybody else, any of the whites, in that dining car. That was an experience.

Those who went on that trip were educated a lot about things that we probably would not have known.

Dad was very critical about food. He would always have the *best* food, and we had to have our table settings every weekend with table-cloths and napkins, and it was his custom that on certain days he'd bring someone home, whether it was the street cleaner or the president— the elevator operator or the bishop, whoever was in town—and have an elegant meal.

Now, my grandma and my mama were both people that learned to scavenge: they could cook common meats—pork chitlins, and all that kind of stuff—and make a tasty meal out of it. But I remember one day we had a meal: it was some kind of steak, and my dad said, "Take it back."

"What do you mean?"

He said, "I work too hard to eat that old stringy meat. I deserve better." And they took it back. In the Great Depression! He said, "I work too hard; I don't need to eat that crap."

There was just something *different* about him.

One time—I wasn't quite a teenager then—he wrote something in his newspaper. He wrote something that offended the Ku Klux Klan. He said: in the future, what did he hope for his children to be? And he said Oscar would be the president of the United States. That's back in 1930! And I would be his attorney general—next to the president. It was out of the question at that time to even *mention* the president of the United States—and he put it in the newspaper.

So he got these letters from the Klan. In fact, they sent him a bullet, a silver bullet. And said, "You're going to have to be out of town" by a certain time "because of what you've written in that paper."

In his next article, he said: "I wish I could oblige you," but said, "I have nowhere else to go." He said, "I hope to be buried out there in Grace Hill Cemetery. If I had another place to go, I would, but I'm staying here.

"So come and get me."

That was his temperament.

I remember, growing up, we had a lighting system in our yard, because we were afraid the Ku Klux Klan would come. He had lights rigged up, all along the wall, and he had trained us, if something went wrong, to click those lights on. He was ready. And he never shied away from controversy.

When my daddy took over the Pythian office, he exposed the fact that somebody had been taking money from the burial funds. One of his biggest jobs was to rebuild that burial insurance. He had to plea to people, and in his newspapers he wrote about it: such-and-such person "Guilty of Stealing Funds from the Pythians."

It all came to a head one day at Peterman's Barbershop, where he would get a shave and haircut. There was a drugstore right across the street, the Temple Pharmacy, and the fellow that ran that drugstore was involved with stealing from the endowment fund. When my daddy came out of Peterman's Barbershop, he was walking down Fourth Avenue, and this guy called his name. He turned around, and the guy threw some *acid* on my dad, or some lye—and that was one of the most vicious fights that ever happened on Fourth Avenue. My daddy knocked that man down and literally nearly killed him. They had to pull him off the guy. He had a big ring, a diamond ring, and he cracked that ring—I have it at home now—he cracked the *diamond*. This man and his father were the druggists, and they left Birmingham after that.

It didn't blind him, but my daddy always had a little scar under his eye where that lye hit him. Of course, between this fight and what had happened with the Klan, people would say, "You better not mess with O. W." It wasn't as serious to me at the time, because I didn't know what it all meant, but he had a fellow who drove the elevator, whose name was Willie Whatley—and for a while he became my dad's bodyguard. Daddy had a gold watch, an Elgin railroad watch, and he also had this .45—this pistol—that he'd take out and lay on the table before he'd go to bed.

Oscar and I would look at it, and we'd dare not bother *that* thing.

My dad was really a student of humanity. He was friends with people who had unusual qualities, black or white. He was well liked in the Jewish community. If something was wrong with my foot, or something was wrong with my ear or nose, we could go to Dr. McGaha. He was a white doctor. He would see that we were taken care of.

I remember when my dad had a painful experience, where he swallowed a fish bone that got stuck in his rectum. He called Dr. Henry Cullen Bryant, the black doctor; Dr. Bryant was gambling and didn't come. So my dad looked in the telephone book, and he called up a guy—a young white guy, Dr. McGaha—and this guy came to the house and performed something on dad that relieved him of the pain. He made a friend of my dad for life, because he relieved that misery. The next day, Daddy was still recuperating, and Dr. Bryant finally came to see about him—my daddy jumped out of bed and knocked him out *flat*—because he was playing poker while my dad was suffering! My dad cried over that: said, "This is my friend, and I called him, and I got to get this other fellow"—but that made a lifetime friendship with Dr. McGaha.

I remember those kinds of incidents that are not recorded in the history of that era. People need to know about that: that all people weren't one way. All whites weren't prejudiced. You had some great people of different colors that would come to your aid, if they respected you. There were people who supported blacks, and they were Italians, they were Greeks, they were Jews; they were all *kinds* of people. It's not a wise thing to say that all people were this way or that way, because there's a difference between "all" and "some." My dad said you couldn't pigeonhole people into one groove. He knew that was a big mistake. He understood that there was a bond between people. So he never hated white folk. He'd say there were some good ones; there were some *real* good ones; and there were some real *bad* ones. Just like everybody else. It's a terrible, defeating, degrading prejudice when you think that all of a certain kind of people are alike. You've always had those that were outside the circle.

There were always some people who saw another way.

People ask me, "Where do you get your musical inspiration?"

All I know is: we had a person in Demopolis, where my mother came from, and his name was Arthur Prowell. He was what they call a roustabout. He was a fellow that played music, and he could *sing*. He was one of these tenors: he could do these Irish songs, with this real keen tenor voice, and played the trumpet, and never had a lesson in his life.

We called him "Finktum." When he was just a boy, he ran off with the Ringling Brothers Circus. He would play, and he'd sing—I don't think he was a blackface comedian, but he was a comedian; he could do all these kind of things. Plus, he would help put the tents up, so he made extra money.

The story was, and I can attest to it, he lived sort of a reckless life. In fact, they said at Ringling Brothers they would *whip* him, if he got out of order—it was right out of slavery times. And when he came back home, he was deathly ill. He had lumbago or whatever it was: a heart condition where your legs were all swollen up. He was my grandmother's half-brother, and he was staying at my godmother's house, over in the Smithfield area. It was my job to go after school to take a basket of food, something to eat for dinner and something for breakfast.

The problem with Finktum was, they said he was a pauper. He had no money. He had nothing; he had just thrown his *life* away; and the church would have to give him a pauper's burial, because he had been a drunkard and a roustabout and all of that kind of thing. Another thing that was wrong with him was that he didn't profess religion. So every day the pastor would come and ask him to praise the Lord before he died. Said, "You got to go to Heaven or Hell, so profess religion."

He would just look at them. They'd have the women from the Missionary Society singing over him, and he wouldn't say anything.

I would be alone with him a lot of times. He was in bed and couldn't get up, and he would say, "How'd you do in school today?"

"I did okay."

"That's good." He'd always say: "Get your lessons. Get your lessons." And he would say, "Tell your grandma, don't worry about me; stop worrying about me, I'm all right."

But they were talking about him: they said he didn't have anything, that "Ms. Eaton's got to pick up *dimes* to bury him," and they said he lusted after women—oh, his reputation was *terrible,* man. Somebody said he had tuberculosis and somebody else said he had this; all kinds of stuff. But he would talk to me, and I would sit there with him until it was time to go. And he'd say, "Tell your grandma, don't worry about me. I'm okay."

Finally, the great bishop, Benjamin Garland Shaw—that was a tremendous bishop in the town. He could kick the devil out of the church and preach these *fiery* sermons. If you did something wrong, he'd jump over the pulpit and *point* at you. And I never will forget, he had this cross that was as big as a horseshoe. Solid gold. I'd always look at that cross.

They brought him finally to Finktum. And Bishop Shaw said, "*Now, listen.* I hear that they've been trying to get you to profess Christ, before you go to Hell."

He didn't say anything.

"*I'm talking to you, sinner!*" Bishop Shaw told him, said: "If you don't profess Christ, you're gonna be put in a rubber casket and *bounce* your way to Hell!"

Rubber casket and bounce!

But what happened is, they just prayed and they prayed and they prayed, and he never did profess religion—and when he died, he died singing: "Life Is Like a Mountain Railroad." See, he could *sing,* man, and he died.

They had the funeral at the church down the street. It was a decent funeral, because Dad put some money into it—it wasn't any pauper's thing.

Two days later, two white gentlemen showed up. They said, "We're looking for Ms. Eaton, the sister of our beloved Arthur Prowell." They said, "We're sorry we couldn't get to the funeral, but here's a check for *five thousand dollars.*"

Listen!

They had a system where the circus workers would put money in this burial association, and they brought all this money down for Finktum. That was as much money as I guess the whole city of Birmingham had *heard* of, back in that day. So Grandma gave some of it to the church—that's the reason the church is there *now,* because they could repair it from Arthur Prowell.

That was one of the things that happened when I was coming up, and I love to tell his story—because his roots are in all of us. We all have that reckless abandon. And these people in those days, like Finktum: they had a thing in them, a *passion,* that drove them to do what they did. The fascinating thing is their honesty of character. In spite of everything, it just shone out through him. He wanted to be with Ringling Brothers: he *went* with Ringling Brothers. My dad wanted to go to school: he *went* to school. Determination. And Bishop Shaw: *he* was a one of a kind personality. He had charisma before this charismatic ministry got going—he was a master of that. You can look back in time and see how he influenced people. These people I knew, back there: they had their values. They had a purpose. They were their own people. Regardless of what situations were, whether it was racial prejudice or whatever goes on, they were determined to do what they had to do. Like my dad told my mom: "They're going to *play* that 'Old Rugged Cross.'" When Dad tells you to do something, you do it. You don't question that.

What I've learned is, you have to have somebody—it doesn't have to be a parent, but *somebody*—that you join with, that's a driving force, to make you want to *do* these things. You have to have a spirit for that— a spirit of excellence.

You have to have a spirit to *do* something.

2

The Church

GOING BACK TO THE LATE TWENTIES, I FOUND myself in the church. In fact, the church I go to now, Metropolitan A.M.E. Zion, is the one I was reared in. I had to go to church every Sunday—my daddy was the superintendent of Sunday school, so there was no doubt about it. The only time I got free from church, really, was when I went to college: I didn't go any, then, at all. I go now, but at that time, I guess, it was just a *freedom* from church. They're probably turning over in their graves right now, because I'm telling the truth. But the church was a great part of my life. And I didn't know any *other* life.

One thing we had at that time, I remember vividly: when you were four or five years old, every neighborhood had its Bible school. Up the street from us there was this lady, Mrs. Guy, who had a Bible school, and you'd go every Wednesday to her class. You had to learn the whole Bible, from the Old Testament to the New Testament. You memorized those verses every week, and you had to get the words just right. She had a cow in the backyard, and at the end of the class we'd get a glass of milk from her cow. That was your reward: warm cow milk and oatmeal cookies. Of course, those who couldn't say their Bible verse would get a lick—but then she'd feed them anyway.

Every Christmas at the church, you had your Christmas speech; Easter, you had your Easter speech. Everybody stopped to listen to you on Christmas and Easter, to see how you were developing. Every child, from the cradle on up, had to recite a verse. They'd write them out for you, and they'd give you a couple of months to learn your speech.

If you got up and recited a long Bible speech—"the valley of the shadow of death," and all that—you would be rated high. You knew from the very beginning, when you're about six years old, who's going to be the intellectual, who's going to be able to do something— because this little girl recites so much until you just want to say, "Sit *down!*" Then there's little Johnny—he would get nervous and run, but they'd get him to the mic, and finally he'd say: "Jesus . . . wept." Well, you're just a dummy if you can't learn more than that! If little Johnny did that for two or three years, they knew there was no hope for him; but they'd clap to encourage him to do better. And you had to say it with a firm voice, too—"*Jesus wept!*"—even if you didn't know anything *about* Jesus, you had to say it. People in the church would see how your family was rearing you. If you spoke in a dialect, they'd say, "There's a lot of bad stuff going on in that house."

My brother got up there one year, and he said, in this deep voice of his: "I'm not going to speak today." Little bitty fellow! When Daddy heard that, he went up there with his belt and whipped Oscar out of the pulpit. Of course, the church people said that was so bad for Brother Adams to whip that boy like that—but when Daddy got after you, once you got your punishment, it was over. There wasn't any aftermath: you got what was due, and now you're free again. When we got home, the phone was ringing; they were asking, "Did he do something to that boy?" No! No, no, no. We were sitting up there eating a chicken dinner, and everybody had forgotten about it. That's the way it was. You didn't have a grudge: you had served your time. It's like you were sick, now you're cured. That's the end of it.

I remember one day we were in Sunday school, and my dad was reviewing the Sunday school lesson. He would do it annually; Peter was his favorite person in the Bible, so when it came around to Peter, he'd review the lesson. I think it was Peter who cut somebody's ear off—Daddy always said Peter was "*full* of fire." Daddy had gone to England with the ecumenical council in, maybe, 1912 or '13, and while he was over there, he bought an English walking suit. This suit was like a tuxedo, but it had a frock tailcoat to it, different colors. Every time he'd review the Sunday school lesson, he'd put this coat on. Over the years he got bigger and bigger, and Grandma had to sew a gusset in the back so it would fit him; but he'd insist on wearing that suit.

He had reviewed the Sunday school lesson that day, and we were on our way back home. We were one of the few families that had a car: we had an old Buick, and it was a *bird* of a car. We were driving home: we passed where the Sixteenth Street Church is, and Kelly Ingram Park.

My dad said, "Oscar"—Oscar was sitting in the backseat—"why did you keep moving around while I was reviewing the lesson today?"

Oscar spoke up—and I think this is what made a Supreme Court justice right here. He said, "I didn't want to sit by that old black gal."

"What did you say?"

Oscar had been sitting next to this real dark-skinned girl. And every time she'd move, he'd move out of the way. He was fidgeting and probably making faces or something, and Daddy had seen him.

"I didn't want to *sit* by that old black gal."

Boy, that car came to a screeching halt. Right there on Sixteenth, where the civil rights museum is now; I think about it every time I pass by.

BAM. It was drizzling rain. He got Oscar out of that car, and took him up into that park. That belt came off just like it came off the day Oscar didn't say his speech—he could pull that belt off quicker than Buck Jones could pull his pistol out.

I've always been what you call an observer: I was always watching. I knew what the consequences were going to be, so I tried in my life to avoid them. I was *watching*. My mom was there; she said, "Oh my God, he's going to kill him!" And—WHAM, WHAM, WHAM, man. When my dad came back to the car, he made a profound statement that I think rang in Oscar's head forever. It changed his life. I know it affected mine. My dad said—and he was fair-skinned as any white person—"Don't let me *ever* hear you say that again." He said, "I wish that *I* was so black I could spit *ink!*"

I said, "Oh, man." It scared Oscar to death. And it took all of the prejudices out of him. "I wish I was so black I could spit ink"—when you're young, you could imagine your father spitting that ink. I mean, you talk about a visual.

That was the way we grew up.

In that day, you had a lot of feeding going on in the churches. You'd come to church, and you'd stay all day. They'd have a thing where you went down in the basement and they would have prepared something to eat between services. They had these specialists: like Miss Sugar

Red, who was a specialist in teacakes. I remember, you had people who were famous for potato salad. They would fix Jell-O, and you had all kinds of meats and things. You'd go down and eat, and then you'd go back to another service. You'd have a morning service and an afternoon service.

Between Sunday school and church there was a little time lapse, and all of us—our big brothers or big sisters and all—would go down to town, to Twentieth Street, where the big department stores were. When all the stores were closed and nobody was on the street, we'd go window shopping: you'd go and buy everything that you wanted. You wouldn't *get* it, but you'd write it down—"I bought a fur coat," and how much it cost; "I bought this pair of shoes"—and when you got back to church, the older children would add it up and say, "Frank, you spent three thousand dollars!" That was "window shopping."

I had two cousins, Lemeriah and Victoria Foster. These little girls were about my brother's age; I was not as old as they were, but they were just beautiful and brilliant girls. Their mother, Alice Foster, was a seamstress with the New York Ballet Company, and she traveled all over the world with that ballet company. They would be leading the window shopping. There was another lady that was very important to us, Miss Katie Lambert: she ran the only newsstand in Birmingham that blacks could go to. She'd have the *Chicago Defender,* the *New York Times,* and all those magazines. You could go in there on Sunday morning, and she'd let you browse them—you couldn't afford to buy them, but you'd look. From there you'd go on up into town and do your window shopping. The girls would buy all kinds of dresses, and they were buying fur coats in their imagination.

One thing you have to understand about the church was that it was right there on Fourth Avenue, right there in the black business district. That was where the poolrooms were—the members that *built* the church ran the poolrooms, and a lot of them were gamblers. The Missionary Society would go down in the poolroom and beg for the church; they'd stop playing pool and give the lady something, to get her out of there. My grandmother was one of the ones that would go into the poolrooms and beg. Nobody thought anything about that: it was a *metropolitan* church, *downtown,* and it served the people in that area. So it was supported by the prostitutes and the gamblers: they all put their money up.

Missionary Society members: Linette Eaton and Sugar Red,
ca. 1930. Courtesy of Frank Adams.

A lot of the money in the church came from the Pullman porters.
The Pullman porters were a class of wealth in the society; if anyone
was well off, it was the Pullman porters. They had money because they
traveled the train, and they got these massive tips going from Florida
to New York, to all those places where rich people would go for their
vacations.

So those were the deacons of the church: the Pullman porters and
the pool sharks.

Then we had people in the church who could fix anything in your
house. If you needed some plumbing, you had a guy that worked for
the plumbing company; you couldn't pay what the plumbing company

would charge you, so this guy would come on his own sometimes and fix it for you. In other words, you were self-sufficient within that church. Everything was there. That's why the church was a big economic engine, and the big organization, later on, that fired Dr. King's movement. He couldn't have gotten off the ground if it wasn't for the church. The church supplied a pulpit for him. The church provided people. All the pastors didn't agree with him, but the ones who did were so powerful that they turned their members' minds and thinking over to him.

All of that came out of the church.

Of course, we had a history of having terrific musicians in the church, too. In the African Methodist Episcopal Church, you had an organization and what they called the Discipline, and the services were universal: if you went to Philadelphia or Detroit, they would have the same format or procedure. It wasn't just picking a song: there would be a certain song that all the churches were supposed to sing on a particular Sunday. Then they would have a place for what we would call anthems: the arranged pieces of music. And then you had the gospel singing: folk singing, and the old spirituals, where there was no written music. Those songs were just passed down from one generation to another.

You always had an instrument in the church, a trumpet or something. The church band was a small band, and they played the hymns for the afternoon services. Sometime in the year, the church band and the choir would give a joint concert.

The Metropolitan Church had some outstanding singers. In fact, we had Vera Colb, who was with the original Gospel Harmonettes, the great gospel group. Each church had its attractive singers. You have, around here, groups like the Ensley Jubilee Singers and the Sons of Zion—all these quartets and jubilee singers—and they were known for their harmonies. And people honored certain singers: they would attend certain churches for their music.

You had people like Mrs. Novella Sims—those people that could really *sing* things. This lady was a natural singer. The church would never be what it wanted to be without Mrs. Sims: because she would lift these old hymns up from slavery. These gospel songs that hadn't ever been printed; nobody even had them in the book.

There's a lady, Beulah K. Hall—she's with her people in Montgomery now—I always keep in touch with Mrs. Hall, because she knows songs that nobody living would know now. Old, old songs, and she can lift them. She's not in good health, so I'm going to put a project on it, where I'm going to get a tape recorder to her, just to sing into, and I can transcribe that stuff. I'm going to have to do that soon, because Mrs. Hall is pretty sick. But she can still sing.

There was one old lady that would go through the church—Mrs. Vye—and she had her own thing: she would say, "My soul's happy, my soul's happy!" and she would walk around the church. And the shouting—people would, as we say, "get happy" in the church, and cry and shout—all that type of thing.

They had something—they don't do it now—called "lining out." A lot of the people in the church couldn't read the hymn book, and they'd need to know what the words would be: so lining out is when I say, maybe, "Precious Lord, take my hand," right before you sing it. You had a person whose job was to stand up in the front and line out the songs.

I observed all these things, and evidently they're still in my memory bank. I remember Mr. G. S. Norman, the choir director; he came in his full World War I military uniform. When the choir would sing, he'd wear his uniform, his khakis with the boots, and he'd stand there and direct the choir. He had a cane—really, it was in place of his rifle— and where you would say, "One, two, ready, play," he would hit that cane on the floor and say, "*Hop! Hop! Hop! Hop!*"

He was the one that knew all about harmony: he had the sopranos, altos, tenors, and bass. He *knew* music. He would do a few Negro spirituals like "Go Down, Moses," but most of his music was *Bach* and the classics. He insisted on perfection—none of this just *shouting* and going on—and he had some people that could *sing*. Most of the time, if you're in church and you say, "I'm not a professional singer, but I'd like to sing in the choir," they say, "Well, come on to rehearsal." You don't want to tell somebody in the church, "Hey, you can't sing in the choir." You're welcome. You're another person up there; if you just mumble and move your mouth, you're okay.

Not with G. S. Norman. You would have to go through a *rigid* audition.

Sometimes you had these talented preachers who sang. Not all preachers could sing, but it was to your benefit if you could. We had some new pastors come, and the very first day, we found out they couldn't sing—so there would be some doubt: what would be the benefit of their message if they couldn't sing? But they recognized that, too, so they'd get somebody to sing *for* them.

We had Miss Elmonia B. Nix—the one I told you about, who didn't know a note if it walked up with an overcoat on—and a defining experience there was that we had to go to her concerts. She sang with a warbly tremble in her voice—and you'd better not laugh at Ms. Elmonia B. Nix or they'd get your behind.

Miss Nix would have her annual recital, where she would sing "Ave Maria" and what classics she knew. That's the first half of her concert, and she would do a good job. But lo and behold, she would have her "modern" concert of popular music. All the young people would have to sit through Miss Elmonia B. Nix's concert, on the front row—or your hide would be tanned, boy. We had to be there, dressed in our finest. She would tell you that she was singing something from Verdi's opera; we didn't know who Verdi was, but we would look up at her. She'd sing it, and she'd be dressed, I guess, in a 1910 gown: it was outdated, but she'd wear it, and she'd sing.

She'd have this brief intermission, about five minutes, where she would change things around—then this would be her popular music time. She would do a song like "Stardust," but she would take on this nauseating vibrato: "*Wooo-ooo-ooo!*" And my brother, Oscar—as I say, I always thought he was a genius—he taught us how to hold our jaws, to keep from laughing. If you made a sound, somebody would come with a newspaper: BAM! Ms. Nix would be standing there, and she said, "I cry for him. But we'll go on." Then she'd start another song: "*Te-ea for two-oo, and two-ooo for te-eea . . .*" And there we would go again—you might get three whippings in one night, before she finished. She would look out in the audience and say that there were more this year than last year—but there wouldn't be more. To this very day, I don't know why she would have that popular music part to it, but she'd insist on it, and she insisted that was for the children: to hear "the songs of today." People would come from different churches to hear her recital. It was terrible, but it was a formality that she had her programs printed, and she discussed the history of each number.

Then, I'll never forget: we had the baseball sermons. They'd have all these preachers at the baseball field: one would start a sermon on first base, and then he'd go to second base. This preacher would recite a brief passage from the Bible and say a few words. Then the next preacher would come around and say something; and the *next* one would come around; *another* preacher would preach around; and they're all coming home, preaching—and people loved it. After they finished, they'd all run home, to home plate, and the people would applaud. You'd have, maybe, the Ensley Jubilee Singers on one side of the field, and some other singers on the other side. People of all races would come to see those things, just like they did when the Black Barons played.

We had a fellow at that time, Professor Wilson, who would come to Birmingham and play in the church. I remember him coming to our house and sitting on our porch. Professor Wilson worked at A&M College—he was a teacher of music—and he would go to the biggest country clubs down there in Huntsville, and he would stand out there on the golf course and play all these beautiful trumpet solos. "In My Old Kentucky Home" and "Carry Me Back to Old Virginny"—he'd be out there, playing this, and people would donate money to the school. People don't know about that now, but that's how they raised a lot of money for A&M. He's buried on the campus out there, and he was the bandmaster of all bandmasters.

He could play every gospel tune that you could want. Sometimes if the church had a choir to sing, he would come unannounced: he would come from the back of the church, playing "Nearer My God to Thee," and he'd go into the variations—the piano could be falling apart, but he could find where it was. One of my mentors, Mr. Lucius Daniels—he was in Fess Whatley's saxophone section—he told me that he was at A&M when Professor Wilson was there teaching band. He said they had practiced for months for this concert. The curtain went back and the auditorium was filled up—but he said, on the very first number somebody made a mistake and Professor Wilson said, "Close the curtain!" If there was *one* note missing, that was it: end of concert. He was *meticulous*—but nobody anywhere could beat him as a virtuoso. I've seen some complete musicians like that: they don't have to tune; they just put their mouthpiece in and they start playing right with you. They're just miraculous. It's like he's a *part* of the instrument; like you pick up your pencil and it just goes to writing.

Not all of them, but most of the educated blacks and some others would be members of the Sixteenth Street Church, which is just around the block from Metropolitan. Even if you belonged to a small church, they would always have something at Sixteenth Street that you could visit and participate in. Sixteenth Street Church had an organ. That was for a church over the mountain to have an *organ;* we barely could have a piano, and our pianos were mostly out of tune. But Sixteenth Street had this organ and the pipes and all.

The band at Sixteenth Street Church at that time was formed by Mr. J. L. Lowe, who founded the Alabama Jazz Hall of Fame. Now, most of the churches had one player or two players, maybe a trombone player or a trumpet player, but Sixteenth Street Church was such a marvelous church—its attraction now is to see where the little girls were killed— it was a church that all churches would aspire to be. And a musician was a musician. If he was a jazz musician, he'd come in and play in the church on Sunday. They're still playing, today, at Sixteenth Street Church.

It was a fabulous place, and it still is. Most of the churches were wooden, but this church was brick. It had a sanctuary with stained glass and all that kind of thing, and it was designed by one of the greatest architects that we knew of: his name was Rayfield. He designed a lot of the white churches, and he was recognized as a genius. As far as the Sixteenth Street Church is concerned, people don't know about its architecture, its acoustics in there. You can walk in there now and snap your fingers—you don't need a microphone to hear that pop. That was due to the genius of Rayfield. He had all the seats arranged, and all of them are equal. You could be in the back of the church and have the same view, because the floor was elevated. And you didn't have to go to the florists on Sunday, because he's got a thing that's still up there, outside, on top of the church: a garden. When you have a service, you go up there and pick some lilies or something, on top of that church. That was Rayfield.

Rayfield was an architect who came from one of the big colleges up in New York or somewhere. He started teaching at Tuskegee Institute but he had a falling-out with the school, so he opened his own business. He designed churches not only for places in the United States, but he sent his blueprints to places in England and France and everything. For a black man at that time, that was unheard of. A lot of the buildings in Birmingham, the big churches: they don't recognize Rayfield, even though he designed their buildings.

Professor Rayfield had a wife, Miss Bessie Rayfield, who sang in our choir at Metropolitan. Miss Bessie lived to be over one hundred years old, and she was still singing. She was a real fair-skinned lady. Evidently, Rayfield really loved his wife, because they had a place out in Titusville, called Rayfield's Folly, which he built for her. He had stained glass windows in the house, and dumbwaiters that would pull up flowers—he had built for her some sunken pools of water where they had goldfish going around in the house—all that kind of thing.

The point I want to make is: the leaders in the black community in Birmingham at that time had this real *professional* thing going on. These people knew what the standards were—but they had standards *beyond* the standards. I'm talking about the twenties and the thirties and up to the forties. The black professionals at that time had so much pride. They may not have spoken about it, but they felt that what they had was even superior to what the whites had.

I used to hear the carpenters, man; they'd start off early in the morning fixing our house. You could hear it—*wood*-saw, *wood*-saw, *wood*-saw—it's singing a tune. We had carpenter called Derricot: Henry Derricot. He worked with Rayfield, and he lost his sight—he was a blind carpenter. But when you wanted a house built, you called on Derricot. Derricot would sit there, and he could figure a three-story house and tell you precisely how many *nails* you would need. If you bent one of those nails, you had him to deal with—he'd *shoot* you if you missed a nail.

But he could make music with that saw.

Another thing we would look forward to in those days was Reverend Becton's tent show. Reverend Becton had what he called the "Consecrated Dime" at the Sixteenth Street Church. He would hold sway there with a revival service for maybe a whole month. Then they would leave out and go through rural Alabama under these tents. It was called the "Consecrated Dime" because if you gave a dime, it would be consecrated, and you were supposed to get maybe ten hundred dollars back, because he prayed over it.

Some of the young musicians would join up with him and play gospel music. Reverend Becton would have young musicians that he got from Lincoln School, and sometimes the parents would allow Reverend Becton to *adopt* the children, because they thought that would give them a better life, to go and play. He would take them back to

New York City, and he would find a place for them to stay. He would take care of them and feed them, and he would make sure that they enrolled in school. He picked up a lot of talented youngsters like that, and that was how some of them really got into music. That's how they got into New York and played at the great clubs there.

These guys out of grade school got on that circuit with Becton, because they could play these songs by ear. One of them was Joe Guy. Joe Guy got to be great in jazz, because he could play what he heard—this *natural* way of doing music. If you had gone through school, you'd have to read the music, but in those old tent shows, they'd just come and hum it—"Onward, Christian Soldiers"—and you'd better pick it up.

That's what Becton did. And he could put on a show.

In those days, they had these *fiery* preachers. They had some women for the first time: I remember there was a lady—it was the first woman preacher any of us had seen, back in the thirties—and her name was Ms. Player. She had a revival like Reverend Becton would have, but she had so many people come because they were curious to see this woman evangelist. She preached a sermon, I'll never forget it, called "The Eagle Stirreth Its Nest," where the eagle is pushed out to fly, and they catch the eagle before it flounders and hurts itself. And she could really *preach*.

Now, my daddy was known as being a great speaker, too. He'd always start up in a very soft voice, and he'd build to a roar. It would be building up—gradually, gradually—and always end with a crescendo. There were people who were great artists at that. They had this *huh*-hooping they did, *huh*-hooping—rhythmic—*huh!* That type of thing would stir an audience.

The greatest one was Bishop Benjamin Garland Shaw. I told you about him and Finktum. Bishop Shaw had more charisma than anybody I've ever seen. Reverend Becton and all those preachers had their style, but Bishop Shaw was the *one*—he was a short man, and stocky, and he looked like a bull. To me, he looked like a Mussolini, with a big, thick neck. He could speak just above a whisper. He knew the Discipline, he knew the laws of the church—although they claimed he violated a lot of them—but he came in the church, and he *demanded* that they respected him: that they would stand, for respect of him. He's the one that had that cross—what seems to come to my mind most—it was real gold, and the arms on it were that thick. There were people who went to church just to see Bishop and his cross.

That was the first time I had noticed this HUH-hooping, what they call "hacking": HAH-huh! Bishop had a thing, when he would get stirred up in his sermons: the other pastors in the pulpit would come and grab him, to hold him back, and he's still preaching. By the end of the sermon, the whole church would be on fire. There were people who were known to shout, who would come from all over when they knew that Bishop was preaching. I don't know whether he canvassed to get them, but they would come and get up and shout. Mrs. Vye would go through the church: "My soul's happy, my soul's happy!" And then you had the smelling salts: somebody would fall out, and they'd use the smelling salts to revive them—then they'd get up and shout again. We, as young folk, would sit there and watch.

Bishop Shaw was one of a kind. It was a fact that everybody in Birmingham, white and black, knew there was not an orator like Benjamin Garland Shaw. He could quote the Bible, verse by verse, and then come from all kinds of angles at it. He knew his history, all about the presidents and *all* that type of thing. And you'd better not challenge him.

He would preach, man; he'd get the church into a frenzy; then he would stop. He would tell somebody, "Go open that back door." He said, "Henry Jones has been knocking on that door for about ten minutes; let him in." And when they opened the door, here comes Henry Jones! People fell out. People fell *out*. We don't know to this day how he did that. It was probably a simple trick, but he had that kind of power and persuasion.

I have learned that if you're around those kinds of people, they can really, without any training in hypnosis, cast some type of spell on everybody. Grandma was talking about how one day he was preaching, and he went through a thing where he *grabbed* the devil—he's in the pulpit—and he *took* the devil down the aisle of the church, and took him to the porch, and *kicked* the devil out of the church. And people said they *saw* it!

Electrifying.

People back in those days were smart, but this is the sort of charisma he had—no matter what they knew was right, people *felt* this man. They felt his power. They felt that if they'd been doing something wrong, they *had* to come to the church, because they couldn't escape his punishment. He was going to tell it, and they knew it. They came and got their beating.

My dad respected him. My dad was a wise person, and he didn't believe all of it, but he respected him, and he was his friend.

One thing Bishop Shaw would do: if you had a relative die, and perhaps you didn't take an interest in this person, but then you were at the funeral; if you were a nephew and you were known to have neglected the deceased; or if you were a son who had been off somewhere, and then came back, just for the funeral—man, you should not be there. Because he'd preach, and he'd point his finger: "You'd *choke* your mama to death!" Then he'd jump back under that pulpit. He'd come back up with somebody else: "You should have *took* her to the hospital, but you were out *drinking* that night!" BAM! He ducks back under the pulpit. He didn't say very much to soothe your soul. Like he told Finktum, "You're going to *bounce* your way to Hell!" People would be screaming.

Bishop Shaw, in his time, was like a king: he was more than just a bishop. That's why he could walk down the aisle and criticize people when he was *burying* them. And he wasn't big, but he wielded so much power. People were afraid of him. He demanded respect.

I remember something had happened: Bishop Shaw felt that he could take certain liberties, and there were some that wanted to take him to account for his indiscretions. So one Sunday, Bishop came in— it was customary that everybody would stand up when the Bishop came in—and on this Sunday they didn't do it. This had never happened before. So he told them: he said, "Listen." He had had people screaming and hollering in that church, and he had baptized all of them. He said, "I'm going back out the door. And I'm coming back in here. *And you'd better stand up.*"

He said, "That's right! Or something will happen to you, right here. Lightning may strike—and it won't be tomorrow!"

He went back to the door. And he took his time walking back up that aisle to the front.

Everybody stood up.

He went to the microphone, and he said, "I want you to remember, the rest of your life: when the *whales* plow the waters, the minnows better hug the bank."

Bishop Benjamin Garland Shaw.

3

Schoolboy

WHENEVER SOMETHING BIG WAS IN TOWN, MY daddy would carry me to see it. I had heard Marion Anderson and Paul Robeson, all those people who would come South and give performances. I remember I went to the Lyric Theatre and heard the band of the Republican Guard of France—and they were *terrific*. They were just impossible. They played things like "The Flight of the Bumblebee," the whole band together, and they were supposed to represent all of France. That was fascinating to a little fellow.

The first time I ever heard Duke Ellington's orchestra, I must have been very small. It was publicized in Dad's paper that it was coming to town, but nobody here put any credence in Duke Ellington because they had never heard him. His records were very few here. We just knew that he was supposed to play what they called "jungle music" at the Cotton Club in New York—and people said, "I don't want to hear any *jungle* music *here.*" When the Ellington orchestra came on their first Southern tour, this thing about jungle music was sort of stigmatized on them. Duke had a Jewish friend in New York City named Irving Mills, who furnished him with something that wasn't heard of then: two train coaches that could be hitched going west, south, north, or east. When they weren't at the Cotton Club, the band lived on those coaches. They quickly established their name in New York and that part of the country, but in the South that wasn't so.

Still, people were curious. So this crowd was out there in front of the Masonic Temple, milling around in line, waiting to see him. My dad was out there and I was out there with him.

Nothing happened for a while. It got to be late in the afternoon: what we used to call "dusk dark." They weren't late, but bands would usually get here a little *early*: you'd see them on Fourth Avenue, or they'd be talking about it on the radio. Duke Ellington hadn't done that. Somebody said, "Well, he's not coming. It's getting dark; I'm going home"—and right before the crowd dispersed, right down on Fourth Avenue, came I think it was two stretch limousines—I don't know where they got them—and in those limousines were Duke Ellington and his orchestra and their entourage.

We hadn't seen anything like that before. When they stepped out of there, the first thing I saw was this *tuxedo*—and I had seen a black tuxedo before, but I hadn't seen a tartan *plaid* one! He had a tartan plaid tuxedo, and—I always think about this—he looked, to me, like a *giant* of a man. I was fascinated because he was so tall: my daddy was a big man, but Duke was towering over my dad and everything. I hadn't seen anybody that tall before.

Instead of saying, "Hello, everybody," he just looked up at the sky—like he was in another world. Because they *were* from another culture: they had nothing to do with us. We were curious about them—we wanted to touch those clothes we had never seen, and we wanted to say, "Hello, there, how are you doing?" But they didn't have any interest in that. It's just like: "We come to play music and that's all. Then we're going to go back to our quiet coaches." To us, I guess it was like going to the circus and seeing some kind of strange creature for the first time. We were just in awe. We had never seen hair slicked back on heads, which was probably common in New York, but we were just—to put it bluntly—we were just kind of *country* folk, and we didn't know the sophistication and all that kind of thing. Of course, a lot of it was pretense and put-on, but they were acting their role. So we went out there and listened.

They were unloading these boxes. They had these fellows doing all the work, and although they weren't band members, they were in uniform, too—we were used to seeing folks in overalls putting up equipment, but these fellows were dressed down in little jackets. The first thing I saw was a big box, and in that box was a timpani. I had seen a drum, but I had never seen anything like this. It was a copper timpani, but I didn't know any better: I thought it was gold.

The next thing I knew, Sonny Greer—this tall, thin fellow—was towering over that timpani. He was known to have every drum known to man. He had a *gong*—I had heard one in the Charlie Chan movies, but I had never *thought* about a gong. He was tuning his golden timpanis up. And on stage he was fascinating, because he was one of those that could twirl his sticks, and he'd hit all these things. He was one of the big features of the Duke Ellington band: Sonny Greer. Later on in life, some of the critics said that Ellington's band would have been better off if they didn't have Sonny Greer, but he was one of the things that really pushed the band. They thought he should play harder: less showmanship. You know how lovers of music sometimes say, "This guy's an entertainer rather than a musician"—but he was *both*. I got a chance to play with him years later: not with Ellington's band, but when he took up residence again in Washington for a while.

Anyway, I was there watching him. Of course, the concert was awesome. The first number they played was "Ring Dem Bells." People were just frantic because they hadn't heard a band play like that. And they didn't have any space in time for anything but that music: as soon as they got through with one piece, he'd hit the gong—*bam!*—they're out there again, and off—*bam!* If you were out there dancing, it looked like he was *punishing* you, because he got through one fast number—*bam!*—another one—*bam!*—another one, right after the other one—there were some sweet numbers, too, but this was a *dance*. They didn't take any prisoners. I mean, they swung. They just swung the folks to *death*—I guess he figured that we wanted to dance down here. And he gave them enough that after about an hour they were soaked. They had no air-conditioning—they'd thrown the windows up and they were perspiring. Men were putting their shirts back in their britches and women were pulling their dresses up. When they found out that the music didn't take any breaks, they just stayed out there as long as they could.

Years passed, and I followed Duke's band and even got to play in it for a while. One time, I was in my early twenties, and we were in the dressing room; it must have been in the Loop in Chicago. The guys in the band were talking, and I asked Duke: "Duke, do you remember me? The little fellow at the Colored Masonic Temple back in Birmingham, Alabama, back in the thirties?"

The Africans call it *ofu*: an *ofu* is something you wish you hadn't said. It's like a pitcher throwing a pitch and he knows, when it leaves his hand, the guy's going to knock it out of the park—but you can't go back and get it. The Africans say *ofu* means "speech comes to life"; if you say something, it lives. It goes to one person, and another person, and if they repeat it, it will mutate or they'll add something to it. But once it's out there, you can't take it back.

When you're around people like Ellington's band—people who are experienced and talented, and who have an organization like a family— they don't have to laugh at you or call you an idiot. They just *look* at each other. And when I said that—"Duke, do you remember me?"—I could feel the pressure. I could feel what they summed me up to be. It just made me seem that I was this little, young, ignorant fellow. "How did Duke put him in here, and he's going to ask a question like *that?*"

But what happened is: Duke spun around in his chair and said, "*You?* Sure, I remember: you were on aisle six, row five, seat *two*"— and turned back around in his chair. It was like somebody passing a card out real quick, like we were both playing games on *them*. Because *I* didn't know where I was seated, and they *certainly* didn't know.

Duke had that kind of charisma. He was the one that always could pull the rabbit out of the hat.

The Masonic Temple, where I first saw Duke, was really a wonderful place. Of course, the fraternities were something of great importance to black people then: the Masons, the Elks, the Odd Fellows—you name them. You can still see where the Masonic Temple used to be, right across the street from where the Hall of Fame is now; and the Pythian Temple, where my daddy had his offices, was just around the corner, on Third Avenue. These were great things in the black community.

The main thing was insurance. There were no black insurance companies in those days, so the fraternities provided your insurance and took care of your burial. They would take up a modest fee for membership; you would pay your dues, and when you died, they would give you a decent burial.

If you were a member of a fraternity, no matter what your status in life or what your job was, you were *somebody*. You could be poor— penniless—but at your funeral you were judged not by your wealth but by how many fraternal organizations attended. All of them had to show up and do their rituals. They would dress up in all their regalia. They'd have their swords and they had the helmets with the plumes on them. If someone lingered over the casket too long, this guy would unsheathe his sword: "Move on!" It was exciting. They would play "Taps" and all that kind of thing for you; they'd burn ashes, they'd say their speeches, they'd go into different languages, and they'd have these *swords*. And that was supposed to spell out the significance of your life.

If you didn't have a fraternity at your funeral, it was like a pauper's burial: they would put you in a box, and that's it. If you had just *one* organization, people didn't think so much of you: it's like you've got nobody there to send you away. But if you're a member of the Knights of Pythias, a member of the Elks Lodge or the Odd Fellows, they all would be represented at your funeral. People would say, "Man, did you know he was a member of *that* fraternity, and *that* fraternity?" That was your goal. You could work on the garbage truck, but if you were a Mason and an Elk, and a Pythian—people didn't want to see you die, but they *sure* wanted to go to your funeral.

My daddy, being the Grand Chancellor of the Pythians, would be in all these ceremonies, and he would usually give the oration. He would tell about Damon and Pythias, who were friends: they were going to execute Damon—they were going to cut off his head—they had his head on the block—then here comes this dust storm. *And who was in that dust storm?* That's *Pythias,* coming to rescue his friend Damon! That was *friendship;* that was the Pythians. My dad would tell that, and he would start out just above a whisper—that's how he got his audience's attention—but he'd be *roaring* by the time the speech was over.

Because he was the Grand Chancellor and had his newspaper, my daddy had two offices over in the Pythian Temple. I got to learn a lot there, because I was the office boy. I would go there and Ms. Mattie B. Rowe, the secretary, would teach me to type—q, w, e, r, t, y, and that kind of thing—and then I had to keep the room clean, and I drove the elevator. That's when he taught me all the etiquette you're supposed to have, how to tip your hat and all; he said, "That's a sign of your having a culture."

I got a chance to go with my dad down in some places that most people never heard of. They would have these meetings in the woods, and they would have big barbecue pits out in the ground, and the chicken would have a lot of soot on it—my mama would say, "I don't want to go and eat that sooty stuff they got down in there"—but we ate it and enjoyed it.

The thing you have to understand is this: these fraternities were before the NAACP, they were before all those things. They were called the "protectionists." They protected the people, and they stood against discrimination as best they could. And one day, when history is told, there'll be a lot of stories where those fraternities prevented a lynching—and really *did* something.

There was one case that was never publicized. A fellow that I taught with later, Joe Jones: his father was on the streetcar coming from Traction Park, over in North Birmingham, where black people would go and have picnics. The conductor, for some reason, got up and *spit* on Mr. Jones—he was probably sitting in the wrong place or something—and Mr. Jones cut his neck with a razor. Killed him. They put him in jail, and they were going to lynch him.

One of the fraternities—I don't know which one it was—raised a bunch of money, and they must have bribed the jailer, because they went and got this guy and sneaked him out of jail. They dressed him up like a lady, put lipstick on him—he was a fair-skinned guy—and he made it all the way up to Chicago. They never did get him. The fraternities did things like that. If they had to pay, they would pay a price to keep you from being killed.

That's something people don't know about, but it happened.

Of course, I was just a little fellow with all these things going on around me. You find out: in your life, you're fed some things—you don't know how they're going to be digested until later on, until you grow older in it. Now I can put them—not all of them—but put them in a perspective: of what did it *mean* to me, and what did it mean to other folks? If you're a youngster, you're hearing things, and you see all of these things unfolding. You don't know what any of it means. But you are having these *definitive* experiences.

In the neighborhood in those days, we used to have what we called "peach battles." We had gangs that would throw peaches. And we had an Italian guy named Tanglefoot Carson, whose family had the grocery store right next to our home. I guess he was a teenager when we were little, and he was our leader, because he knew how to win peach battles. We did what he said to do. He was older than we were, so he took care of us.

We would organize against the enemy. Other neighbors from not too far would come, and we'd get into a peach battle. They couldn't beat us because Tanglefoot was our strategist. He'd tell us to "Hide over in the churchyard till they come," and all that. And he'd have flanks: one group would go out front, and they'd think that was all of us—then here comes another group! You would see *him* in the fray, too. He'd call command from a post somewhere, but then he'd join in the group, throwing these peaches. Every year when peach time came, when the peaches were green—and everybody had some trees—Tanglefoot Carson devised the *rubber gun*. That was a big piece of wood, and he cut little notches in it, so you could pull a rubber band to this notch here, or that notch way back there, the highest power; you'd cut old inner tubes up, car inner tubes, and make the rubber bands for your rubber gun. Tanglefoot would check them to see if they could fire.

I remember one day that I realized that my brother was really my brother. We were having a *rock* battle—it was a terrible thing, man; instead of peaches we were throwing *rocks*. And a fellow across the street, Walter Bolden, was older than I was and he was known, really, to be *bad*. He threw a rock and hit me right on the side of my head. I still have a scar from it. My brother, Oscar, ran at Walter. Walter's grandmother lived across the street, and we thought she was some kind of witch; we were scared to even go over there. Oscar took off—and those shotgun houses were just one hallway, all the way from the front to the back—he ran all the way through that lady's house and *caught* Walter, and knocked Walter *down*. Oscar had never fought before. But they had to pull him off Walter—and Walter's grandmother, who we thought was such a witch: she was afraid to come out.

My daddy, when he got home, said: "Well . . . that's what brothers will do." I was sitting there with a big hole in the side of my head; but I had the satisfaction and appreciation that my brother, who was three years older than I was—that he was my *brother*.

Birmingham, so far as the black community goes, was divided up into certain sections: like the Enon Ridge section and the Smithfield section, where we lived, and Titusville. These sections were the first ones in Birmingham that had blacks buying their own homes and being able to finance them. As I said, Tanglefoot Carson's family had the grocery store, and they lived right there in the store: the Italians were the ones that owned the grocery stores, and they lived among us. There were great entrepreneurs, like the Brunos, who developed a whole chain of grocery stores; they lived up the street and had a house for them and a separate building for their store.

It was a camaraderie. The Italian grocer would have a horse and wagon, and he'd pick you up and talk with you. At that time Smithfield was evolving. That area was mostly populated by Italians who worked in the steel mills, and they lived right in the community with the blacks. The Italians were not accepted by the whites at that time; they were put against just like the blacks were. So when they would have an Italian feast, where they had all the breads and cakes from the old country, they'd invite their customers. I remember going to an Italian wedding down the street, and seeing *all* kinds of breads and cakes—and they invited you to partake of it. They respected us and we respected them. Friendships were built then. Sometimes I thought *I* was Italian.

In our neighborhood we had two notorious young fellows: George and Blue. They were ferocious. If I were to see one of them today, I wouldn't be comfortable. They were brothers, and they would jump out of trees when we would come home from school, and they would take our lunches.

George had *fiery* red hair, and red-looking skin. And the other one was "Blue" but just as black as my shoe—Blue was just *dark*. And it was a combination that was absolutely frightening. They could outrun anybody.

At that time we didn't have a paid lunch; we didn't have a federal lunch program. You brought your biscuits and eggs; whatever you had, you brought it from home. A biscuit or a piece of meat or something— that was your lunch, and George and Blue would take it.

They would take it from *everybody*.

George and Blue must have been about thirteen or fourteen years old, and nobody knew where they lived. They didn't go to school, but they would be on the street all the time, and they would prey on you. You couldn't walk four or five blocks from home before somebody would say, "BLUE!" And you started running. When they'd take your lunch, they would hit you—with a *brick*—to intimidate you. They ran rampant in that neighborhood for years. And they would beat the *girls*—they would stop *anybody*, they didn't sympathize. No matter how small you were, how big you were, if you had a lunch, George and Blue would take it. You couldn't *pay* them. You couldn't bribe them. The more you tried to bribe them, the bigger brick they would hit you with.

I don't know where they are now, but they left their imprint on people, like Dr. Lyle at Alabama State. We were section mates, as we called it, through grammar school and through high school. We *still* talk about them. He says, "Are they still out there?" I say, "I don't know!"

I say that to say that in my time I have met some people—not many, thank God—that are just *bad*. Just bad, just bad, just *bad* to the core. No remediation for them. If they go to jail, they'll come out and they'll be bad all over again. No elixir, no pill, no nothing. Even Bishop Shaw couldn't save them. We told the truancy lady, but she couldn't do anything with them—Miss McQueen—she had a pearl-handled pistol, but she couldn't stop them from jumping out of those trees. And the thing that was so unreasonable was they would take enough lunches to feed an *army*. I could never understand how they could eat them all.

Nightmare—George and Blue.

At that time, we had games that they don't play now. On every corner you could find men, big men, playing checkers. Fourth Avenue was a place where they played checkers, and pool—and my dad had a chess set. He had an ivory chess set he'd brought back from England; I guess he played it all by himself, because there weren't many people interested in chess. But he had all these things he'd brought back from England.

Of course, this is during the Depression—and I think the Depression lasted longer for our folk, in our community, than it did for other folks—but we had a toy called a roller-packer: that was a tin can that you stuffed with dirt, and you had a clothes hanger you stuck in there. You rolled that up and down the street. Every little boy had his roller-packer. And we had kites; you *made* your kites. You could make your own paste, and take some newspaper and some sticks and make your kite.

The biggest thing was: on Christmas morning—early, early in the morning—you would hear the skates. Everybody had a pair or skates. I guess they must have stayed up all night waiting to put them on. And you had to do what they called the "eagle split": that was a rite of passage. You were supposed to be a *brave* fellow if you would go to Center Street hill—that's what was called Bomb Hill in later years, or Dynamite Hill—and you started going straight down that hill, and then you'd *jump* around, backwards. If you didn't hit the ground, you were accepted among the teenagers, or among those who were gifted. But Christmas would be a day when you saw a lot of kids coming home with tears in their eyes, holding their legs where they'd been injured, jumping off of Center Street hill.

Across the street from Tanglefoot Carson's store was a fellow that was real tall, and he was the one that mastered the eagle split first. His name was Nathan—Nathaniel Young—but everyone called him "Man." Because Man could fix everything—Man could fix toasters and make baseball gloves out of old rugs—and he devised a thing where you took a two-by-four and took apart a worn-out skate, and made the doggonest *scooter* you ever saw. We called them "skate-a-mores."

One of the things I remember the most: Mr. Carson's grocery store used to sell what we called a Black Cow sucker. Now, a Black Cow sucker—you never had one of those; I hope you never do—was a great big piece of malted chocolate. Didn't have any sanitation wrapping on it at all; you just bought the raw sucker. It was made out of the cheapest malted chocolate, that would rot your teeth out in a month's time—when you're young, you get two sets of teeth, but the first ones would always go with the Black Cow suckers. We would chew on these things, and it was like an everlasting piece of candy. You'd go out and you'd suck on it, and then you'd put it in your pocket. You're playing marbles, and when you wanted that sucker, you'd pull it out, no matter how much grit had gotten on it; another little guy was next to you, shooting marbles—"*Hand me your sucker.*"—he'd suck on your sucker, and pass it back. A lot of times you'd get some thread off your clothing, and you'd suck that down, too. Sometimes, if you had any left over, you'd put it over by the bed—*to be continued*—and pick it up in the morning.

Man, that was a time of life. It's a wonder we all didn't die.

I was just beginning my schooling at that time. And one group that was highly respected in those days was the teachers. The general populace of uneducated blacks respected highly those teachers who had graduated from school or had made some success. They understood that their children had to do what the teacher said. If a teacher gave you an F, the parent would give you an F at home.

In the black community, we had people who didn't get to go to school and earn advanced, doctorate degrees; so sometimes, without any credentials, they would give you an honorary title. If you were highly respected in the profession, they'd give you the name of "Fess": that's an abbreviation for "Professor." You could have Fess Jones as a football coach—*Fess* Jones, that's a high title. And of course, at Industrial High School, they had the famous Fess Whatley. He was called that because he taught music and his bands were so good: John T. "*Fess*" Whatley and his Vibraphone Cathedral Orchestra.

Some of those people in that day had so much respect for the schools that they named their children after the school superintendent, Erskine Ramsay. Ramsay High School is named after him. Erskine Faush—a great minister and a great radio personality—his name is Erskine *Ramsay* Faush. Erskine Hawkins was Erskine Ramsay Hawkins. Ramsey was a white superintendent. And that was a commonplace for people to name their children after outstanding people, whether they were white or black.

The first principal I ever heard of was a Mr. Dobbins. He was a fair-skinned fellow, and from what I could see, he was very well educated. They had a place out below Bessemer called Pauline Bray Fletcher Camp—this was just a wooden frame building, but we would go there for picnics because they had a swimming hole behind the property. It had what we called "suck holes" in it, where something would pull you down—and this was one of the first things I knew that was a tragedy. Lincoln School had a picnic, and this little schoolboy was swimming in that pool, and it sucked him down.

This fellow Mr. Dobbins was the principal. He tried to get the boy out, and he drowned; Professor Dobbins drowned trying to save this boy's life. They wrote about it and sometimes they mention it now, but that was a part of the history back there.

Mr. Dobbins was followed by Mr. William Moore—"Professor Moore." Now, if you were at Lincoln School, you had to know all the multiplication tables. At lunch time, Professor Moore would walk up and down the hall, and he would stop you and say: "What's two times two!"

"Four."

"What's eight times eight!"

"Sixty-four."

If you said sixty-three, he'd say: *"Who's your teacher?"*

"Miss Wimberly."

"Come on, go with me . . ." He'd say, "Miss Wimberly, this brother does not know his multiplication tables. He's not going to the lunch room anymore, until you teach him his multiplication tables."

That was it. You never knew when you would have to do without your lunch. Of course, it was nothing but a little cup of milk and some oatmeal cookies—and George and Blue would *steal* all your baloney sandwiches. But that was one of the ways Mr. Moore would test you: *"Spell* that word!" He'd walk the halls, and everybody tried to hide, to get in the lunchroom before Professor Moore could get to you. I remember, he would make the raids in the toilets. They said he pulled somebody off the commode to ask him how to spell *Connecticut.* He was fanatic.

In those days, you had the Bama Preserve Company right down from the school, about a couple of blocks, where they made Bama peanut butter and preserves. Alaga Syrup was another place they had down there. And in the spring, about two o'clock, you couldn't stay in your seat, because the Bama Preserves is going to can all those jams and jellies, and the aroma would come into the classroom. You're so hungry, you can't stand it. You smell those peaches through that window—how could you pay attention to what the verb said to the predicate?

Then we had, down from the school, what they called the "tater chip house." You could go to the tater chip house and buy a bag of cracked potato chips. They were stale, and they would be cracked—there'd just be pieces of them—so you could buy a big bag for about a nickel. You'd sit there on the railroad track and eat these old potato chips till you just fell out. You'd go home, and Mama'd say, "He got the greasy mouth"—you'd have to take a laxative. But you'd sit there and eat those chips—*you* don't know.

I started at Lincoln Elementary in 1934. And when I got to the band room, Mr. Handy—William Wise Handy—was the band director. He was the nephew of William *Christopher* Handy, who wrote the "St. Louis Blues." And he was a brilliant musician.

Mr. Handy told me that I couldn't be in the band, because I was so small and didn't know anything; but he recognized the fact that I was already playing the pieces, so he said, "Well, when we march, you can march on the side of the band." I had this little, small, E-flat clarinet that somebody gave us, and I did that.

Mr. Handy was an absolutely magnificent person, because if you played a saxophone and you broke a reed, which cost a dime—if you couldn't get a dime, Mr. Handy could *make* you a reed. He'd sit there and cut it with his knife and make you one: "Try that." And all the broken instruments, he didn't take them to the shop: he fixed them. He had a torch and he could weld things together. I remember one of the first clarinets I had he put together from two old, broken-down clarinets. It was a hybrid.

He'd give private lessons at his home. He lived in a tremendous home that the great architect, Rayfield, built. He charged a quarter for a lesson that would last an hour; if you didn't have that quarter, he'd say, "Come on anyway, just pay me later." He would insist on giving you the same amount of time, whether you paid him or not.

I remember, he looked like Toscanini. In fact, when I first saw Toscanini's picture, I thought he was related to Mr. Handy. He dressed like a real musician. He had a little goatee, a little beard—I hadn't seen anybody who looked like Mr. Handy. And he talked in that kind of manner, too: if you turned him upside down, he would still be the perfect gentleman.

Before he got to Lincoln School, he taught at the Mount Meigs Reformatory, near Montgomery, a sort of a little prison for bad boys. He came from Alabama State University, and he would take his elementary school band back to Montgomery, to Cramton Bowl, to play at the halftime event between Tuskegee and Alabama State: one of the big, annual college events. I had never been away from home— *Montgomery* was like going to California then. So one day this great bus rolled up on the campus and all of us were packed to go. We stayed in an open building where they had put some cots out, and you had to wash yourself and bathe yourself; some little idiot was making noise all night, and somebody got scared and couldn't wait for home. But there we were. And we simply played music. You know how the college bands will make all kinds of formations on the field—they'll spell out the temperature or something—we would just go round in a circle

Lincoln Elementary band, ca. 1938. Frank Adams is in the second row, ninth from the left, with clarinet. Courtesy of Frank Adams.

and round in a circle and wind all up and then come out. That was our half-time show: a circle.

Then there were the wonderful band concerts and variety shows produced by Mr. Handy and the Lincoln School teachers. We would have the variety shows at the high school, because we didn't have an auditorium to accommodate us. We looked forward to this event because it gave us a chance to visit and perform on the stage of the great Industrial High School. Every year, that was our main fund-raising event. We would play complex stuff like "Princes of India"—things that the *high school* band couldn't play. We would play something like an excerpt from Tchaikovsky, and Mr. Handy would introduce one of his own compositions, like the "Zenith Overture," or the "Twentieth Century Overture," which I still remember now. Mr. Handy would be in his uniform, and we would play this classical music.

What I remember most were the parades. We played in the annual Armistice Day parade—we call it Veterans Day now—and they would have all the bands come out. All the black bands were placed in the back of the parade, and although we played with fervor, the big problem, with all the horses in front of us, was how to avoid stepping in horse manure. Eventually Mr. Handy stopped the band from participating in the Armistice parade. Our parents understood and appreciated Mr. Handy's decision. He said that that was an insult.

The fraternal societies would also have their annual parades—and the ones I loved the most were the Odd Fellows. They rode horses and were completely attired in Roman armor, including breastplates, helmets, and spears. I can see them now. They had these horses, and the horses would rare up. This was scary to me—they were just doing it for show, but this horse would rare up, man, and you didn't know whether you'd be stampeded—everybody's jumping out of the way— then all of them would unsheathe their spears. Good God almighty. You can imagine if you were a youngster and you hadn't seen anything like this: "Look-a-there! Look-a-there!" We could hardly parade with them.

Spectators, I don't care where they would live—they could be in Mountain Brook or Pelham, or wherever—when they found out that there was going to be an Odd Fellows parade, white, black, blue, green would come to watch. We all enjoyed that.

These parades would be an all-day affair. They would go from Eighth Avenue North to where we have UAB South now—block after block after block—that was a long, long parade. But it was all happiness. You didn't get tired, because there were so many exciting things to see. You'd get to the church, and it would be at least a four-hour service after you had several preachers preaching and all the ceremonies that went with it. The Masons or the Pythians would have a song— like, they would take "My Country 'Tis of Thee," but it would be:

God bless our knightly band
Firmly they ever stand
From storm and rain

Something like that. The band would play and they would sing. And the parades didn't just end at the church: the grueling part of it was that you had to march back to the place of origin! It would take you two and a half hours or more to *get* to the place, and then two and a half hours coming back home. But that was exciting to me, because I had so much energy. And it was exciting to the people, because they got to see the parade twice. They took pride in the duration of those programs. And I guess it's in some people's nature to want to celebrate. So it wouldn't be over until the last band would get back. Then, if the spirit was high, the bands would meet up and blow—they'd challenge each other.

We had a fellow, they called him "Black Jack." I don't know how long he stayed in elementary school, but he was our drum major for years and years. He would take the mace, this huge baton that's in front of the band, and he would throw it up; it would go up above the telephone wires, and he would *catch* it on the march. He never missed it. We had what we called the second line: youngsters and parents that followed the band, and watched Jack throw that baton. Everybody would be waiting to see if he'd drop it, or if it would go back behind him, but he was always in front, and *boom,* he'd catch it, right on time.

I don't know how Jack stayed in school for so long, but he was our superstar.

The thing about it was: the parade gave us, really, a chance to see humanity. They had some people that would have these little wagons, these little push carts, and they had what they called tamales, a beef that's encased in a corn shuck. I remember the guys who had the popsicle wagon, and there was one man selling potato chips, popcorn, candy, whatever they could get their hands on—so you could get a hot tamale or a taste of lemonade.

There was a trumpet player in Mr. Handy's band—he was *such* a trumpet player—Elliott Knox. They called him "Blue Jesus." And I remember, one of the most impressive things that I ever heard was they had a song called "My Old Kentucky Home," and he played a thing, "Massa's in the Cold, Cold Ground." He went out one day, it was drizzling rain, but Mr. Handy sent him out there on the school ground and he played "Carry Me Back to Old Virginia" on that trumpet. It was raining down—all the people in the building came to the window, looking at him playing all the variations. I said, "Great God"; it impressed me. It impressed everybody at that school. If somebody got out there now and played "Massa's in the Cold, Cold Ground," or "My Old Kentucky Home," or "Swanee River"—"where the darkies all play," or whatever it was—if you did that today, they'd say, "What kind of idiot are you, playing that, or having my *child* play that?" But it was beautiful music, and it's still beautiful music. Your life would have been changed if you heard that boy. He must have been in about the sixth grade, seventh grade, and he had mastered that trumpet like a virtuoso. He could triple-tongue and double-tongue, and Mr. Handy had trained him. Elliott Knox: Blue Jesus.

Mr. Handy had his own way of doing things. Some people didn't like

William Wise Handy, ca. 1940s. Courtesy of the Birmingham
Public Library, Department of Archives and Manuscripts,
J. L. Lowe Collection.

Mr. Handy because he wrote his notes backwards: on a staff, where the
note goes to the left, his notes would go to the right. But we learned
that way: it was backwards, but it was right. And Mr. Handy had a different way of counting music. Usually if you have a triplet in music,
you say, "da-da-da," or "one-two-three"; but he said, "That's *down*, and
this is *up*. And in between that you turn your foot to the side—that's
mash. So it's: *down-mash-up; down-mash-up*." That was his method.
Move your foot, *down; mash* to the side; then *up*—it's exact. When I
got to Duke's band, the first night we played "Caravan"; I was doing
that, *down-mash-up,* and the guys were watching my feet—they said,
"Yeah, he's got it!" Mr. Gordon—Amos Gordon, who did the arrange-

ments for Louis Armstrong's orchestra and is in the Hall of Fame—he played that way, too. *Down-mash-up:* Mr. Handy's method.

The biggest thing was: Mr. Handy would instill in us that everything we played, we had to *remember*. People said that they wouldn't promote Mr. Handy to the high school because he didn't teach the reading of music. But that was not the case. Mr. Handy had the first audio-visual aids: he had written the notes on a screen, a pull-down shade, and he'd pull it down. We had never seen that before. Then he had a wire recorder. Every time we would play, he'd tape it on this wire recorder, and we could hear it back. Professor *Whatley,* over at the high school, didn't have all that.

Mr. Handy did teach reading—he just insisted on drilling and learning things to memory. His thing was, if you're parading somewhere, and you're looking at the music, you could fall in a ditch. Most people thought that if you could read the music, that was intellectual—to sit there and *read* it—but he was saying that you have to *own* the piece, and you can't own it unless you memorize it. So we trained our memories.

Mr. Handy was sort of an unsung hero. He was a tremendous teacher. In fact, if there hadn't been Mr. Handy at the elementary school, Professor Whatley never would admit it, but there probably never would have been a *high* school band. Because that's where we got our formal training and technique together: with Mr. Handy. He taught us the fundamentals.

When I got to the high school, I could play everything I could hear.

4

"Fess"

WHEN I GOT TO THE HIGH SCHOOL, IT WAS DURING the forties, during the Second World War. Professor "Fess" Whatley taught printing at the school, but he was famous all over the country for producing these great musicians like Erskine Hawkins—and his band, the Vibraphone Cathedral Orchestra, played all the dances in Birmingham. When I got there, all of Fess's musicians had gone off to the military—the Tuskegee Army Band, the Navy Band, all across the country they volunteered for those places—so he had to find somebody to take their places in his orchestra.

This was where I think a big change came in my life, because I had a good passion for music, but I had no interest in playing *jazz* music. I didn't even listen to it. But Professor Whatley called me in his office and said, "You're going to take the place of Mr. Amos Gordon, my lead saxophone player." I didn't know what he was talking about—but I knew that I didn't want to be in his band. I had heard never to even go *near* Fess Whatley. All the disciplinary problems at the school would come to him, and I'd heard about how ferocious he was. So when he gave me that *demand,* he said, "Go tell your mother that she's going to have to buy you a saxophone. I heard that you could read music pretty good . . ." Well, I had a good *memory,* really: I couldn't read that much, but I could memorize what I played.

I went home and I told my mom. I made up a story. I said, "Mom, that man wants me to play in that orchestra, his Vibraphonic Orchestra"— I couldn't even pronounce it—"and they stay up at night and they're much older than I am, and I don't want to do it, because"—this is the biggest tale—"*I want to make the A-B Honor Roll in high school.* And this is my first year, and I really just want to play in the *marching* band. But *those* fellows stay out late, and they're sleepy all the time, Mom . . ."

She was knitting and didn't pay much attention—I didn't *think* she paid much attention. I thought I could *win* this one, because it was during the aftermath of the Depression, and I said, "Times are hard, Mom, and my brother, Oscar, and I have *clarinets,* and we don't want saxophones. I don't know anything *about* a saxophone; I don't want to *learn* anything about a saxophone. And they *cost* too much, Mom." I said, "You and Dad *sacrifice* for us . . ." I could make a speech, you know.

She put down that knitting and she said, "Listen. Not only are you going to play sax—we'll get you a saxophone—you're going to go back and tell Professor Whatley you're going to do *everything* he tells you to do."

I was utterly, utterly defeated. It felt like I had received a prison sentence.

As I say, Professor Whatley was the disciplinarian supreme. He was like a legend in the community, and his longevity really made him respected. And he had something nobody else had: he had three Cadillacs. He had three *long* Cadillacs, man, and he would haul the band in these Cadillacs. He loved them; it was a passion with him. If any little thing touched on one of them, he'd take it over to Drennen Motors, and Drennen would be proud to fix it. And Fess was a stickler: you couldn't eat any peanuts in that car. That was bad luck. If he had two or three cars driving somewhere for a performance, the one in front had to be the leader. If it swerved just one iota, he would stop it and change drivers.

Fess had these Cadillacs parked around the school when we were getting ready to go to Tuskegee or somewhere. He'd have his students shine them up and put wax on them. Those were his precious gems. And he was the first one to have an alarm in his cars—so if a kid would come up, look at it, and touch it, a horn would blow. He'd be in that printing shop, and that was it: you just stood there with your hands in the air, waiting for him to come. He had this fraternity paddle; he'd come out with that paddle, and you'd get a lick for every time that horn blew. He wouldn't say anything to you at all; he'd just come out with that board—WHAM! And nobody in the school would complain about it. You might think, maybe somebody in the community

Fess Whatley and Cadillac. Courtesy of the Birmingham Public Library, Department of Archives and Manuscripts, J. L. Lowe Collection.

would say something about this guy, but it wasn't like that. They respected him so much that if you went home and told somebody that you touched on Mr. Whatley's car, they'd probably hit you *again*. You had no logical way out of it.

I was at Alabama State years later, talking to my friend Dr. Lyle. He was a good player. He went off to Florida A&M and got to be a terrific band director. He came back and he developed Alabama State's band. The first year he was there, he sent for me, for one of his workshops. And he said, "Remember that time we were playing 'Stars and Stripes Forever' and it had that little middle part for a clarinet?" He said Fess Whatley had come up from the basement—like somebody *flying*—and threw him down on the ground, and started *hitting* him. "He claimed I made a bad note. And," he said, "that was so embarrassing!"

You have to remember, Fess Whatley was never officially the band director. The whole time he was at that school he taught printing. The director was right there directing the band. My first band director was

Wilton Robinson, an excellent teacher; he got drafted in the war and was followed by George Hudson, who taught there for many years. Now how would you feel if somebody would come in your class—say you're teaching English, or math—they come in and beat one of your students for making a mistake? You're supposed to be the director, teaching them, and here comes somebody over you, sailing through the air; just jumps, *bam,* on the students.

But that was Professor Whatley.

He was a person that everything, *everything* had to be in order. He was committed to the school. And one of his responsibilities was to get everybody in class. Some stragglers would come and he would take that paddle and run them in there. If his band didn't get back until early in the morning, he'd just go down to the school; he'd change clothes and go to sleep on top of the composing slab in the printing room. Then he'd be up at seven o'clock to catch those who were late to school. That was his dedication. If you were in his band and the band had gotten in late, he would go around the building to make sure you weren't sleeping in your classes. He'd hold your money until the end of the day, and you wouldn't get paid if you fell asleep in class.

I didn't like to be in a situation that was so autocratic. I couldn't understand why he was so demanding, but I found out that that was the way he had to be, to discipline all those students who went on to greatness: because he insisted on certain things like punctuality and neatness. He insisted on perfection. The way you dressed had to be just right; the time you got to a job had to be *precisely* right; the time you *finished* had to be precisely right. He was just like a clock. And we had to practice and practice.

Professor Whatley's discipline—so far as the *reading* of music, and the *exactness* of it—was what appealed to Benny Goodman and Cab Calloway, and Duke Ellington and all those people; because they knew that if you had been trained by Whatley, you would be well disciplined. You wouldn't cut up crazy, you would be on time—because you would think about Fess Whatley.

The main thing was you were able to read the music quickly. At that time, bands were expanding. And Fess always insisted on having a large band, like Fletcher Henderson or Duke Ellington. The thing about the size of a band was: the more people you put in there, the more importance on reading music. You could take just a clarinet and

Birmingham's first jazz band, the Jazz Demons, 1920s. Fess Whatley, second from left. Courtesy of the Birmingham Public Library, Department of Archives and Manuscripts, J. L. Lowe Collection.

a trumpet and a rhythm section, and you could each go your own way—like a Dixieland band, it's got all these contrapuntal parts going at the same time, different instruments going up against each other—but when you had a *big* band, when you had one saxophone and you added two more to get a certain sound, every man couldn't go for himself. You had to have harmony. You had to be in a section. You had to have an arrangement, and that called for the reading of music.

That's where Whatley's forte was: in teaching reading. Whatley saw all that coming. After he got to the high school in the early twenties, he developed that reputation that got across the country: that "this man here, in this one black high school, he's teaching the guys to *read.* So check with Professor Whatley." The other thing was the discipline. Those guys who had been having a lot of problems in their bands with alcoholism and dope, all kinds of things like that—they said, "Well, let's get this guy from Birmingham."

Improvisation—making things up—*wasn't* his forte. His thing was *not* making up things. But that was why he was so successful, because he insisted on you being mechanical. If you played "In the Mood," you played it just like it was written.

You have to understand: Industrial High School was started around 1900, and it was a school where the industrial arts were taught, like sewing, cooking, and woodworking, and then band—which was not an *industrial* discipline, but it was taken and taught in that manner. Of course, they had more conventional courses, too—reading and writing and arithmetic and history—which were all taught in the main building. All the industrial work was done in two separate buildings, one for girls and one for boys. You would have band every day; or workshop every day; or cooking, sewing every day. And Industrial High School was known all over the world for its curriculum.

Those things that we call "frill" courses were *major* courses. When you got to the high school and took music, it wasn't just playing in the band, or going to this elective, maybe, once a week: they were teaching a *vocation* in that study. Music was just as important as history—because, they said, this may be your life! If you don't have to a chance to be a doctor or a lawyer, you might get to be a schoolteacher—that was a high place in the professions—and if you didn't do that, you had your band; you had your music; you had your sewing or your woodworking or your printing to survive on.

I guess it followed the theory of Booker T. Washington, who felt that you should do those kinds of manual disciplines, and then develop into other, more scholarly areas. It was not like you were being prepared for college: you were being prepared to go out and *work* after the four years of industrial training. If you couldn't get a college education, you had to survive. Like Booker T. Washington said, you let down your bucket where you are. You had DuBois, the other philosopher, who said, "No, you're supposed to have a full education: forget about all that *hand* stuff"—but the people had just come out of slavery, to a certain extent, and they needed to be taught a practical skill. So Fess Whatley and a few of the others were so smart, they put band in as a manual-arts discipline. And this music thing was serious business.

In the school system, so far as music was concerned, segregation actually worked to our advantage—because you had more time on task. If Fess Whatley assigned you to the auditorium period and you were in charge of the band, you were a professional musician. Listen: you went to the class, the regular band class; you went to the band practice that was scheduled during the day; and if you were directing something, you did *that* for an hour a day. So you spent three and a half hours working on your craft: your music. If you had a football game, you'd be there *after* school. Now, that's ridiculous, that's too much time on it, but it was what they wanted to do with you. People may say, "This is out of balance." But it's not out of balance when you're looking at the end result. If you want a plumber, everything else is nice, too, but you concentrate on his plumbing.

That's the difference with an *industrial* high school.

Of course, the schools in those days were separate and unequal. But even though it was unequal, sometimes something that's not the way it *should* be can work to your advantage. If it had been equal, I wouldn't have learned as much about music as I did. I wouldn't have had the opportunity. Those were times when certain people would say, "My goodness. I'm going down in the mines and digging coal, and this guy's going to New York City—playing a doggone horn!" When the parents saw that, they said, "Uh-huh. My child is *gifted.*" Gifted for what? "Gifted for what he's trying to do. He's motivated."

In that school and in that community, there was a seriousness about *being* serious. They had a certain spirit about education. They felt at that school, for years and years, that they were not equal to Wood-lawn High School, the white high school up the street—they felt they were *better.* They *were,* because they concentrated on what they were doing. They had oratorical contests all the time, and an assembly program where they put these plays together—Mr. Jones, Bobby Jones, would put on these Shakespearean plays. You had those who strived so hard that it became unequal on the other end: Philips High School, Woodlawn High School, could never produce an oratorical team like Parker High School. They could never produce a choir or a band like Parker High School, because it wasn't *necessary* for them to do that. It wasn't a life-or-death situation like Professor Whatley had.

I remember, vividly, every day there was an assembly program. We had these slogans—this year's is "Making Work Worthwhile"; "Being Honorable"; "Count on Education"—every year there was a slogan. And Mrs. Roosevelt—Franklin Delano Roosevelt's wife—and even W. C. Handy and Mary MacLeod Bethune would come and talk to the students. We'd have people come and speak on these slogans.

There was a band up in the balcony that played for the students to march in, and if you got a chance to lead that band, that meant that you were really successful. I was leading the band, maybe about nine of us up there. Professor Whatley would come in, and it was embarrassing to me, in a way, because he had that paddle, and he would hit people with this thing. I don't care if the *president* was there, he was going to come in with this paddle. Everybody had to stand up together, and they had these folding chairs—if the chair made noise when you stood up, you didn't pass out after the assembly. You waited for Professor Whatley with his paddle. And I was so embarrassed at him doing this.

Eleanor Roosevelt came and she made a speech, and the high school choir was just magnificent. Because if you went to school there, you had a certain section to seat yourself in—the altos would be in one row, the tenors would be in another row—and that went for the whole school, thousands of students. You'd know that you were a soprano, so you'd sit over here; if you were a bass, you knew that you sit in the back somewhere. They had these little young voices, they had the tenors and all—and that was organized in your schedule, for thousands of youngsters.

At most schools, in an assembly program, somebody just comes up and sings "My Country 'Tis of Thee," and it sounds good. But when Eleanor Roosevelt stood up and heard this mass of people—the whole school, singing in *harmony*—that was such a thrilling sound that she said on stage she had never, *never* heard anything like that. It sounded like a cathedral choir.

No other school had thought to do that.

I remember, for W. C. Handy, when he came for one of these assemblies: Professor Whatley would just pass the music up for his "Saint Louis Blues"—and you'd *better* not miss a note. You have W. C. Handy down on the stage with his trumpet, and we're playing "Dah dee-dah daaah!"—the *"Saint Louis Blues,"* baby, looking at it for the first time!

When I left there, I was probably as knowledgeable as I am now about instruments.

It would surprise you: we couldn't afford to see Erskine Hawkins's band when he came to town—the tickets were probably a dollar and fifty cents—but because he'd been a student there and taught by Professor Whatley, Erskine Hawkins would bring his whole band, *in uniform*, to play at the school *before* the big dance. And that was so inspiring. We worshipped those guys, because they were so well dressed—very few of us had tuxedos—and they had their hair processed and all. They were treated like gods. When they played at Parker, it was that they were *home*. And when those big pieces would come out, like "Tuxedo

Junction"—nobody could play them except Fess Whatley, because he had these copies from Erskine Hawkins. Erskine Hawkins would copy those pieces by hand, all those great pieces, and send them to Professor Whatley.

If you were Fess Whatley's student, he pretty well demanded certain things of you in your personal life. I know a certain instance where a musician was mistreating his wife in Chicago, and Fess Whatley got word of it . . . you might find him at the door of your house—*boom!*— he'd knock you out. A former student! He'd check up on them. He would go to New York City every year to find out what they were doing. He had so many up there. And if they needed something he would help them out.

Haywood Henry is one of the examples of that. Haywood Henry played with Erskine Hawkins for many years. He would send for Fess Whatley and give him a two-week vacation in New York. He'd take him to the productions, like *Phantom of the Opera* or *Annie, Get Your Gun,* because he was playing in the pit.

Once you were a student of Professor Whatley, you were his student for life.

I see some musicians now in New York City and California: they mention Fess Whatley, and they'll *lie* and say, "I played in his band." A lot of musicians claim him, but some of them didn't get to know him until later. Now, Whatley's influence is shown by all those people that are in the Alabama Jazz Hall of Fame. He has about 90 percent of them, but there were some who never got to Fess Whatley. Some of them went off with Reverend Becton, straight out of Mr. Handy's class. Some of them were at the high school, but they never got a chance to be in Whatley's band. The thing is, you didn't have but thirty-five or forty uniforms in the band, and he would only take as many musicians as he had uniforms. So here's a little guy that started school with you: he's still there at graduation time, and never got a chance to play. But he was *there.* He could probably rehearse in the band room, but he couldn't go in a public performance, because he had no uniform. Probably a lot of the students that could have become great musicians didn't have a chance to play.

Now, in Mr. Handy's band, he had a way you could *make* the uniforms. He had improvised uniforms: buy some white trousers; you've *got* a coat; put your tie on, black—a little bow tie if you've got one; if not, a string tie. You've got some black shoes—that's it. A little Pop-eye cap costs twenty-five cents; that was some money then, but he'd buy them by the box.

Some schools today would spend thousands of dollars for a uniform. But there's a certain thing about life when you have to get your little trousers and sew them together, shine your shoes, and all that kind of thing. That's part of it. Somebody took your cap, you've got to buy another twenty-five-cent cap. Now, that's a big deal.

The point is: in Mr. Handy's band, if you wanted to play, you could play. If you couldn't get an instrument, he had his own instruments you could borrow—or he'd make you one. So where Professor Whatley would have, maybe, forty pieces at most, Mr. Handy would have a hundred and fifty. The Lincoln band and the high school band would meet up at the Elks parade every year—Mr. Handy's band would be there waiting, and they'd blow the high school band away! The Lincoln students were so small, but there just were so *many* of them.

Another difference was that, in Mr. Handy's band, he had the little girls and he had the boys; he didn't discriminate. Whatley had no girls in there. He said that marching was just too much for the girls to do. After I started teaching school, some years later, I thought about that, and I didn't exclude *any* students.

I learned that when you exclude people, you can make an awful mistake.

All the time that I was in high school, the students had to wear khaki trousers—until your last year, they let you wear black serge. The young ladies wore blue dresses, and when they got to their senior year, they wore white dresses. You had to be in uniform all the time. And—*guess who*—Professor Whatley was in charge of all that. You would come to school, and if you didn't have your uniform, you had to go back home. There weren't any excuses. If you came and they noticed the uniform wasn't clean, they would make you go in the restroom somewhere, and they would send it to the cleaners across the street and have it cleaned for you. If you were that pitiful, that you couldn't keep your uniform clean—you don't stay away from school because of *that*. But they're not going to let you sit up in here with the wrong kind of thing on. That was the discipline.

Of course, the uniforms were designed so no one would feel inferior, or one student wouldn't seem more affluent in dress than another one. That worked out well. But in society as it was at that time, there was always the desire to be a little different. So you would attempt to add something unique to the uniform. Students would buy the most expensive shoes, which were Edwin Clapps. Edwin Clapp shoes had white strings around the soles. And you were judged by how clean you kept those white strings. A girl would look down and see your shoes, and if they weren't Edwin Clapps and they weren't clean, you were out. So you would take peroxide or something and go over them, and they had to be of a very high quality. Some would work a year or two years to get a pair of Edwin Clapps; you could pay down, pay down, pay down, and in a year you'd get the shoes. Of course, it would be horrible if somebody *stepped* on your shoes—you're ready to fight if somebody steps on them. That seems to be a rather simplistic way of thinking, but that was important then.

We had some who were affluent and some who barely eked out a living, but they all took pride in that uniform. I look at the children going to school now with their shirttails out and wearing their hair all different ways; I say, what would happen if Fess Whatley saw that? He would probably drop dead or have a stroke. He would be sincerely angry—everybody would. If you came to a high school today with a bow tie on and your shirttail in and a suit on, they'd run you away before class is out. They don't know about Fess Whatley. You can't tell youngsters to keep their shirttails in if they don't know that years ago it was an *art* form tucking your shirttail in.

It was strict discipline in those days, and you just conformed. It *had* to be strict discipline because it was the only school for blacks, and the enrollment was up in the thousands. When you were walking the halls, you lined up in pairs—you had so many students they couldn't do it any other way. It was a given that you had to line up, or you'd crash into somebody. Your clothes had to be clean, or else you'd have a *plague* in school. People were afraid of things like tuberculosis—all kinds of disease—chicken pox, and measles and mumps, and everything. When I was going to school, we had what we called tetter: your hair would come out and you'd have sores and you had to wear a stocking cap, and everybody knew you had the tetter.

I was thinking the other day about two things that really plagued black people for many years. One was a kind of gum disease: people would die because their system would be poisoned from teeth that should have been extracted. The blacks didn't have dentistry anywhere near what the others had, or anywhere near what we have today. If you had a tooth abscess, it would poison your system. People were dying every week, just from that gum disease. The other thing was tuberculosis. Later on, when I taught at Lincoln, we had big games, football games and basketball, dedicated to getting money to eradicate tuberculosis. I've got trophies in my house now, where the band played for the TB Games.

We had something, in those days, called an asphidity bag: it was common in the school, when they had these outbreaks. This would be a little bag that you'd wear around your neck, that had chicken gizzards, or rotten cheese, or whatever it was—whatever they could put in there that would *smell*. That was supposed to get rid of all the vermin and diseases. Then they had a thing called eight-day pneumonia: if you hadn't died after eight days, you would survive. For the eight-day pneumonia they had some *cow-dung* tea. You would have a terrible fever, and you'd drink that, and the Missionary Society sisters would come and sing for you, like they did for Finktum. They would sing, they would sing, and the poor person would usually survive.

Grandma was one of the ones in the Missionary Society that was supposed to have some knowledge of medicines, and she would take me with her. When I was a little fellow, I would carry water or something and be standing by the bedside. She knew all these weeds and things that would eliminate those illnesses. Those were the kinds of medicines they had; I guess it came from tribal times. Sometimes they made you *wish* you were dead, so you wouldn't have to take that cow-dung tea—but you'd start perspiring, perspiring, perspiring, and the choir would sing.

All of that was just a part of my growing up. And so the schools knew: if everything wasn't exactly in its place, you would just about have a plague breaking out.

I remember at the Elks Rest, they had the senior prom. And guess where I was: sitting up there, playing in Fess Whatley's orchestra. I played in the band my senior prom. It was understood: you're a musician, you play. That was first. It was like, "Hey, you can dance some other time." No matter who the girl is, you can't dance; you've got to be sitting up there playing. But I understood that.

Fess instilled in all of us that the music, that was what you were supposed to do. When we would go to rich people's houses and they would offer us food, he said, "No. Don't forget what you came for. You're not the guest, you're performers." You were at, say, the Jewish country club, and they would offer—"Listen, have some of this food, fellows"—and you couldn't do it. You had to go hungry until you got home.

Professor Whatley played for all of the dances, white and black. He would always say that the reason they called him to play the celebrity dances and things in the rich neighborhoods was because he did the best job. You could have a cousin who has an orchestra, and he goes up to you: "Can't you hire me?" You'd probably say, "No, we just prefer Professor Whatley." Because they are perfect. They're professionals. They could play waltzes, they could play mazurkas and that kind of thing. If they played a Jewish club, they'd play some of the Jewish music, and Fess would have music prepared for the Bar Mitzvahs. He knew the ceremonies; he knew what music was called for the dad and the mother to dance, and the son and his wife to dance; he knew all that to a T. He would even tell *them* how to do it sometimes—that "this doesn't go here, this goes here"—and they'd thank him.

Another thing about Fess Whatley: he insisted that every musician carry an ax. There was a group of musicians—I think this was in Natchez, Mississippi, somewhere—they had a fire that broke out and they couldn't get out of the ballroom, so they were burned up. Fess Whatley read it, because it was on the head of the newspaper in Birmingham—so he bought these axes. They were in boxes, about four boxes. He would take those into the place before the instruments, because he said you might have to cut your way out. He was always very, very enlightened about safety.

Fess would always play at the Elks Club and the Masonic Temple; that's where he had his matinees. He had a number called "Kokomo." "Kokomo" was a slow blues, and he had a herald trumpet, a long herald trumpet that would reach across the bandstand, out into the audience. He had this little break: he would play, "Doo-doo-doo, *bomp,* doo-doo-doo, *bomp.*" He would take this trumpet, it would be out over the audience, and the boys would swing the girls out—when he made that little break, that little "Doo-doo-doo, *bomp*," you'd pull her back to you, and squeeze her, *close.* They would do that, and he would stop right in the middle of it and call them "nasty little rascals." Now, they'd *paid* to come to this event, but because he was a schoolteacher, he'd say, "You nasty little rascals! Get back, off of that girl!"

Of course, I sat up there, I didn't know what it was all about; I wasn't into sex or anything. I just wondered, what in the world are they fussing about? *I* didn't know what the nasty little rascals were doing. But he'd holler at them. And Mr. Caswell, the drummer, would say, "Fess, let 'em have some fun!"

It dawned on me, after I had matured a little bit: I thought, now why would he have the audacity to go and *make* that break—and then scream at them? He didn't have to do that. Then, before the dance was over, he'd do it again! He'd go to the edge of the stage, and that trumpet was *long*—he'd bought that thing for that occasion—and it would be out in the audience: "Doo-doo-doo, *bomp!*" The students who had been there earlier, instead of grabbing their partner and pulling her close, they'd walk up to her, scared: "*I'm* not going to do it!"

Another place I got to play in Birmingham was the Tutwiler Hotel; it was a fabulous hotel for whites, and it had the Gold Room, with these gilded gold ornamentations. They had these big dances, and Professor Whatley would go there all the time.

One day we were playing a dance there. I had been playing in the band for a good little while. And with Fess, you had to have a tuxedo; I had this tuxedo on that I bought at the pawn shop. I paid a dollar and forty cents for it at Cohen's Pawn Shop. The rest of them had good tuxedos, too, but mine was different. It was fabulous. It was a rich man's coat, because it had a little flower in the lapel, and a vest. The others just had regular tuxedos, like the one I have now. But this one had a frock tailcoat to it, like my dad's—I don't know why anybody pawned it, he must have been in some pretty bad shape. I got that coat, and every time I'd turn around, the little flap tail would spin out. Everybody'd say, "Good God, here comes the preacher!" I kept that tuxedo through graduate school.

We were going up the service elevator to go to the Gold Room.

And Professor Whatley looked at me—I thought he was looking at my tuxedo—but he said, "You are late. And I'm going to take all of your money for the night's engagement."

Now something boiled up in me. I was scared of Fess Whatley, but to take *all* my money? It wasn't much, but I wanted that money.

I said, "Mr. Whatley, why would you take *all* of my money?"—this is logic, man—I said, "Why don't you just fine me like you do some of the older musicians?"

He said, "You are *late!*"

I couldn't figure this out. I wanted to tell him, "How could we be on the same elevator, at the same time, going to the *same* place, to play the same gig—and I'm *late?*" But if I said that, I'd be dead. So I asked him, "Why don't you just fine me?"

I saw a look on his face that I had never seen before. He said, "You're late because I *said* you are late." And said, "I want to tell you, little man, something"—*little man;* he just defrocked me, you know what I mean?—"that you remember for the rest of your life."

He said: "If I had a date with the devil, I'd get there fifteen minutes early, to find out what the *hell* he wanted with me!"

There wasn't any way in the world for me to comprehend that. Fifteen minutes early to find out what the hell he wanted. This was Professor Whatley.

I said, "My God, this is the end of the road. There's nothing I can do to change his thinking about me." I went through high school with him and learned so much, but there wasn't that closeness between us, like some students had: it was like there was nothing I could do to satisfy him. Others could do it, but I'm not his preferred people.

I found out in later years that he meant well, and he helped me. When I got ready to go to Howard University, he told me how to transfer my union card. And in fact, I was a pallbearer—he picked the ones he wanted—at his funeral.

As far as the unions go: Fess and Pops Williams started the first musicians union for blacks in Birmingham. Now Pops goes way back; he was one of Birmingham's first jazz musicians, and he and Fess Whatley really believed in the union. The unions were segregated then—the black local was 733, and the white local was 256. You had to join the musicians union when you were twelve or thirteen years old; whenever you picked up the horn and started playing, Fess insisted on you joining. I've been the vice president on the executive board for many years now with the union, and the way that came about was playing for Professor Whatley. He made you get a union card.

Fess had gone to the national union conventions, and they embraced him. He loved the national union. And whereas, probably, the white local would be a little lax on some things—not Fess Whatley. It was just like religion to him. You had to have your deposits on time and everything.

When I was coming up in high school was the beginning of those bands like Louis Jordan and the Timpani Five, that had just five pieces in it. That was when I heard Fess Whatley complaining. He called them "bobtail" bands—because he said their tails were cut off. He thought a band should have at least fourteen pieces. "How are you going to pay all that money to just *five* musicians? Where's the female singer? Where's the male singer?" He begrudged them, because they made a lot of money, and he said that they were going to kill it. A band like Louis Jordan would come in there with five or six pieces and clean up, and because Fess was a union man, he didn't think it was fair to the other musicians. He couldn't stand Louis Jordan. So when I went to Washington, DC, he said, "Go transfer your union card so you can work and help pay your way through college. *But don't get in one of those bobtail bands.*"

In all of his greatness, Professor Whatley believed in a certain amount of conforming. He didn't want you to be a troublemaker. He said of Benny Carter, of his playing ability: "He's first class, first class, nothing like him. He's the last word. But," he said, "he's a devil." Benny Carter was a master musician, and it got to be in all the black papers that he was going to arrange music for the movies. "He's going out there in Hollywood: you'd better *watch* that man, he's going to tear it up. He's going to be a troublemaker. No, Hollywood's not going to be the same after that rascal gets out of there. Watch and see, watch and see."

I remember Fess talking about Duke Ellington when he would come to play at the Masonic Temple. Duke had this elaborate contract. He had to have a Steinway piano, and he had to have it tuned thirty minutes before the performance. Not before that. That Steinway had to be tuned on stage. That was in the contract. He had everybody's name on there: what is *he* supposed to get, what is *he* supposed to get. They have to have some kind of food after the program, and they would end at precisely one o'clock, and it would start at nine o'clock, precisely on the hour, eastern standard time or whatever it was. They had to have these bottles of water—nobody else did that. It was all that detailed: they had to have a certain kind of chair in a certain area, and they didn't want anybody drinking within twelve feet of the band, and it had to be checked out by the fire department. All that kind of stuff. And Duke had some people with him to check to see that that was done.

Fess wasn't so pleased about that. "How is he going to come down here and tell us how to tune *our* piano?"

He could never understand that.

When I was playing with Professor Whatley, he would have these trips to Mississippi; to Tuskegee; to all these places. We were going up to Columbus, Mississippi, on the weekends. The distance was pretty long at that time; cars didn't go as fast as they do now. But Fess had this big Cadillac, and if you look at those old cars, they had a little seat in between the backseat and the front seat that you pull out: a little bitty seat you could sit in. Anytime we would go somewhere, he would write down: you sit here, you sit here, and you sit here. He would always have this seating arrangement for the band: where you sit, who would drive, and all that kind of thing. That was good up to the point that he put me *between* two of these little seats, which was *severely* uncomfortable—and I was small, but you're sitting there going to Columbus, Mississippi, and back. And it occurred every time we would go out of town—just about every week. So it got in my mind—I guess it would get in *somebody's* mind to say something—in that instance I suffered so much, I did a thing that probably changed my whole life. I asked Mr. Whatley: why could he not *rotate*.

Little fellow—the *great* Fess Whatley! He was speechless.

I repeated: I said, "Why don't you rotate the seats, Mr. Whatley?" I said, "I've been in this seat for five months now. And it hurts."

Man, he didn't say anything.

I came home the next day. *My mom was crying.* I said, "Mom, what's the matter?" I had never seen my mom cry like that.

She said, "Mr. Whatley was by here." This was during the school day. "And he said what you said to him. And said that you're just an awful little brat, and you're not going to be successful—that if you don't change your ways, you're going to bust Hell wide open!"

Man.

When my *dad* came home, he said: "What did you say he said? *Give me the phone.*"

Uh-oh, boy. I didn't know what was going to happen.

He didn't hesitate. He called up Professor Whatley. He said, "*Whatley.*" He didn't say, "Professor Whatley," he said, "*Whatley.*" My dad was a terror when he got upset. He said, "What the devil are you coming up to *my* house telling my wife?" Said, "You'd better not *ever* do that again! If that boy hadn't said something to you, he wouldn't have been a son of mine!" And he said, "Don't you ever, as long as you live, come by my house for *anything,* especially telling my wife something about my son. You need to keep your behind up there teaching those children."

Now nobody talked to Fess Whatley like that! But he did. Good God almighty—I didn't know what was going on.

"And another thing." He said, "My son, I understand, is a *good* little musician. And he doesn't have to play with your band any longer."

BAM, man.

I said, "Wow."

The next day—I don't know how it happened—but the phone rang. Guess who it was.

Sun Ra.

Sun Ra from outer space! And he said, "Mrs. Adams, I want Frank to play in my *Intergalactic Arkestra.*" Man, Sun Ra had been banned from walking the streets with his crazy outfits on. And to my surprise, my mom said: "*Of course.*" Now Mom was Missionary Society president and—nothing *wrong* with Sun Ra, but everybody knew he just wasn't normal. He was *weird,* man, and for my mom to say that . . .

Dad came home. You never could tell what Dad would do. Dad said: "*I don't see anything wrong with the boy playing with Sun Ra.*"

I thought my folks had gone crazy.

5

Outer Space

THE THING ABOUT IT WAS: YOU WOULD KNOW FROM the very beginning that you were in an *unusual* organization with Sun Ra. Even though I was a youngster, I knew I wouldn't find anybody like that again. You meet some pretty weird people, but not like Sun Ra.

Sun Ra lived across the street from the old Terminal Station in this rickety, raggedy house: I mean, it was terrible. But when you got in there, he was so full of what he was doing. He really *believed* in this outer space thing, and he talked about it all the time. He would say this was this and this was that, and he rehearsed, rehearsed, rehearsed, 'til his band was just a jewel—I mean, it was just a jewel—and he had people in his band that weren't great readers of music, but they could catch on quick. They had this complete musicianship about them.

I first heard, like most people in Birmingham, that there was this *weird* guy—there was always some talk about this fellow that lived near the Terminal Station, in this broken-down house. Nobody would say he was crazy, he just had a reputation for being different. In certain neighborhoods they knew he had a tremendous band, but he was a bandleader that nobody knew where he came from.

He was just *there*.

In those days he was called Herman Blount, or "Sonny": Sonny Blount. And you just couldn't figure him out. Did he have a mother, or did he have a brother? Everything was a mystery about him. We never heard of him eating any *food*—he survived on grapefruit. He would go to Mr. Forbes's music store, the biggest music store in town, and look through all the new music. He would probably be eating on a grapefruit, and he'd take his pen out and a piece of manuscript paper and copy the music. He'd stand there for maybe an hour, and drip grapefruit juice on the music and write it out by hand—he never would *buy* the music. People would be standing back, waiting to be waited on, and no, he wouldn't move. Mr. Forbes would stand and watch him. When he finally got his music, he would say, "Thank you" to the wall or something, and go on out. And everybody understood that.

You would say, because it's segregation and everything, "Why don't they stop you from going in the store?"

He'd say, "They like me."

"Why would they like you, when you're messing everything up?"

"They understand. That I'm a *power*. And really," he said, "we are friends."

He thought about white people that way. He said, "They are my brothers. They are my brothers, but some of them don't know it yet."

Sun Ra would walk the streets of Birmingham with all this crazy garb on, these Egyptian robes and peculiar hats. People would stop and look at him. In the course of time, the police would stop him and they'd say, "Listen. We understand that you have a nice band, but you've got to get off the streets of Birmingham. You've got to get off the streets, because you're *scaring* us."

This was flower power before flower power was ever thought about. This was Dr. King before Dr. King. He walked the streets, so they decided to do something.

They stopped him. "We have told you, time and time again, to get off these streets. Next time, we're going to put you in jail, and we're going to leave you in jail for a long time."

He never said anything.

The very next day, there he was, walking the middle of Fourth Avenue. So the policemen stopped him and said, "Now, we've *told* you that we're going to take this billy club, and we're going to slam it across your head, and we'll put you in jail for a long time."

That was the first time he spoke to them. He said: "No, you won't."

"Yes, we will."

Sonny said: "If you pick up that stick, you'll be paralyzed from the top of your head to the bottom of your feet." He said, "You *try* to do it. Go on and try it!"

He was screaming at the police—they had never heard anything like that, back in 1930-something.

They said, "*Why* won't we hit you?" And he whispered in a soft voice:

"*I'm from Mars.*"

They knew nothing about the planets. "I'm from Mars!" They got out of there—the police were so afraid—they went back and they told the chief. The chief said, "You're just chicken. Why don't you throw him in jail?"

"Well, why don't *you* go, Chief? He said we'd be paralyzed!"

There was one policeman—they should have made a statue for him—he said: "We're just not going to bother him." And finally they left him alone.

This was back in the early thirties, my elementary school days. I was born in 1928, so he was already on the scene back there; I had heard all these things about Sonny Blount.

When I got to high school, I had some contemporaries, Walter Miller and Big Joe Alexander: they were high school students, but they were playing so much *jazz,* and they were in Sun Ra's band. I loved to hear what they were doing—I couldn't *understand* what they were doing, but I knew they were making so much progress in jazz. I remember going to the Masonic Temple and Sun Ra would have a gig there sometimes, and I remember Walter Miller playing one of these great Roy Eldridge solos, like "Twilight Time," and Big Joe was just tearing that tenor saxophone up. In Professor Whatley's band, it was generally known that we were a notch above all that—because we had our tuxedos and played in the Mountain Brook Country Club—but really, although we were in the top band, we secretly wanted to play with Sun Ra. Because they were learning so much *jazz:* how to really *play* jazz.

I had heard a lot about Sun Ra from Big Joe and Walter, because we went to school together and they were our peers. Big Joe called me up one day—this is before I started playing in Sonny's band—and he said, "I heard you playing with Professor Whatley. You need to be playing in my band. We're happier over here." Said, "You're not happy over there with Whatley. I can hear it in your music. You're a wonderful player, but you're not happy."

Blount's band was real unique. Everybody in there couldn't read music real well, but he could put them together: I admire Sonny for being able to mold his musicians together to do things that he did. His orchestra would consist of maybe three trombones or five, it didn't make any difference—he wanted to know how you sounded and how *you* sounded. If two bass players showed up, they were both on the job: he'd have two. Some of the musicians might have complained, because they'd have to split the money more ways, but Sonny wanted to hear what each one of them could do: how it all sounded together.

As I said, he lived in this rickety old house, and his whole world was in that place. It was a wooden frame building. As far as we got, and anybody got, was the front room, and that was where he had his bed and where he rehearsed. I think he took his meals in there. We understand that he had a sister or somebody, but nobody ever saw anybody there in the house. He would always be there, and he had these records stacked about five feet off the ground, these 78 records, and he had his piano in there. I remember that the hallway was about to fall in—you could step down in a hole or something if you weren't careful—and the furniture was in shoddy shape.

Always it was very crowded. Whenever we had a singer, after he set the drums up, the singer would have to be out in the hallway, and he would call that person in whenever they would do a vocal number. The saxophones would be up against the wall over here, and the trumpets would be somewhere back in there. But you didn't think about it. There was never any talk about anything but the music. He had a wire tape recorder, and he had a shortwave radio—I don't know how he got it—and he could get music out of New York, like from the Savoy. He would have all these wild players on there, like Don Stovall. They were playing bop before bop was even heard about. He'd listen at night to that, and he'd play that back for you. It was the craziest music, but he would say, "That man's not crazy. You just aren't able to understand it yet. He's trying to tell you something, but you don't know what to do. He's just trying to tell you he's *free*—okay? So listen at it." And if you listened long enough, you'd get it.

He would say, "I was born with x-ray ears; I can hear all these things you humans can't hear yet."

He had people like Henry "Red" Allen on that transistor radio, and they would be playing the trumpets: they would be playing very differently than you would hear them play in a concert, in a ballroom, or even on a record. It was a wild thing, and they would be playing number after number after number.

Sometimes if there was a big band like Jimmy Lunceford or Benny Goodman, he would transcribe that off the radio; he'd copy his arrangements right off the radio. If a band would come to the Masonic Temple, I don't care who it was—Duke Ellington—he'd put that little wire recorder down there, and in about two or three days, he'd have all those parts written down, by hand. Nobody knew how he could do that.

Of course, Professor Whatley called me back after reflecting on what he had done. So it wasn't but a couple of weeks before I was playing with both Fess Whatley *and* Sun Ra. That gave me two bands—and there was a great difference between Fess Whatley's band and this Sun Ra experience. I know that sometimes I would look at Whatley's music, and I would compare it to Sun Ra's. If a vocalist would be singing, Sonny's background music would be much simpler to play, lots of whole notes and things. Professor Whatley would have bought and copied out arrangements that would have these cascading runs like the pros would play. On the "Swanee River," you'd have maybe a sixteen-bar reed chorus—Sun Ra didn't have that type of thing, but he'd play a lot of *blues*. He had a fellow named Teddy Smith who played saxophone—a natural. They would play this "Hootie Blues" that would go fifteen minutes. Teddy Smith would be out there playing, playing, swaying from side to side; the people would be hot and sweaty and *perspiring*, and he'd go on and on and on.

Sonny was very popular because he had these soloists, and if you got out in one of those public housing projects where he played, your three-minute record wouldn't do. If you played Glenn Miller's "In the Mood" and had to stop after three minutes, like the record—those folks want to stay out there *eight* minutes, perspiring. That's what they call *dancing*. Even a blues band like B. B. King: they could play what they recorded, but that's not enough for dancers. They want to get out there and dance until they fall out. So you had these soloists who could carry on all night. That was one of the things that made Sonny's band so popular in certain areas: Sonny could play the thing through once, twice, over again, and add something to it—and people liked that.

Now, Professor Whatley's band: he'd play a dance, and we'd play a number—maybe "Tea for Two"—and then the number would be over, and people would sit down. When I left Birmingham, I found out that people don't do it that way in New York and other places: you play *sets* of numbers. You'd have a set of four or five numbers before people would sit down. *Sonny* would take just *one* number, and play it for thirty minutes if he wanted to, as long as he saw people out there dancing.

Of course, Professor Whatley believed in the strictest interpretation of things. Sun Ra would take liberties—and he was composing his music, so he had a say-so in it. Sun Ra took pride in who he was as a *creator* of music. And that was *all* he did; morning and night, it was music. He'd say, "I can't afford to be sick, because my music demands that I'm working twenty-four hours a day on it." Said, "I wish I didn't have to do that, but—it's my mission. And even if I am sick, I'm still creating."

So Sun Ra was in demand, because his band could improvise. They could start from the back and go to the top, and all that type of thing. And they had some showmanship—they could *move* a little bit. In Whatley's band, you just stood there; he didn't want you to move. Whatley had all these rules, that if you were playing a wedding or something, the band was not to eat the food—because, he said, "You're the servants." But in Sun Ra's band, during intermission, if there was some food out there, they were going to *get* it. And with the people they were playing for, it was okay.

Man, Sun Ra: that was jazz music. Those guys didn't wear tuxedos, they wore what they could. He didn't tell you certain things to wear, like all the other bands would, and as a consequence, they said he never got those jobs over at Mountain Brook Country Club—because his band would be in their BVDs or whatever. *Somebody* might have a tux on, but the next guy might have his T-shirt on. And Sun Ra wouldn't discuss that. It was all okay.

He played all over the housing projects—on the street, anywhere he could play. And when I finally started playing with him, that was a change in my life. I found out there was a discipline in Sun Ra's band that you wouldn't necessarily perceive. Whatley's thing was this *rigid* discipline, which was okay, but in Sun Ra's band, he had his own concept. With Whatley we were strictly doing what was proper. The dynamics wouldn't be changed; you weren't allowed to get up and play a solo unless it was written down. But with Blount, you could stumble over something, and then go back and try it again. And it was the sort of thing where you could *talk* to each other; you could have fun. You would sit there sometimes all night. If somebody was making a mistake, you could stop and help him—there isn't anybody getting mad about it.

Sun Ra had discipline, but he had a thing where you would want to discipline *yourself.* If you messed up, he might say a little something and just pinch you with the fact that you should know better than that: you're disrespecting the *music.* He wouldn't talk about it so much, but *you* know; you know you didn't play your best.

When I was playing with Whatley's orchestra, it was mathematical, precise—and I marveled at that. Everything Fess Whatley did had its place: when to get up, when to go to bed, what to read. I would organize my thing, and it was good.

But I knew there was something else out there in this jazz music.

When I was first starting, I asked some of the musicians who were older, who could really play—improvise, that is; I could do most of the things that were popular because I could memorize things, but they were real *jazz* players—I said, "Show me how you do this. How you play a jazz solo. I want to be a jazz player, like you." And they said, "No. Can't do it."

I said, "Why can't you?"

"Well, it's just a gift. Some of us have it, some of us don't. *And you don't.*"

Wow. I started thinking. I said: "Well, is something wrong with me?" I saw a light-skinned person playing jazz, I saw a dark-skinned person playing jazz, I saw one that was in between; and I saw a young lady playing jazz—Grace Chambliss could just play anything she heard—so, I felt that maybe . . . maybe my *hands* were too big, or whatever. It was a terrible thing to be told you can't do something—and then see other people around you doing it. I had not been too interested, really, in jazz, until they told me I couldn't play it. I began to like jazz when I was drafted by Professor Whatley; I saw these older musicians were doing things, and my interest grew. I didn't *love* it at that time, but when I was told that I *couldn't* do it—that's a challenge.

So I tried my best to learn what it was all about. I would practice in the closet, so nobody would hear me: in the closet, the sound is absorbed by the clothes. I practiced over and over again, up and down those scales, and I'd try to do little things, but it just didn't sound like *jazz.*

One day I was doing this, and this little finger on my right hand struck this key—and it made a sound I'd never played before. I jumped up and I said, "I've got it! I've discovered jazz!"

I ran through the hall to the front room, and my big brother said, "Wait, wait, brother, you didn't discover jazz—you just discovered one note! You hit one note that *sounded* like jazz. That's a blue note."

I said, "*Blue* note?" And I found out later that he was right. I just had one little thing—but I found out that if you can find something small, it might open the entire door to other things for you. That's what happened to me when I got to Sun Ra. I found out some of the things that the musicians were doing but just didn't know how to tell you. When I got into Sun Ra's group, it was an *altogether* different ball game. He could explain: if you flatten the third note in a scale, it sounds like this; if you flatten the fifth note, it's going to sound like that. He could explain these things to me that the other guys couldn't.

I remember I would be traveling, perhaps from Mississippi, with Professor Whatley. He'd have a few older people in the band, and they'd be talking—and I remember one time they said, talking about me, "Yeah, he's going to be fine, but he just doesn't play loud enough: like Mr. Gordon or somebody. He does all right, but I miss that big *sound* of Mr. Gordon's."

So Fess went and bought me a mouthpiece, an Otto Link mouthpiece, Six Star; I never will forget it. It did make a little bigger sound, but it was too open for me. I'd bite my lip trying to play it, and all—one of the first things I threw away when I got to Howard was that mouthpiece.

In Mississippi we'd make a little bit more, but a regular gig with Fess Whatley, you'd make about six dollars—which was pretty good at that time—and I had it divided down where I loved barbecue so I'd buy myself a barbecue rib sandwich from Palmer's Barbecue, and I'd buy my mom a pork sandwich. That was a ritual. That was heaven on earth, and I felt like I was really doing something. The rest of that money I'd keep. But every time I'd get my check, until just about the end of high school, Professor Whatley would take something *out* of my check to pay for that mouthpiece that I didn't want—maybe a dollar, or fifty cents, out of it—until I guess he finally figured I'd paid for it. *My* calculations were, I paid for that mouthpiece three or four times.

The point I'm trying to make is: that was a casual conversation that could make you feel that you're not getting there. "He's going to be fine, but he doesn't play loud enough." You hear that, and you're depressed by it—especially a little fellow—and there was no technical or logical solution that they were capable of giving you. They'd say, "Well, you just can't do that. You can't play loud like Mr. Gordon."

Then I remember a conversation I had in elementary school. Mr. Handy said I had a "silver tone." *Silver,* that's good. And he said I had an "Italian tongue"—"a *Dago* tongue," he said. I didn't know what it meant, but it was positive. And one of the things that I want you to remember about Sonny Blount: he would talk about me and he would say, "Yes. He's brilliant." He's talking to somebody and says, "Not only can Frank read music, and he can play, but he comes from a noble family. He's going to be a great musician—in fact, he already is, but people don't realize it. They don't know about him yet."

I was listening to all this—and when you get that kind of thing going, it puts you in a place where you have a respect for *yourself,* and nothing adverse can change that. Then you look back and say, this guy, weird as they say he was: the others told me I couldn't play jazz, but he was the one that said, "He's *playing* it." And said, "He's excellent." And said, "Not only can he do this, but he has a good *background.* He's not in the heathenly group." Like you've got some sort of pedigree. "He's going to do great things, because that's just the way he is. He has the ability to do good. And he'll probably be the one, when we leave this planet, to get to Mars first!"

Sonny said, "What's in you is going to come out. And you'll be able to hear it."

So, one day we were at the Masonic Temple. And he looked at me and said, "You got it." That meant to take the solo. Well, I thought I could do something, man: I had discovered a few things—I knew little marches and church songs, but that didn't fit in with *jazz.* I got out there to the microphone and I thought I was going to do everything, but . . . everything just locked up on me, and I couldn't do anything but repeat over and over again one little passage. One little scale, over and over. I couldn't even reach for my blue note. People started leaving the dance floor. It was horrible. I looked over at Sonny, and he just waved his hand: "Stay out there."

I was out there so long you could have gone to lunch and come back before I sat down. They had four trumpet players in the band, and all of those trumpet players could have blown the stars out of the sky—they had those high ranges, and they could really play. They were angry because people were leaving the dance. Here I am squeaking and squawking, and he's insisting that I stay out there. I don't think all trumpet players are like this, but some trumpet players can be *mean*, and these were *monster* trumpet players. They could set a piece of paper on fire just looking at it, and I could feel the pressure coming from them—at least I thought I did. I knew when I sat down, it would be terrible. They would not only be losing money on me, because people were leaving, but all the good players would have a bad feeling toward me, which could ruin his band. When I finally sat down, I knew that would be the end of my playing with him.

But what happened is: he looked at me, and after everybody left he told me, "What you played was wonderful." Now, that would *have* to be a tale—because all I did was play the same thing over and over again. That wasn't beautiful at all, that was just a monotony of sound. When he told me that, it confirmed for me that, absolutely, he is just as crazy as anybody says he is!

But he said to me that it sounded perfect, it sounded magnificent. And I was so hungry for something like that, that it made it real. I felt something I'd never felt before: that what I did was valuable. It was appreciated. I didn't believe in levitation, but I just came up out of my seat, and I floated all the way home. I walked by the barbecue stand, I didn't even smell the barbecue, man. I ended up at home in bed, tapping my foot. And I said, "Hey—I'm a real jazz musician!" Because *Sun Ra* was a jazz musician and I respected him, and *he* said it.

That built up my confidence. So I started going around him and playing. And he said what's in you will come out. This thing about "You can't do it" just went away. The very next day, I felt different. Because when you're around somebody that you really respect—and they've done marvelous things and you've seen them, and you've watched them compose, and you've watched their actions—you're hungry for this. And when they give it to you—*wow*, you become a different person.

I started going to his home, this—well, I hate to call it a "shack," because it wasn't a shack; it was *heaven* when you got in there, and he had all these records and everything. It was never, "Hey, we don't have but two people, Frank, we're not going to practice." You'd practice if it was *one* person, two people, or people all over the room, sitting all over the bed and maybe somebody out in the hall, waiting to be called in.

These practices went on and on and on. You didn't have to have a gig coming up; you just practiced. You practiced.

If you did play somewhere—I don't care where it was—it was still a *rehearsal*, because the band would mess up, and he would *stop*. And start all over again, and never have any shame about doing that. People on the floor would just have to stop dancing and wonder what he was doing.

He had some outstanding musicians in that band, people that nobody has heard of today. Walter Miller, trumpet. George Woodruff, the saxophone player; he sat next to me. We called him "Jarhead"— and then "Jarhead" became "Jarhee." He didn't solo, but he was a good person to have in your section. He was the third alto player. I told you about Big Joe Alexander, tenor sax—he was my cousin, and he was a *furious* little musician. He could play everything, and he was *rough*. He played "Stardust," and it sounded like somebody beating on a brick. He had torn up his alto saxophone, and Sonny said, "I think I need to put him on a bigger sax, a tenor." He put Big Joe on a tenor, and he blew himself all the way up to the big time. Sun Ra saw that in him. Big Joe played with Woody Herman for a while and Tadd Dameron, but nobody knows much about him today.

We had Warren Parham on tenor sax, too. He was phenomenal. When my brother was in high school, he would always talk about Warren Parham's tenor playing. He was a quiet player, but he could *play*. Smooth as silk. Then we had a tenor player called Warfield. He had the palsy; he had the shakes all over. His fingers would settle down when he played, but other than that, he'd be shaking. And Fletcher "Hootie" Myatt, drums and vocals: Fletcher "Hootie" Myatt was the star.

Sonny had several of these natural musicians in his band—like I told you about Teddy Smith, the alto saxophone player. I ended up taking his place in the band. We called him "Velt," because he had a velvet tone. The only thing about him, he stayed inebriated most of the time; but I watched him one night, he just stood up there and played about forty choruses and never repeated himself.

It was sort of like a family. There was a one-armed piano player at that time, Dan Michael: he was connected a lot with Sonny and all of us. Dan Michael came from Homewood, where my wife was reared. I think he taught school. He was a tremendous player, and he did vocal coaching. He had this artificial arm, but he could play one of the most complicated things, which was "After Hours," by Avery Parrish. He could play it with one arm. And he wrote some real complex music that he gave Sonny for us to play. We played at the Masonic Temple, and he introduced this piece of music; we did our best to get through it. There were people waiting to dance, but Sonny kept going over Dan Michael's piece until we were able to give it a decent performance. That's how Sonny was: you're going over that piece of music 'til you get it right.

In his early years, Sun Ra had this thing called the Solovox. This was before the electric piano. It was an attachment onto his piano that made organ-type sounds, before the jazz organ was popular. It just attached, a little thing about the size of a cigar box, and you'd plug it in there and you'd hear these ghostly sounds—*woo-oo, woo-oo*. That was one of the things that got him this outer space business, because you'd hear this eerie sound coming through. It wasn't amplified much, but he'd always attach it to his piano.

I remember, he would go sometimes to hear bands like Ellington when they'd come to the Masonic Temple. And he wouldn't fraternize—he wouldn't attempt to meet anybody—but he would make sure that someone would point *him* out: "That's Sonny Blount over there." Then, if you were in the band, *you* wanted to meet *him*. He's not going to come up and force himself on you, but he'd set it up so you'd introduce yourself.

He had, I guess, a mystique about music. He would remind you that you had to listen to Shostakovich: "He was one of the blessed angels." It would have made no matter trying to *talk* to Shostakovich about his music, because he couldn't have told you; it was just a thing that came from one of his planets. Toscanini, the great conductor: "Well, he was just one of the blessed ones. He *has* that. No matter what you try, you can't do that. *But*," he said, "there's another place for you. All of you are in heaven, but there's another seat for you, and you should accept your seat."

Sun Ra believed that there was a spirit of excellence in some musicians. And there were some—no matter how good you would think they sounded—to him, they were fakes. Although they could execute something real well, it was phony; it didn't come from a deep, sincere force. He would speak about the purity of the music.

I asked him about one great musician, who was married to Billie Holiday: Joe Guy. I said, "Sonny, Joe Guy can *play*." And Sonny said, "Well, that's true. That's true. But he only plays for himself."

"What do you mean, he only plays for himself?"

He says, "Listen at him. He's not trying to play for anybody but himself. He doesn't care whether his music is good or valid for you. It's *him*."

I had never heard anything like that. I said, "This is weird. This is really weird."

There were—what was it?—"real prophets" and "false prophets." You might listen to Benny Goodman. And he would say, "That's a great musician, but he's not playing true New Orleans music: listen at it." What he was doing was nice, but it was commercial; it wasn't the real thing. He talked about Louis Armstrong: "Well, it just wasn't meant for him to read music." It was *meant* for him to go to the waif's home because he shot a pistol off during some festivity; and they put him in the juvenile home; and there was this bugle there; and he picked this bugle up—according to Sun Ra, that was all just preordained, that he was supposed to do that. He always had this sense of predestination. He would say, "My music will probably be sought after and understood in"—how many centuries?—"maybe next century. You'll understand it better by and by." And it was like: "Although you don't have a crowd tonight, you're playing for some holy people. Your sounds are going somewhere that people hear you."

I'd play something. He would say, "Did you *need* to make all of those notes to *say* something?"

If I said, "Yes, I did—"

"*Okay!* It's all right. Leave it in."

He'd say, "Listen at that." And, "Listen at that." You'd listen, and all of a sudden, you don't know what day it is, but when you're in the right environment, around the right people, you're like a sponge. You just take it, take it, take it in—and you get better and better. An exchange goes on between you and someone else. Then you've got it. You've got what you need.

That was the environment he provided in this broken-down home, with all of these crazy things in it.

Sometimes he would lecture—I guess you would call it *lecture*—he would talk about outer space; about the moon and Mars and Jupiter. And he'd say, "Everybody, if you get to fussing and fighting, that's okay: because I'll just call my spaceship, and go to Venus, and leave you all here. And you don't all know, it's a blessing to have *me* around, because I'm the *true* maker of music." All that kind of stuff, and you know it's not all true—you *think* it's not all true—but when you see the guy *living* like that . . .

A lot of people ask me, "Did he really believe all this space stuff?" He *absolutely* believed it. There was no trickery with Sun Ra. He knew that this planet was not his home.

He would say things like, "I know you can't see it now"—he had this soft voice—"but people will be traveling in spaceships to different planets; they'll be going from one planet to the other. And what I'm going to do: those of you who don't listen to me, I'm not going to give you my address. Some of you will be looking for me, but you won't know what planet I'm on."

We would look at each other. "What *planet!*" He would call out your names and what star you were born under, and what would be your inclinations. He would talk about somebody like W. E. B. Du-Bois, who wanted blacks to have full education, and then Booker T. Washington, who wanted them to do menial things and "let down their bucket"—and he would appreciate both of them. He said, "How could you do without one or the other? It was just a fact of the gods that they put them both here at the same time." Or he would say, "What are you talking about, segregation? They probably got more segregation on *Jupiter.*" He'd explain how the rotation of the planets would make things a certain way, and you couldn't understand it. Some of them would laugh and say, "My God, what's he going to come up with next?"

He had it all worked out. Here's a guy that plays the trombone, and he'd say, "He's an excellent player. He's going to be all right, but," he said, "he's in love right now; he's just mooning. He'll come back to himself." He'd stop and tell somebody: "You could play much better if you weren't thinking about women all the time."

"How do you know what I'm thinking about?"

"It comes out in your playing. But they were here before man, and they'll be here after you're gone. You're laying down your life with thoughts like that."

Somebody might say, "Why does Velt get drunk all the time?"

"Well, it's the gods that say that Frank is supposed to play lead tonight; that's why. *Velt* had nothing to do with it. He would have to get drunk tonight, whether he wanted to or not, because it's his time *not* to be here."

You see?

If you tell somebody about all that, they don't understand: they say that he's "off" or something. But he wasn't off. He just had this pre-determined way of what he was. He was that way because *he was that way*. He didn't conceive himself as being a part of the world. So his evaluations *of* the world were not the evaluations we have.

I remember one day, when I really got to play—I got to be a good player, and I could play pretty well—Sonny called me early one morning, and he said, "Come up here. I want you to hear something. It's real important." When Sun Ra wanted you there, you needed to be there.

I got my bicycle—I don't know how I did that, to carry a big saxophone case on a bicycle—I rode all the way up to that old tenement where he lived. The first thing was, you had to be careful going into his house, because the porch had holes in it, and you could fall down in there. When I went up on the porch, I could hear all this fantastic saxophone playing. I said, "Man, that must be a terrific record."

Like I said, I thought I was getting to be pretty good. I opened the door—*listen!*—and there was a little midget, about that tall; he had rubber bands all *around* his horn, all wrapped up; and he was just *killing* it, he was playing so much.

First of all, it shocked me because he wasn't any bigger than this, and I could hear him playing all the things I wished I could do. You know what I did? I closed the door, got on my bicycle, went back home, and started practicing. I never even let Sonny know I was there.

He didn't say anything to me about it for two or three weeks. Finally he said: "How did you like that?"

I said, "What?"

"You know: you came by my house. How did you like that little fellow playing?"

Oh. I said, "He was terrific."

"I know. Because I can see it in your playing."

That's how he taught.

I found out that this fellow was a saxophone player with what they called the Carolina Cotton Pickers; that was a real great band, and a lot of the guys, like Cootie Williams, went from there to Duke Ellington's band. This little midget was sensational. And that was Sun Ra's lesson to me: not to think you are so much, because this guy is *really* playing.

To tell the truth, I was glad when that little fellow left town.

Sun Ra never trained to be a teacher. In his situation, you learned by observation. Whatley would tell you, "You're cutting the note off too short," or "Do this; do that," but Sun Ra was more of a feeling. "Can't you *feel* that? Listen at that—feel that." Or he would suddenly change the key, and if you couldn't follow it, he would look at you like, "Why didn't you hear that? You should have heard that!" This would make you stay on your feet. Professor Whatley would never try anything like that. He'd tell you exactly what to expect.

I learned that with bands like Sun Ra, there is a sort of looseness—a sort of *controlled* looseness. Sonny didn't appreciate too much imitation, or copying somebody else's thing. He would say, "What do *you* say? Let's hear from *you*. I don't want to hear from Charlie Parker, I want to hear from *you*, what *you* do." He would tell you to put a little of yourself into it. And I found out that the best enjoyment from music comes from the fact that you have some creation in it, going on all the time.

Sun Ra had that.

Did I tell you about when he came here to get his award? He came back here to be put in the Hall of Fame—in fact, I was the one that recommended him. In Birmingham they knew about him, but he was just a weird entity to them. He came here and he brought one drum, a little snare drum, and a fellow with him that, if you saw them both, you would determine that they were crazy, right off. But there he was, at this Hall of Fame thing.

This was back in—let's see—it must have been 1979 that Sun Ra was inducted. It was a beautiful affair. They had Jo Jones, the great drummer; that's the night Jo Jones was inducted. They had a lot of the big ones that are in the Hall of Fame now. It was just an awesome day, and everybody was so proud. After the event was over—I hadn't spoken to Sun Ra for years; in fact, I doubt he knew I nominated him—but on the way out, I saw him at the piano, still plucking at the piano a bit, like he used to do after a performance. His back was turned to me.

I said, "Sun Ra"—"*Sonny*," I called him—"Sonny, do you know who this is?" He didn't say anything. I said, "Do you know who this is?"

He said, "Of course. You're my saxophone player. You're Frank Adams." Then he turned around in his seat. And this is where I had to unload a lot of things on him: ego, you know. I said, "Listen, man, I have played with Duke Ellington's orchestra; I'm supervisor of music for Birmingham schools; and I made these records and all; and my wife is a teacher, she's out in the county teaching fifth grade." And I said, "I've got a *son* since I saw you; my son, he's at Boston University, playing in the symphony." *Blah, blah, blah, blah, blah.*

He looked at me. You want somebody to say, "Oh, that's wonderful!" But you know what he said?

"That's a disgrace."

I felt like a corkscrew going down in the ground. My ego had been shattered, man. I went down, down, down. I kept looking at him. He said, "What a waste." *What do you mean?* I said, now he's going to tell me—this *weird* creature—he's going to be telling me something about how my life is a *failure?*

We're staring at each other. And I started thinking: *he* thought that I should never have been away from his band. That was all that mattered with him. I should still be playing in his Intergalactic Arkestra. That was what I was here for: *not* to have a family, *not* to do anything. That was his world.

It didn't take me too long to analyze the fact that what he believed in *was* me, and he felt that I should have stayed, regardless of everything, with his orchestra. That really touched me. But then, I wouldn't have met my wife; I wouldn't have been anything but what he wanted me to be.

And I remember, my mind started going back, years back, when we played a dance in Talladega College. He had an old raggedy car that he had rented from somebody, and he had one of these things that had a trailer to it, an old wooden, broken trailer with a top; and all of the instruments were put in that trailer. He drove all the way out to Talladega College. He had one car, so it was cramped in that car.

We went out and played. And instead of waiting around awhile after we finished, everybody ran and jumped in that car, and squeezed in there. By the time he got the money, there was no room for the leader. So he crawled back in the back of that little wagon back there, with all the cymbals and drums and everything falling on top of him.

I guess I wasn't the only one, but I felt bad about that. I had had some religious training, you know, and my folks had taught me to respect leadership, regardless of race or whatever—that was the *leader,* man.

And here you've got him back there like somebody going through Jerusalem on the back of a donkey or something! So I said, "This is going to get everybody terminated. Everybody in this band will be fired tomorrow."

When we got back—*listen!*—he said not a mumbling word about it, man. He didn't say one word. And I always try to put things in perspective. I've been around Lucky Millinder, Andy Kirk, Duke Ellington, Fess Whatley, anybody you can name—but I've never seen a person like that. Duke Ellington was a tremendous guy. Fess Whatley was, too. Count Basie was. But there never was another Sun Ra. And in your lifetime, if you ever meet a person like that, that would ride cramped in the back of an old trailer, and do everything in his life to succeed—*he can't be stopped.* You understand? You can't stop him. He's not interested in any *clothes;* any *wives;* he's not interested in anything but his music. That's why he could conceive of himself coming from another planet: because nobody's like him.

Like I was saying about Joe Guy—I could say, "Sonny, I'm impressed with him; he can really *play.*" He would say, "Yes. He's fine. But. *He only plays for himself.* He doesn't care whether you like it. He sits there and gets paid for playing for himself."

That was an insult, that Joe was *selfish.* If you trace his life with Billie Holiday, he was selfish, and he took dope because *he* wanted to get high. He didn't care about you—this was selfishness! Even to *die* before your time is selfish, that's what Sun Ra would say. He said, "That's the biggest thing; people *need* you."

And see, he needed me, perhaps—and I betrayed him. I left. So if you look at it in that perspective, you can see where he's coming from.

That was Sun Ra.

He was a free flower. He was just blowing in the wind.

6
First Gigs and Birmingham Clubs

WHEN I WAS STARTING OUT, THERE WERE A LOT of opportunities for a young fellow to play music. In fact, I need to back up here to describe some of my very first gigs. The earliest of my playing was with a woman named Theo Carr. She was a pianist and a singer, and she had some little clubs she played over the mountain—*little* places, like a bridge club; they would call on her to bring some music. She couldn't really hire professional musicians, so she took me and my drummer friend, Herbert. We were just little children, out of elementary school. She gave us a few dollars and she'd pick us up and bring us home.

I don't think we knew but one or two songs, like "Mairzy Doats and Dozy Doats," and we could do "Sentimental Journey"; we could play a little song like that, and people liked it. Then somehow, right at the end of my time at Lincoln School, she hooked us up with this carnival: Heeny Brothers Circus, right down on Eighth Avenue. I don't know if you've ever seen these, but they had these little neighborhood circuses—not like the big circuses Finktum played in; not like a county fair. But they'd have, maybe, one little Ferris wheel, a little place where you could throw something at the rubber dolls; balls to hit the rabbits or whatever—just a few things. And they'd have a tent where they would have a comedian, and maybe two or three dancing girls.

Carnivals were always low-key so far as a lot of people were concerned, but if they came to a black community, it was like jubilation—because they had different dancers in there, and they had black music. They would have somebody come out and beat a drum or play some music to draw the crowd in. And that was my first gig, really. We'd go out in front of the place. They called it "balleting"; that is, you're drawing a crowd. You'd go out front and you'd play a little tune—at that time, in the thirties, "Tuxedo Junction" was popular, so I probably knew how to play "Tuxedo Junction" already and just a few tunes, but that was all. We'd be finished around nine o'clock, and I think you got about a dollar, maybe fifty cents or something. So we'd look forward to that.

One time we played at this tent show. And my friend Herbie was more streetwise than I was in elementary school. We were leaving and he saw Theo with one of the workers in the show, a white guy, and they were in a sexual position he could see from outside of the tent. He saw them having *sex*—you could see their shadows in that tent. I didn't know what it was about. But it hit Herbie as being horrible: this *miscegenation;* this guy with Theo.

I didn't know anything about race relations. I knew that there was segregation—every kid would know that, because everything was separate—but Herbie had, I guess, a sense of race. He had more knowledge of worldly things than I did. Maybe I had been sheltered; I just hadn't seen that. But this thing about race was big in his mind at that time.

Herbie picked up a big brick and threw it at them, and *hit* them, in that big tent—and ran.

I said, "What'd you do that for?"

"They were doing the nasty!" I didn't know what the nasty *was*. But naturally I ran, too, and I didn't know what became of that.

The next day I saw Theo. She had a big bruise mark on her arm, where she'd been hit. I never said anything about it, and Herbie never said anything about it.

I had no sexual awareness whatsoever. Even when I got to high school, and Professor Whatley would play "Kokemo," and they'd come together close—I guess they called that "shimmying"—I just thought it was peculiar. It didn't arouse anything in me. I had no idea.

I remember, back then, we had this large house on the corner, and there was a real *shapely* woman that would come down the street, and my brother and I would go from room to room watching her, you know what I mean—but that's all. We didn't know too much about things.

I got the chance to play with Mantan Moreland's Hot Harlem Revue a few years later, before I finished high school. It must have been the first year that I really got away from home. We would travel, and we were in New Orleans, and we were doing pretty well. I walked backstage—you know, it's dark behind those curtains—I walked back there, and all of a sudden one of the chorus girls kissed me. Out of a clear blue sky, just walked up and *kissed* me. I didn't know whether to hit her in the head, or what. It did arouse some kind of emotion in me; I said, I wonder what that was about. I knew from common sense that most people on a show like that were attached to somebody—you could get yourself *killed* by that kind of thing. But I said, I'll find out what this is all about.

I approached her. I said, "Why did you do that?"

She said, "I think a lot of you. But don't mistake that for anything. You're a nice little fellow. And you're a good-looking little fellow. And you play a lot of horn; I like that. But," she said, "I wouldn't want to have anything to do with you, because it would just mess your mind up."

I said, "No, it wouldn't! What are you talking about?"

She said, "You don't want me. It was just that I felt an affection for you, and I kissed you. You don't know it now, but," she said, "you're going to go far. I'm twelve years older than you; if I did get involved with you, I'd ruin your life."

I must have been about thirteen or fourteen—and a grown woman! It took a long time to convince me. I said, "Well, can I try?"

"No!" She said, "You don't want to try!"

Then I started looking at life. I started thinking, what are these things all about? And thank God, thank *God,* she didn't take me on. I had no experience. No experience at all.

After I'd been playing with Theo, I got to play with a fellow named Banjo Bill. He was an excellent guitarist. Nobody ever remembers Banjo Bill, but he made his own equipment, his own guitar, and he had it all electrified. His amplifier was made out of wood—the only time I ran into another one of those was playing with Howlin' Wolf; he had his own homemade box, like Banjo Bill.

I remember, when Banjo would turn that amplifier on up, it sounded like somebody sticking a nickel in a jukebox. It would go *ploop!* and I knew we were about to play.

He called me to play with him at some white establishment, a little club or something out there on the highway. A lot of times the over-the-mountain group would come and patronize these blues players. They liked authenticity. They would have a blues player at the Birmingham Country Club or something—for the college students—and Banjo was on that circuit. He played the guitar, never a banjo. I don't know why they called him "Banjo Bill"—that must have been before my time, that he played the banjo.

If he would get a job, say, at Mountain Brook Country Club or one of the big places where they wanted "Tennessee Waltz" or "The World Is Waiting for the Sunrise," he hired me, because I had gotten to where I could play those songs. He wouldn't know those kinds of things. He'd just say, "Play it," and he'd turn on his amplifier and play behind you. You'd play "Stardust"—it had no relationship to what he was playing—but people would even clap for it. He advertised that any song you want, he could play it.

One outstanding thing about him that really stuck out was that he paid better than anybody else: it wasn't but a few dollars difference, but that *was* a difference when he handed you five dollars. For a little fellow, that was a lot of money, man. In fact, this was admirable about him: he would get tips and he would halve the tips with you—most bandleaders put it in their pocket. And he would always thank you for playing with him.

He would pick you up at home, like Theo would do. He evidently dressed pretty decently, because Mama wouldn't let me go with anybody that looked shabby. He'd say what time he'd get you back, maybe eleven o'clock or something, and you'd go with Banjo Bill. He had a pretty decent car, and he'd bring you back home.

He lived over on what they called Bice Hill. Some people still call it that. When you go up there, if it's raining and muddy, you can't get back down from Bice Hill. You go way up high; if you keep going, you get to a little peak and you can't turn around, it gets so close up there. You had a lot of musicians—the blues players, the ear players, the house party players—that were in North Birmingham, and they lived on Bice Hill. Particularly piano players. That's where Banjo Bill lived, and that's where Robert McCoy lived, who I played with later; that's where Frank Hines, the piano player, and so many of them lived. In fact, Avery Parrish, the great pianist who wrote "After Hours" for Erskine Hawkins, lived in that area. North Birmingham was known mostly for its musicians and its blues players.

Banjo would call a singer that was pretty popular, Sammy Mayo. Sammy was a little youngster, not much older than I was. I don't think they went there together, but eventually Banjo went to Cleveland and Sammy migrated to Cleveland, too. I'm quite sure that they played in some of those blues places out there.

Sammy Mayo was already in high school before I got there. When I was at Lincoln School, we would go to the high school for the variety shows, and that's how I first knew Sammy. They had a number by Lil Green, called "In the Dark"—something about "Your fingertips touched my knee, in the dark"—and they would turn the *lights* off, and Sammy Mayo would be singing it, and people would *scream*: "Ohhh! In the dark!"

I didn't know what they were screaming about, but it was this suggestive song. In those days, they didn't come out and curse, but it was such innuendo you'd know what they were talking about—of course, *I'm* sitting up there in the eighth grade or seventh grade, and I didn't know *what* she was singing about, "when your fingertips touched my knee." And why did they cut the lights off? I had no idea.

But nobody could sing those blues like Sammy Mayo.

In Birmingham, at that time, there were several places where you could go to hear music.

I told you about the Colored Masonic Temple on Fourth Avenue. That was a stretch above the others. You'd have to be *dressed* to go into the Masonic Temple, because they would have the big names: Benny Goodman would come in to play to a segregated audience, and you'd have Lionel Hampton and all. They had a Gold Room that was modeled after the Gold Room at the Tutwiler Hotel, and it was just magnificent.

I heard some tremendous musicians at the Masonic Temple. I remember going there a couple of times when some of the modern jazz groups would come in; a lot of people here didn't appreciate modern jazz, but all the musicians would go and listen. There would be just a few people in the audience, and that gave me a chance to talk with the musicians. We had bands like Benny Carter, the great saxophonist—I remember talking to him and asking him some things. I asked him, "What kind of mouthpiece do you use? What kind of reed do you use?" He had a plastic reed, and it sounded so good. I said, "Where can I get one?"

He said, "What kind of reed do *you* use? How long have you been playing?"

"I've been playing maybe a couple of years," I said. "I use a wooden reed."

"Hm." He said, "I'd just stick to that, because this right here pinches. I wouldn't want you to go around here with cut lips—wait a couple of years, but don't bother with that now."

You'd get advice from them. They would all want to talk to you, and they took a great interest in you.

There was a man at the Masonic Temple, Monroe Kennedy: he was the one that did all the booking. He and Fess Whatley would put all these things together, and he was blind. Monroe Kennedy would come through the dance hall, and he'd bump into you—"Excuse me"—and we never knew, but he was *counting* the people. He could tell you how many were there: "It's a hundred and ten." He never would miss it, and he couldn't see. But he's like Derricot, the carpenter; he had that sixth sense.

The Colored Elks Rest was on Eighth Avenue, and that's where a lot of musicians played. I remember one Christmas they had a jam session. I had never heard of this type of thing, but they had Joe Guy and they had Nelson Williams, all these trumpet players. Shelton Hemphill. They would all meet up on a Christmas. They'd arrange something where the musicians would get together and listen and play.

The Elks Rest had a balcony overseeing the dance floor, and the band would be up top there. I heard some of the most outstanding music being played in there. They would take one number and go through all the keys with it. If they played a number like "How High the Moon," they'd play it in one key, then go to another key, in what we call a cutting session: each of those trumpet players would try to outplay the other. They'd go on for thirty or forty minutes, man, and that was fascinating to me: the first time you get to hear this *complete* musicianship. One guy'd get a high note, the other guy'd go *higher*. Nobody in there but just musicians and a few friends listening.

Then, of course, on Fourth Avenue, there was Bob's Savoy. Bob's Savoy had international recognition: anybody that came to Birmingham wanted to go to Bob's Savoy. It was a huge place. They had beer and alcohol in there, and usually they would have a band. People would get off on Friday night, and they'd come there—Friday, Saturday—they'd stay in there and drink beer and beer and beer. From all parts of Birmingham—Fairfield, Bessemer—they would come into town.

See, this *was* the town. Fourth Avenue was just the heart of everything. You had all these barbershops; you had all the poolrooms and everything; and Bob's Savoy was just the center. It was the centerpiece where everyone would go to be entertained. Any time at night, you'd see people crowding into Bob's Savoy. Bob was a popular person and people always liked him. We would play in there sometimes in Professor Whatley's band, and of course you couldn't hear, because of the beer bottles and everything. But they always tried to have some kind of a band in there.

There were two other major clubs here at that time. One was the Madison Nite Spot, and it was run by a man by the name of Monroe. I can't remember his first name; we just called him "Monroe." He had a big restaurant out on Fourth Avenue—I think it was called Monroe's Tavern—and he moved out to the Old Bessemer Highway. That building is still there; you can go out there now and see an old wooden building where they had it. Monroe made a fortune because he would bring bands in like Louis Jordan. The Bessemer Highway was real narrow, so when Louis Jordan would come to town, you couldn't even get *down* the Bessemer Highway. Bull Connor was incensed about that. He said, "When he gets up there dancing like that, my negroes get to cutting each other *up* down there—I don't want him to *ever* come to Birmingham!"

That was Bull Connor: he said "my negroes" like he owned them.

Monroe would have these dances at the Madison Nite Spot. I don't think Fess Whatley ever played there, but local bands like Jimmy Chappell, Jesse Blackmon, Montrose Baker—those were bands that I'd sit in and play with at times. When I was at Howard, I would come home during Christmas and Monroe would hire me; he'd always give me a little job to play during the Christmas holiday, and I enjoyed that. Of course, these were what Fess called "bobtail bands"—the ones that had their "tail cut off."

I remember, I played a dance at Monroe's for something called the 7–11 Club. 7–11 was the name of a whiskey, and they called the club "7–11" after this drink. They brought the whiskey up, and they had the bottles on the tables. Your table would have about eight bottles, a pint for each person. They had so much they couldn't consume it all, so everybody got inebriated—by the time we finished playing, early in the morning, they were all just passed out on the tables. There would be bottles half-empty, there would be bottles completely empty, there would be some that hadn't even been opened, because they would over-buy. In the end, I guess, the bottles defeated them—they couldn't get up from the table. We played "Home Sweet Home" and left; everybody was crouched over the tables, like they'd been shot, like it was a scene in a movie. Just collapsed. I remember getting home at just about day-break from that kind of thing.

The Madison Nite Spot was a good opportunity for me, because Monroe liked my playing, and he would call on me. But Monroe was vicious. His reputation was that he got mad and killed a man with an axe. So I didn't ask too many questions.

Ray Charles would come to town, and Ray Charles at that time wasn't the Ray Charles that people know about now: he imitated Percy Mayfield, and was really an exact copy of Charles Brown. "Bells will be ringing," and all that kind of thing. In later years he changed his style, intentionally, to be rough. He developed his own type of sing-ing, with that little growl in it; that was his creation. Before that, he was trying to be a smooth singer.

He idolized Louis Jordan: that's why Ray Charles played the saxo-phone. He would carry that saxophone with him everywhere, even after he got famous, and he would get up and play some blues on it. A lot of people don't know that. Later on, he changed to the Ray Charles that you know about.

One time he had his group in there, and one of his members said something that was insulting to one of the workers at Monroe's Tav-ern. Monroe came and nearly beat the poor musician to death, man—nearly killed him. I wasn't there that night—I think I was in college at that time—but I heard about it. Everybody in Birmingham knew about it. The musicians union came to see what was happening, and they made Monroe pay for the fellow's hospitalization and everything. Monroe was a vicious person, and he was very arrogant. When you got to the door, to make sure you didn't have any behavioral problems, when the guy sells you a ticket he shows you his gun: "*What do you want?*" If you're afraid, you'd turn around and go somewhere else. They'd do that to intimidate you. "You know doggone well what the cost of a ticket is! Put the money up or get away from here!" You're with your sweetheart; you don't want that to happen. But that was how Monroe ran his club.

The other night spot that gave youngsters, and oldsters, too, a chance to play was the Grand Terrace. The Grand Terrace is going out near Forestdale, out on Highway 78 West. That's where B. B. King and the blues bands would come. It was named after the Grand Terrace in Chicago. The person who ran the Grand Terrace was a person they called "Foots." Foots Shelton. He lived out there; he had a bedroom and everything in that club. Of course, like all those places, they had the little cabins where you could go and have sex: you'd get up off the dance floor and come in there and have sex. And Foots was just as vicious as Monroe. In fact, there was an altercation where he misplaced a fellow's hat. You know how you check your coat and hat: this fellow was waiting for his hat. He was looking at it—said, "There it is, right there!"

Foots got mad and shot him. "*That's* not your hat." BAM!

That was the kind of thing that went on.

There's something else that I really want to tell about: because people—no matter how depressed they are, or how uneducated they are, or how *whatever*—you can mistreat them until it reaches a point where they rebel. I don't care what group it is: it's common to all races of people, and it's probably common in the animal world, too, that if you abuse them so much, they break.

This was during the war, and everybody was saving money. You had tokens, you sacrificed for the war, gas is rationed, and all that type of thing. There was no money. But one night they had a big party at the Grand Terrace, and it all ended in a terrible situation, because the band was about to play, and the people started turning the tables over.

Dances would not start until around eleven o'clock, and they would go on until morning. At that time people were working in the steel mills, and they had what they called a triple shift. They would get off at eleven, and they would have time to go home and put their clothes on, and then go to the dance. The TCI workers and the miners would go home and put on all their finery, their tuxedos and everything; they would get their wives who had been slaving all day and dress them up and come out there to the Grand Terrace.

What Foots had done: instead of having ashtrays, he had cut sardine cans and put them on the table. People were in their tuxedos. And they couldn't take it—it was *insulting*. A sardine can on your table for an ashtray! That's what I mean about reaching the boiling point: where you take so much, and then you can't take it anymore. Even the most weak-minded person would rebel against that. He's gone home and gotten his bath and gotten his tuxedo on; he's got his wife that he's bought a beautiful dress for, and she's probably got perfume and all that on; and he comes to sit at a table, with no tablecloth or anything, and a big *sardine* can sitting in the middle of it. That was just the pits. And they turned it over; they turned it out. They said, "I'm not going to take this." They started turning over the chairs—Foots was back in his room—and they said, "Come on out of there! Bring your guns! We're going to kill you!"

Foots suffered because of that for a while—until he could bring another big band in there, like Louis Jordan, and everything was forgotten.

When I was coming up, I was always interested in knowing who the musicians were. And Birmingham had some musicians that nobody's ever heard of. One was named Charlie Cox—he was a wizard reed man— and then there was Delmas Means, whose interest was the clarinet. At first, he was a student of Professor Whatley, but he wasn't interested in jazz. He didn't sound like us. I remember my brother used to come home and say, "Listen, you need to hear Delmas Means." He was practicing all these great pieces of music—concertos and things—and it didn't even *sound* like a clarinet. He was the projectionist at the Famous Theatre, but finally he left and went to California and got with the symphony.

We had a man—Hurlon, I think his name was—and he was teaching violin. Nobody knew anything about a violin but Pops Williams, and Pops was interested in jazz. But Mr. Hurlon would get a group of youngsters together to play the classical violin. He didn't have many players, but there were some—like Hampton St. Paul Reese III—who took lessons from Mr. Hurlon.

Hampton St. Paul Reese III: *he* was a different fellow. Fess wanted to kill him. He would come to school in his pajama top, and he was just *weird*. He'd insist on you calling him *Hampton St. Paul Reese III*. His mother was a widowed woman and she did everything she could for him. He learned violin when everybody else was learning the trumpet or the clarinet or saxophone—and then he learned those instruments, too. In fact, he was the first one that would transcribe some of Dizzy Gillespie's music for us in the bebop era. He went off to the Navy Band, and he took lessons in New York and learned the Schillinger System of writing music. That's a mathematical system of writing—you had to be a mathematician to do it, but those formulas worked. He got to be a great writer of music, and he wrote all the music for B. B. King's orchestra for years. He could write for a small group, a large group, a symphony group—and he could do this without the piano. He could just sit on his porch and write, and he knew what he was doing.

There was one drummer I remember, because he played with me later on, called Cat Summerville. He had a huge cat drawn on his drum. He lived right across from where the jazz museum is now, in the fraternal hotel. You could play a show—the dancing, and the intro, the exits, and whatever's in between—Cat would just listen to it once, and his head was like an encyclopedia: he remembered all those things. That's why he got to be the champion—he was the champion drummer around here. If you wanted to play a show, you'd get Cat Summerville.

Birmingham had several families of musicians. Johnny Grimes and his brother, Baby Grimes, were both trumpeters; they went on to play with some of the big bands in New York. Then you had the Clarkes—Richard, Chuck, Peter, Mary Alice, and Babe Clarke—and of course, the Lowes: Sammy and J. L. Lowe and their sister, Leatha.

At that time, there were twelve or thirteen bands in Birmingham, other than Professor Whatley and Sun Ra. And they would always have somebody absent, where they'd call on you to come play. The musicians were interchangeable: you see this guy in that band and that guy in this band. But all of those bands were exceptionally good bands. They were *precise*—I think in some ways Whatley set the example. You had those that were copy bands—they played Count Basie's music, or they played Lionel Hampton's music, or whatever was popular—but Whatley had a band that could play just about anything.

Jesse Blackmon had a band in the forties, in my high school days. He had been around since the thirties. He was a piano player, Jesse Blackmon, and he played *everything*, everything. He idolized Count Basie. Jesse Blackmon had a *complete* band, and everybody in that band could read music, except Jesse; so he would depend on somebody else to rehearse his band. There were amateur arrangers, like a fellow named Bull Simpson—Charles Simpson. His mother was a schoolteacher. He had a brother; we called him "Little Simp." Little Simp played the saxophone, and Bull would write arrangements. He took a correspondence course in arranging, and he was very talented. He was a drummer, but he had to stop drums because he had hemorrhoids—so he picked up the saxophone and played it. He was one of Sonny Blount's early players, too. Jesse Blackmon would pay him a small amount of money for arrangements, so he could play just about anything that Professor Whatley played.

I don't know how true this is, but when Joe Guy came back to Birmingham, he and Bull became great friends, and I think Joe might have introduced Bull to narcotics. They played for years at a little jazz club, and they were able to do the things like Monk was doing, and Joe was doing, in New York City. They carried on that same kind of experimental thing here. The fellow that sponsored the club was an Italian guy—I think he's still around—and this club ran ten or twelve years. Joe played in there, and Bull Simpson.

Then we had a player, a phenomenal pianist, John L. Bell: he was another one of the ear players. I remember playing at the Grand Terrace, and what he would do with young musicians was try to throw you off. One Christmas I was home from Howard University; we were playing "Body and Soul" and he modulated into another key, which was very confusing to me. That made me go back to Howard and practice—so the next time I saw John L. Bell, he changed and I changed right with him.

He was one of those phenomenal guys that couldn't tell you what he was doing, or didn't *want* to tell you what he was doing. He and Joe Guy and Charles Clarke played at Bob's Savoy. It was a group of them that had been in the big time, had played with big bands, and they were back at home. Joe was sort of like a spiritual leader to them—but the spirit was in the wrong direction, with the drugs and everything. Later on, after I came back from Howard, in 1950, Joe worked for me for years and years at the Woodland Club.

As I say, the musicians here were a common pool: you'd be playing with me tonight, and if somebody needed you the next night, *they'd* call on you. That's how you got a chance to see and play with all these people. I was fortunate, because I was there, and I got to witness all this. And that got me, probably, out of my protective environment. I wanted to see how things *were,* on the other side of the street—because I was always curious.

I wanted to find out what people were doing out there.

7

Summers on the Road

WHILE I WAS IN HIGH SCHOOL, I GOT A CHANCE TO play with Sammy Green's stage show. Sammy Green was out of Atlanta, but they called him "Sammy Green from New Orleans." That was one of the first stage shows I played, because they would come to the Frolic Theatre every Tuesday and every Friday, and one night they called for a saxophone player: they sent to the union, to Fess Whatley, to send a saxophone player to play the show. Professor Whatley recommended me.

I guess Fess was under the impression that that band was something like his band, that read music—but it was a different scene when I got down to the Frolic Theatre. I wasn't doing any solos with Whatley's band. And I really wasn't prepared for what happened to me. I was expecting them to give me some music to play for the show, and I was looking for the conductor to come out. They had no conductor. The guy in charge was a fellow named Snake. He was one of the comedians in the group. He was an obese guy, and mean as the devil.

When he came out, he said, "Ready! We're going to bring the girls on with 'Rockin' the Blues.'"

I said, "I don't know 'Rockin' the Blues.'" So he hummed it—*doot*-doo, *doot*-doo—that's how he rehearsed, he'd hum it one time and expect you to play it. I'm sitting there dumfounded. I said, "I wonder what *key* it's in."

"I told them to send me a *musician!*" he said. "This boy can't even blow his *nose*."

I found out that there was another side of the world I hadn't been exposed to. So I started listening, trying to hear those things. There was another fellow in there—his name was Shaky. He was a trumpet player, and he shook all the time, just like the fellow in Sun Ra's band. He took me back in the corner and he played some notes for me and said, "Don't worry, man, you'll get it." I was able to get it, but it scared me to death.

The next time I saw Fess Whatley, he said: "How'd you do?"

"I did just fine." I didn't tell him what was wrong, because it opened my way to learning something nobody else had showed me.

I ended up doing real well with it: I was able to keep the job, and when they would come back and needed somebody, they'd send for me. I played a couple of months with Sammy Green, going back and forth to Atlanta. They played these shows at the 81 Theatre, on one of the tough streets in Atlanta, and they were drawing people in there. I got to do a good deal of traveling with them.

They had two brothers in that group. One played alto saxophone—they called him "Bummy." I forget his brother's name, but he played the trumpet. They were good musicians. I think they were from Birmingham, but they hooked up with this show long years ago, early on, and they'd been back and forth. I remember hearing them playing Duke's "Jeep's Blues." They played some pretty smart stuff.

Then they had a comedian called Sweetie Walker, and he played this *blues*. He played the old clarinet, just like a New Orleans player, in one of those weird keys. Those old blues guys didn't care *what* key it's in; just wherever they heard it, they'd play it. You'd have trouble until you could adjust to that. When I heard them, I'd go home and test them, and try to find out what in the world they were doing.

You find out: if you get around a road situation, you get a little glimpse of what it's all about. I was on the road with this fellow Shaky, in Sammy Green's band, and he had a wife named Lewessika—I never will forget it—she was a Creole from New Orleans, and they would sit on the bus and they would *cut* each other. With beer bottles—a broken beer can. I never could understand it; it was sadistic. And nobody but me paid much attention to it. They wouldn't cut each other's throat or anything like that, but their side or something; you would see their shirts would have blood on them. The next morning they'd be all hugged up together. Bleeding together. Somebody on the show—it wasn't Sammy, because he didn't ride with us; he rode in his own car—somebody on the show would say, "Well, don't bother about that. They do that all the time. Don't stop them, because they'll join together and get *you!*" In other words, "It's our business, leave us alone." That's one of the things that you experience when you're out there.

They just *mangled* each other.

You have to process those things in your head. You say, "Well, why did they do that?" But you can't judge them on any kind of moralistic standard—you just say, "That's one of the things that he did," or "she did." That's just part of their being. And you go on.

Before I finished high school, I got the chance, in the summers, to play in some of the big bands. The summers were divided by different jobs, particularly after I got to college.

One of the most important experiences I had was playing with Mantan Moreland's Hot Harlem Revue. We would play different theatres, and they had some sheet music, but most of it was head arrangements; you had to hear and memorize what you were playing. They had some pretty good performers—musicians and dancers and comedians. They traveled all over. Mantan was one of the greatest entertainers I knew, because no matter where he would perform, people would come. He had been in Hollywood; he had been in movies with Charlie Chan. He was Charlie Chan's sidekick—they called him "Birmingham." He was a real fine actor. A great comedian. He was the head of the show.

I think the show went as far as San Antone, Texas. They'd start off with a cast of people, musicians and all, and as they'd go along, people would quit and they'd get somebody from the next town to join up with the show. The big bands were like that, too: they'd go out and somebody gets fired, or somebody walks off—so they call on another musician to take their place. I got a lot of work like that later.

When you go on a tour, you might start with this band and then get into that band, and after that you get another band. When things die down with this group, there's always somebody else cranking up that needs a musician. I imagine it happens to a lot of players: you go out there in, say, September, and you connect with somebody else in, maybe, November. You might not get back home for a couple of years. When your name is known out there, guys like Duke or Basie or somebody would send for you, even if you're playing for somebody else.

I had some experiences in Mantan Moreland's group. Sometimes the show would make money, but it wasn't enough. They had a manager called Donaldson; Donaldson would handle all the money. We were out somewhere where they were coming up short—not on paying the musicians, but the chorus line. The girls hadn't been paid. That's when I overheard a conversation between Donaldson and Mantan: I walked into the restroom and they were fussing. Donaldson was saying that he wasn't going to pay the girls, and Mantan would say, "*Pay* them! What's wrong with you?" I heard Mantan say, "All *I* want is enough money to send home to my daughter. That's why I'm out here." In other words, "If it wasn't for that, I'd be out of here right now."

Mantan had this tremendous talent. He would never come out looking bad; he would always be neatly dressed. And he would say that, no matter where you are, you're not supposed to use profanity. He said that we had some on the show that would use curse words and that type of lowdown thing. We had some comedians that were just *nasty*. They have them today—using profane words and all that. Mantan said, "I don't do vulgar shows. I'm an artist." He said, "I don't have to stoop to that kind of thing. I can walk out on the stage and just *move*, and people will laugh." And that was true. He could come out on stage, and bulge his eyes, and make his clothes shudder—he could do all that kind of thing.

He said, "When you have to curse to get your audience's attention, that wears out quickly. When you do that one time, it has an effect: you'll have to keep doing it. Then it gets lower, and lower, and lower—and then you're not really a comedian. It's like seeing a naked lady walk into the room: the first time, you're shocked. But the next time, it's just like so much meat at the grocery store. The shock value's all gone." So he said, "Never do that to your audience."

They had one guy on that show—speaking of professionalism and artistry in the comedian world—this guy was called "Iron Jaw." His act was: he would pick up chairs in his mouth—one chair, two—and he would swing these chairs around. You were standing on the bandstand playing—and naturally, I didn't want to get hit by one of these chairs. I would be playing, and I would step back.

Iron Jaw called me aside. He said, "What's wrong with you? I'm a professional!"

I didn't know what he was talking about. I said, "I know you're a professional, and I like your act."

He started cursing. He said, "I'd better not ever catch you stepping back when I'm doing my act!"

"Man," I said, "you think I'm going to let one of those things slam into my head?"

He said, "I'm an *artist!*" I mean, he was mad—and I was just trying to protect myself! "I'm not going to drop that chair. You move, and people don't respect my act: because they think, what is *he* afraid of?"

He said, "The next time I see you moving on my act, I'm going to *kill* you."

Wow.

So I found out that they take pride in what they're doing. That's his livelihood. I guess I hadn't seen that.

I wanted to go tell Mantan about it, but I decided, no, I won't say anything.

A couple of days passed, and somebody said, "Iron Jaw wants to see you."

"What does he want to see me for? I don't want to go down there!"

"He won't bother you, man, he just wants to talk to you."

I went down there. When I walked into his room, he had a great, big hookah—he's smoking opium or something. He said, "We can be friends." He's puffing on this thing. Says, "I'm sorry about what happened."

I said, "I'm sorry, too." And I got out of there, quick.

One time we were playing at this theatre—it must have been in Louisiana somewhere—we were about to play, and there was no drummer. I looked around and said, "What are we going to do? We've got to have a drummer."

Just before the curtain came up for the dancers to come out on the floor, we looked out in the audience, and our drummer was sitting there—he had gotten so high he thought he came to *look* at a drummer. He was supposed to be playing on stage, but he thought he was there to *witness* the band. They jerked him up on stage, and he shook his head and went on to play the show.

That was the first indication to me that everything wasn't just kosher in the band.

The leader of Mantan's band was a guy named Jimmy Hines. Jimmy Hines, I think, came from Washington with his wife, and he was a good saxophone player. I didn't know, at that time, that he had any kind of a habit.

We played Mobile one weekend and everything was going fine. It was Friday night, and we were supposed to get paid on Saturday—but they arrested Jimmy, because he went and stuck up the teller at the door. Jimmy always had this hypersensitivity that he wasn't going to get paid—so he held up the *teller,* to get his money!

This bizarre behavior was going on all around me with Jimmy and his band.

They put Jimmy in jail, and Mantan said, "That's okay, I'll fix it."

We went to the police station, and oh, man, they're going to put Jimmy in jail for *life* down there in Mobile. Mantan talked to the police: he said, "Here we are on the road, and there's his wife over there, and you know that boy"—called him "boy"—said, "he ain't got good sense; couldn't you look at him and tell?" The police went for that, because that's *Mantan Moreland.* Said, "I'm out here on the road; I don't want to be out here, but I got to feed my family, and here he is going to tear up my show—and no doubt he was smoking one of those funny cigarettes—and in one way I think you *ought* to put him in jail, but can't you *see* he ain't got good sense? He probably didn't go to the second grade . . ."

The police looked at Jimmy: "Let him go. Get on out of here."

So, Jimmy: now he wanted to be *angry,* because Mantan got him out of jail. He never got over the fact that his pride had been hurt, because Mantan went down there and got him out—and had to be what Jimmy called "an ignorant black clown" to get him out of there. Mantan *had* to do that to keep himself afloat. Jimmy said, "He says what the white folks want him to say"—but Mantan had to be a superb actor to get him out of there. Mantan had to prove that although Jimmy was a nice-looking guy and could speak intelligently—more so than most people down there, in fact; he was probably more literate than that policeman—he had to make a plea because of Jimmy's wife and the show, and act like Jimmy didn't know any better and would just be more trouble for them to keep in jail. So that kind of talk he used—

"that boy" and that type of thing—was what the Southern people in Mobile looked for; they said, "Here's a good boy, he wants this other boy out of here, let's let him go."

After that, it was like Jimmy sort of faded out. In fact, the other players faded out, too. Jimmy's manhood was insulted, so he found a way to get off the show. Some of the guys were quitting anyway—the piano player got disgusted because every night it would be one thing after the other. Pretty soon the whole band was gone.

I was out in Dallas, Texas, with Mantan, and all the band had quit. We were what we called "deadheading" back from Texas—all the way from San Antone back to home. When bands go out on the road like that, they do the original tour, then they deadhead back to home base, picking up jobs on the way back.

The band had quit, so I had to pick up musicians along the way from different unions: I'd go out in the morning and get a drummer or a trumpet player. I'd go to the musicians union and find out if they had some players to play the show. I'd get them and I'd pay them what their union scale was, per man, the minimum scale. Some towns were twenty dollars a show or for two shows, and some were eight dollars. Mobile, I think, had the lowest one.

We were in this restaurant. I was eating and Mantan was in there, and the musicians that we picked up were in a booth. They were all talking—they were talking about the diminished seventh chord, and "the flatted fifth goes to the augmented eleventh," and "here's a minor ninth, man, what would you do there?" And how they studied with somebody, and they had finished their work at Juilliard, and all—just *talking*. Mantan overheard it. He said, "Juniflip"—they called me "Juniflip"—"We *got* somebody, man. Now we got some *real* musicians for a change. Listen at them! I'm so glad we got somebody that's gonna really *cut* this show."

The very first number, the chorus line came out to dance—the timing was so bad, the girls were tripping all over each other. The drummer dropped his sticks; the dancers had to do double takes because the tempo was changing; it was a disaster. We had to close the curtain. They had to talk to the audience—"Settle down, now"—so the people wouldn't want their money back—a *full house* of people—but we finally made it through the show. And these were the "superior" musicians! We struggled through that show. We cut out *half* of it.

Donaldson said, "I'm not going to pay them anything!" But they were union musicians and they had played; they were supposed to get a certain amount of money. Mantan said, "You *got* to pay them!"

"I'll pay them what they're *worth!*"

I overheard that—I said, "They've got all kinds of guns out there, man." I said, "You better pay these guys what they *ask* for."

They went out there and paid them.

It all ended as a great experience. All in all, I got a chance to be around some pretty mature musicians. In fact, once I overheard a conversation coming from some players. I was young. They were talking about me and they said, "He'll be okay once he gets his breathing together." I didn't know anything about *breathing*—I said, "I *am* breathing, have I got asthma or something?" No: that meant making sentences out of your solos. If you say, "I, went, to, town, yesterday," you're ignorant: it's "I went to town yesterday." You want it to flow. Otherwise, it's going to sound like you're just shooting at stars—*doot, doot, doot; doot, doot, doot*—catching a breath here and a breath there. That doesn't put a carpet down; it doesn't have that flow.

When I started listening to what other players I admired were doing—like Johnny Hodges and Charlie Parker—I found out they had gotten their breathing right. If you listen to the master players, they all have a certain place where they catch a breath. They don't cut a phrase; it comes out in a complete sentence. If they're very good, it comes out in a complete paragraph. In music, the most simple sentence is four bars—the greater the players, the longer the length of the sentence. It's like going from elementary school to writing a novel or a poem. You want to be fluent.

If you're playing a solo, you're like a preacher preaching a sermon. You develop, like you're developing a thesis, or telling a story: the story gets bigger and bigger, and you end up with a climax.

That's what they were talking about, "breathing," but they couldn't explain it to you. It's hard to explain to a child that "your phrases are too choppy."

Mantan really took me under his wing. On the bus he would advise me about things. It seemed to him that I was a young little, innocent guy. Once I was talking to one of the chorus girls, and he came to me and pointed out that he didn't want me to have anything to do with this particular person, because she was notorious—you're riding the bus at night, she'd probably go and have sex with somebody on that bus. He said, "You have to be careful, because that one there has been on this show for a long time, and she's never sent a dollar home to her mama." He said, "You watch that. How could she care about you or anybody else, if she doesn't even send her *mama* a note?" He knew I was vulnerable. He said, "When you're around somebody, find out how they treat their parents. How are you going to make such a big difference in *love* if this person wouldn't even feed her own mother?"

Another thing: he said, "Now, you see a woman—some people look real good when they're young—but if you're going to marry them, you need to look at their mama. Look what's going to happen." That was knowledge; worldly knowledge. "They're going to swell up; you could be with this beautiful little doll, but this little doll is going to expand! Will you still love them after they get five or more years on them and look like they're going to explode?" That was an education for me, because I didn't know anything. I probably thought that Shirley Temple would look like Shirley Temple after she got fifty years old—with the little locks and everything. I didn't like Shirley Temple anyway, but those were words of wisdom. And that was the thing.

He'd tell you: "I'm a professional. And you're a professional." He would always dress real well, and I remember one time he bought this beautiful brown suit; tailor-made suit. He *believed* in tailor-made suits. He lived like he was in Hollywood. And he convinced me to save up enough money so that when he ordered another suit, I could get me one.

I got a brown suit and kept it for years.

Mantan.

I remember in Dallas, we went into this place, and everybody's dressed up in devils' suits: all women dressed with little devils' suits, and little tails behind them. The whole place was full of them. I was sitting down at a table, and two or three of them descended on me. I was young—I didn't know what it was—but they all sat at the table and they were going to set me up to buy drinks. I don't know how we got into this place. But Mantan came up and he said, "No, no. When you're out here on the road, you don't buy anything. *They* pay. They pay to entertain *you*." So you learn things. "You're their guest. The rule is, you make money; you send your money home."

I did what Mantan said: I was sending my money home, because

I wanted to have something saved—so I could just do nothing for a couple of months. I thought I would get to rest when I got off the road. So I'd go to the Western Union in Shreveport, Louisiana, or in Columbus, Mississippi; I'd put my money in there, whenever we got paid.

When I came off the road, Grandma said, "You did such a nice thing, donating your money to the church." I found out my grandmother had given *all my money* to the Missionary Society. I wanted to curse, but I looked at her—that's my *grandma* . . .

I said, "Praise the Lord for good things."

It must have been a year after I played with Jimmy Hines and Mantan that I went on tour with a fellow by the name of Sax Carey. Sax Carey was not a saxophone player, he was a guitar player—like Banjo Bill, I don't know how they got those names. I think he came from Florida, and every summer the musicians from Sonny Blount's band would go off with Sax Carey. Man for man, it was the same musicians in that band.

Sax Carey was not well known, but he had a good band and they traveled all over and went all through Mississippi and up through Memphis and ended up in what we call "Nap Town": Indianapolis, Indiana.

He had two cars, two pretty good cars, and he was a very nice fellow. Had a good book of music. And his band was entertaining: they played a mixture of blues and big band stuff, like Basie's. They didn't have a featured singer or anything; I think Sax did some singing.

We ended up in Davenport, Iowa, where Bix Beiderbecke came from, the great white jazz player with Paul Whiteman; this was his hometown. Somehow or another, Sax Carey had a booking there, and we arrived early one morning. We were sleeping on the bus, and I woke up—I saw this little kid peering through the window at me. He scared me to death. I looked at him: he was a little youngster, maybe twelve or thirteen years old, and he had never seen a black person before, in his whole life. He just stood there looking. He had no prejudice, he had nothing—he had just discovered something. He's looking through that glass at me, and I looked at him. I finally got off the bus and I went out and said, "How you doing?" He said, "How *you* doing," and we talked.

We were the only blacks in this town. And we wondered, should we play this dance at all? Do you think they'll do something to us in a place like this? In certain places, if you don't know a lot about people, you expect trouble where there is no trouble.

It was in a little barn that we played. And that was one of the most beautiful things we ever did. People appreciated us. They clapped after every number. And they knew a lot about jazz. They *welcomed* us in Davenport, Iowa.

We did okay in that band until we got to Nap Town, and we were sort of waiting for something else to occur. While we were there, I got a chance to hear and meet some of the fellows in Dizzy Gillespie's band, like Max Roach; they were young then, and they were playing in this hotel ballroom there. I saw some people there that I wouldn't have gotten a chance to see: Billy Eckstine, Art Blakely, and Dizzy. I got a chance to hear them, because our band wasn't doing very much.

There was a band there called Joe Webb. These are what we called territory bands: they'd never make the big top, but they traveled all around a few cities, and that was their territory. They might go as far as Colorado. A lot of them were riff bands, where the bands would mostly play the blues. You would repeat one riff over and over again, so they didn't call for much reading.

Joe Webb's band had this real stout woman singer, Big Maybelle. Joe Webb needed an alto sax player, so I went on tour with them. That lasted two or three weeks, and in the meantime, they made some recordings.

As I say, when you're out there, you'll connect with other musicians. On that trip with Joe Webb I got a chance to play with Lucky Millinder and two other bands; then I came back to Nap Town and got back with Sax Carey, the band that I started out with. They were stranded there, and when I came back, I had enough money so the whole band could get back home.

That was the way that went.

Road conditions are very exciting when you're in your teens and early twenties. You get a chance to see all kinds of places. But you'll find that the Holiday Inn in Jackson, Mississippi, is just the same way it is in Birmingham. You know where all the soap is; you know where the beds are. You go to Paris, the same thing. You won't get to see the Eiffel Tower, but you'll know what's in the Radisson. A lot of people think, "Hey, he's traveling; he's seeing the world." You're not seeing the world, you're seeing the inside of a truck, of a van, or the inside of a bus, if you can get one. And that's it. You ask somebody, "Where's a good place to eat?" and they'll probably put you in the Waldorf Astoria. No. You have to say, "Where's the *cheapest* place to eat?"

Now, musicians are guilty of even *having* money and not buying good food. Even if they could afford a steak, a hot dog would do. So we ate at a lot of the places they called "greasy spoons." There was one in Atlanta, across the street from the 81 Theatre, and their popular food was pig ears. You'd go and buy a pig ear sandwich: they'd fix it up with a lot of seasoning and everything, and it tastes really nice. But the only thing with a pig ear sandwich is you can eat it at ten o'clock and at ten fifteen you're hungry again. You had no nutritional value. "Give me a pig ear sandwich"; "Okay"; *boom;* and you'd sit down and eat it and before you got out of the place you're hungry again. Because it's nothing but a little gristle, a little fat, and that's all—well, it's a pig's ear. No substance. So I try to avoid eating pig ear sandwiches. They put onions and peppers and all that stuff on it. But it's still a pig ear.

Musicians might say, "If you want to get a stomachful, you buy you some peanuts and drink a Coke"—because the Coke will swell the peanuts in your stomach, and you'll get the false feeling that you're full. But not with a pig ear sandwich. No—you're just down the river with a pig ear sandwich.

I could hear at night on some of the busses—particularly Tiny Bradshaw, who I played with later on—around twelve o'clock you hear those cans of sardines pop. Somebody getting their nightly meal. The bus would be so full of odor that you could hardly stay in there.

Any town—say, Greensboro, North Carolina, or Atkinsville, South Carolina—when you get to town, you'd know the richest person in town—and this is a fact, I found this out myself—was the undertaker. The undertaker usually was the one that booked the bands. In all those towns you had a Carver Theatre and a Booker T. Washington Theatre. That's where you played. And you could depend on all the blacks living on one side of the railroad track, and the whites on the other side.

So: if you go to the black community, you know you're going to cross the railroad track; if you want to find the person who has the money, it's the undertaker; and the place you're going to play is either the Carver Theatre or the Booker T. Washington Theatre. Okay? Those are the rules.

The bands at that time traveled in cars if they didn't have buses.

Now, you have to separate this from the big bands, like Ellington or Jimmy Lunceford and some others like that, who had their own transportation and great sophistication. In these little territory bands, you had to cramp up in a car or something.

Sax Carey and Mantan Moreland's revue, and Tiny Bradshaw: they always had these cars or buses that were in ill repair. I remember traveling through Texas with, I think, Mantan's show. The roads were so flat you could go to sleep hearing that *flap, flap, flap.* It looked like they never had a turn: it was just straight for hundreds of miles. No curves, no nothing. And that would put you to sleep. I remember on that bus, we had a lot of chorus girls and things on there, about thirty people in all—I woke up once and the *driver* was asleep. I had to run up, and he pulled over and shook his head to wake up and thanked me. I don't know how long he had been sleeping, but the roads were straight, so thank God he didn't have to make a curve. Those are the kinds of things that you don't write home about. You just say, "All is well, we're having a wonderful time!"

Meanwhile, you got a chance to stay in all kinds of places. Of course, segregation was really tough during those times, so usually there weren't hotels; you had to stay in somebody's converted home that would be a rooming house for coloreds. No matter how big the band was, you all had to stay there. I was out there on the road, and as I told you before, I wasn't too sexually savvy; I didn't know about a lot of things. We were somewhere near Atlanta—Macon, Georgia, or someplace like that—and we went to this lady's house. Listen! It was filthy, as most of them were then. People didn't change their bedding and all that, but you're on the road: you get used to that type of thing.

I was trying to disrobe, and every time I would take off a short or something, somebody'd say, "Ooohh!" I said, "What's going on here?" Every time I'd take something off, I'd hear this sound coming from the next room.

I looked across the bed, and there were these three little *peepholes.* I guess I was stupid. I picked up a pencil. I went to that peephole, and I stuck that pencil in there.

"*Aaa-ahh!*"

The next thing I know, I had to get out of there. It was the son of the lady downstairs. I don't know whether I ripped his eye open, but I hit him with that pencil. Everybody in the band got mad at me, because they had to leave, too. *I* didn't know what it was, I just heard these noises. I didn't know it was a *sex* predator, I didn't know he was perverted. I didn't even get a chance to see him. And the lady—she had seemed so nice—she started cursing everybody: "Get out of my home!"

That's what you get when you're out there on the road. You get all these experiences. Just like with Jimmy Hines: you didn't know whether he was going to be sticking up the place to get his money, or whether Iron Jaw would kill you—but that's the excitement you go through. Now, if I wasn't *young* then—if something happened to me now like the time Ironjaw threatened me—I would have caught the next bus home. If somebody said that today, I'd catch an *airplane* out of there.

So I guess youth has its curiosity.

The summer before my last year of high school, I worked on a tobacco farm in Hazardville, Connecticut. We were up there three months. It was supposed to help you make some money to go to college: they'd send the money home to your folks, and you could get a good pile of money. In fact, that's the first time in my life that I got to file my income tax reports.

We packed up—you didn't have to bring a lot of clothes, just things to work in—and we traveled. I took my saxophone with me. A good friend of mine, Jesse Champion—he died just recently—he knew all of Duke Ellington's songs: "I'm Beginning to See the Light" and "A Train" and all of them. We played all the way up there, on the train. When we got there, we got our bunks and everything, and we were anxious to see the city.

They had one black guy in Hazardville, and he was a graduate of Tuskegee Institute, where he had studied horseshoeing. He took his family up there, and they honored him so much in that little community. I can't remember his name, but he was the one who took care of all the livestock. One Sunday he came down to the farm, and he took us all to his church. It was a Catholic church. The people were so welcoming to us. We had never seen anything like this.

But the thing that really got me was we went to Springfield, Massachusetts, and that's where they had this big pavilion. And guess who was playing when we were there:

Duke Ellington.

I must have been about sixteen, getting ready to finish my last year in high school. I know I hadn't graduated yet, because I remember going back to school and talking about this. I looked up there: it was an open-air dance pavilion—it looked like it was the size of Legion Field—and I had never seen that many people together. That's a great experience when you can see a *thousand* people dancing. That was Duke Ellington. They had their summer uniforms on, and white jackets, and they were *playing,* boy—I stood there and watched. I was just watching, *watching* what was going on in that band. Just watching them, man. He was featuring the soloists, like Lawrence Brown and Johnny Hodges, and that just penetrated my soul.

When you have a breathtaking experience like that, it leaves an impact on you. You can see all the dramatic plays on television and movies, but it's not like the experience of going on Broadway and seeing one of those real plays. I've played in a lot of them, and there's nothing that can beat the live performance. The New York Philharmonic, man, Orchestra: you go in there, and just to hear them tuning up, getting ready to play, is an awesome thing. Just to *see* it, visually.

I got close to Johnny Hodges. He was one of my idols. I had never seen somebody who's so detached: he didn't smile; he didn't move. He looked like he didn't have any rhythm, he's just standing there—and notes *flying* out of that horn. You're talking about *cool.* Everybody was perspiring, but he was just standing still.

At the end of this thing, it looked like Duke was trying to tear that band apart. They started blowing their guts out, man. One number after another, RAWR! They were relaxed most of the time, but when it would end: the *power* would come down. All those trumpets would be blasting.

I said, "Wow. What in the world is *this?*"

8

Howard

I GRADUATED FROM HIGH SCHOOL IN 1945. ALL MY contemporaries were going off to the colleges, and I didn't have a scholarship. So Sun Ra wrote a letter to Howard University, and it was a letter that was so unusual. He said that he had a player—that he was my mentor—and that if they furnished me a full scholarship to Howard University, room and board, then I would *certainly* make their institution a viable place to go.

Howard University, of course, is over a hundred and some-odd years old; they've got a school of law, ministry, chemistry, medicine, everything. But he didn't see it like that—this was Sun Ra—he told them that if *I* got there, *then* they would become famous! He was saying what I could do for them at Howard University, not what Howard University would do for me. That was his concept: the world depended on them giving me everything. If not, they're going to miss out.

Of course, they sent a letter back that wasn't very commendatory to him, at all. They reminded him that they were one of the greatest black institutions in the world. They didn't have a jazz band, and they didn't want to *get* one. Those music schools—in particular the black ones—were traditional. They taught the fundamentals and theory; they were aware of jazz, but it didn't have any prestige. All the schools have jazz in their curriculum now, but during my time there was no recognized jazz program. There wasn't such thing as a course in improvisation—no, no, no. It didn't exist.

They said that if I came up there, they wouldn't give me a dime, a scholarship or anything. But the drop line was that if I got there, they would *listen*. And that's how I got in.

My life changed when I went to Howard University and met other people: we had a diversity of races there. There were people from Africa, from Germany, from Czechoslovakia—and I didn't know how I would make it, because they were so far advanced. Some had knowledge of Latin, German, Spanish, *all* those kinds of things—they came out of high school speaking *three* languages! I thought I was well equipped the first year I got into college, but I found out I wasn't: there were people from other parts of the country, and all over the world, who knew more about music and English and history than I could ever have imagined. They seemed to be thirty years ahead of me. I had to understand: how could that be? How could this African—who was supposed to be with some kind of spear in his hand—know more about philosophy, and about your *American* philosophers, than you? I had thought they were supposed to be savages.

I had always heard about Chinese people, because I would go to the movies and they'd always be swinging on a rope with a knife in their mouth. They were supposed to be so sneaky-eyed and slow: they could sneak up on you with knives, but you were faster than they were and could knock them out. If it was hand-to-hand fighting, I'd beat *five* of them, because I'm an *American! Bam,* "Get out of here!" I really thought that. But at Howard, I had to learn that there are all types of people, and things are not always what you thought.

Howard University was just an explosion for me.

The first musical experience I had there was: a group of musicians met down in the rec room at Cook Hall. They had a jam session, and everybody was playing. I knew a *few* things, but there was one fellow that I am still acquainted with, he really made his mark: Benny Golson. He played the saxophone—the big sax, the tenor sax—and I played the alto. He got up and played, note for note, a *masterful* solo that he had gotten off Coleman Hawkins, the greatest saxophone player. "Body and Soul"—that thing is still one of the greatest tenor saxophone solos. And I just stood there wondering how he could do that.

We had another fellow, Carlton Drinkard, who later played with Billie Holiday. He was a pianist and a trumpet player, so he had two things going for him. He got up there and he played Bunny Berigan's "I Can't Get Started." Cracked a few notes along the way, but then he played this *solo*. I was awed at the fact that these guys could play these terrific solos, all this jazz, just out of their heads, the first night I got there. That was a defining experience for me.

When I got to Howard, I experienced young people, my age, who had just taken a different route to music; it seemed like their approach had been quite different than mine. Mine was strictly academic: playing the songs exactly as they were written. No improvising. But when I got to Howard, a whole world started opening up to me.

When we did our first rehearsal, I had a clarinet, and I didn't have what we call a tray case that you could put two instruments in. I just had the saxophone case, so I had stuck the clarinet down in the bell of the saxophone—which is a terrible way to do things—and since my case was broken, I had a belt wrapped around it. Shortly after the jam session, I think it must have been the next day, I opened up this case, and they looked and said, "What's that?" They hadn't been around clarinets. "Can you play that thing?" I said, "Yeah." Professor Whatley's music required you to double—clarinet and saxophone. "Well, hey, man, we got some music for that." They had Artie Shaw's "Begin the Beguine," which was all clarinet, and they had Benny Goodman's stuff. They watched me play a little something and they said, "Man, let's try 'Begin the Beguine.'" I had played that with Whatley, so I played it—"*Wow*, man." "Begin the Beguine" required the trumpets to have mutes. They didn't have any mutes, so they said, "Let's go *get* some."

The only thing that I was superior in was that I could read music—and the other thing was I could double. That gave me a job. In fact, I became the lead saxophone player—not because I was the best; there were other guys that could blow the *bell* off those horns, man—but they had problems in reading. Although they were *awesome* players, I found out I was needed, because I could show them something about reading music. They would stop and say, "Show me how this goes." They were quick to catch on, and they were appreciative. And they were masters at playing.

We had a fourteen-piece band—the Howard Swingmasters—and we had some of the greatest young musicians, who really became famous. Eddie Jones, the bassist, played with Count Basie. The trombone player, Bill Hughes, became the leader of Basie's band after Basie passed away. Rick Henderson was our saxophone player; he played with Duke. Carlton Drinkard went to California and made history. Carrington Visor, tenor sax. And of course, Benny Golson: he's the one that wrote "I Remember Clifford," one of the jazz masterpieces, and a lot of jazz standards. Famous person, man. Those were the kind of people we had in that band.

We practiced down in the basement of Cook Hall a couple of nights a week, and we were getting better and better. We had a thing going where the dean—the caretaker for the dorm, they called him a dean— he told us one time, "You know what? You guys in this Howard Swing-masters: you won't be here when the grass turns green." In other words, it was winter, then; by the spring we'd be flunked out.

There's a fellow, he was from Dallas; his name was Summerville. He played the bass, and he had a stutter in his voice. He said to us, "N-n-n-*no*. N-n-n-*no*." Said, "W-We're not going to flunk. W-W-We're not going to flunk. I-I got a system; I got a plan."

We listened to him, and he told a guy: "Y-You're good at history. You tutor." This guy from Philadelphia: "*You're* good at math. You tutor." So within the band we had a tutor for all the subjects. If you weren't doing well, they'd find out about it: they would lock you in your room, and throw the books over the transom. And you had to get it. Your tutor would report you. They'd have a band meeting, and you had to show your midterm reports. If it wasn't above average, you'd be in bad shape, man. They'd make life *hard* for you.

We had four years together. Graduating from Howard was a wonderful experience. It was in 1949—they called us the "forty-niners"— and everybody in that band, in 1949, graduated from Howard University with honors. That's the actual truth. Because you couldn't quit. I've got a thing they gave to me, it's like a Roman jug with two handles on it; I look at that sometimes and think about what you can do. It's *nothing* impossible. All of those guys got to be successful. Some of them went into dentistry; some of them went into music, like I did; some of them went into law.

At that time, in the forties, you had some older people come into college on the GI Bill, and some of them were famous, like Sir Charles Thompson, who wrote "Robbins Nest" for Illinois Jacquet; that was a piece we all talked about. In fact, one of the first things I remember about Benny Golson: he did an arrangement of "Robbins Nest," where he put some bell tones in his part, and I thought that was unique, even then. Sir Charles did a lot of writing in the bop form. Then there was the saxophone player Charlie Rouse, who played for a long time with Thelonious Monk. All of those people were outstanding, and they were all there with us.

One of the guys in that band—we called him "Prof Green"—he came from Boston, and he was a little fellow, about that tall. He was the one that managed the band, and he wanted to be known as "The Little Giant of Song." He wasn't a musician, but he could sing a little, and he loved Billy Eckstine, the big baritone singer—great, *handsome* guy. Prof was nowhere in the world *near* handsome—he had this long nose and this weird part in his hair—but he would get out there and say, "*Aloooone from night to night, you'll find meeee!*" Just like Billy Eckstine. "*I'm just a prisoner of looove!*"—and he'd say, "Watch 'em swoon, watch 'em swoon!"

But he had brilliance. He had attended all the classes with Alain Locke, the great philosopher. Anybody that was real heavy—he called it being *heavy*—he'd go there and take notes, man, and he'd be in that class. He could have finished Howard University already—he'd taken all the courses he needed—but he had so many resources. He didn't present himself for graduation because he wanted to hear what Dr. Locke was saying. He'd tell you: "You need to know about Goethe, man, and *Faust*." And tell you, "Take the course, man, you'll be okay." He could tell you all kinds of things about astronomy; then he would go into Socrates and Plato; he would discuss the "I-Me" circle, and all that kind of stuff, and he would tell you, "Listen to Dr. Locke: he's heavy."

He could tell you things—like, about Alain Locke: that he lived in a house in Washington, one of those brownstones, that he'd lived in when his mother was alive. And that he kept all of her clothes just *intact;* her umbrella was in the same place she left it—Prof knew that kind of stuff.

Another thing: he always had money—but he could never go home. They didn't want him to come home, but they sent him this money. He had all the little English suits, wore big thick glasses, and they called him *Prof Green*. He'd say, "Let's go out and get some *note*"—going round in a big group of people; at Howard, they called it *notin'*—and he could speak all these languages and everything. But on Christmas, New Year's, any of the holidays, he could never go home. So he just stayed there.

He would say, "If you want to get some note"—some recognition— "with this young lady over there, you go speak to her in *Spanish*." Little Spanish words of love. He would go to this Italian girl and say some Italian. He had all these sayings, if you wanted to get some note: for instance, you could tell a girl, "My love for you will cease when a two-month-old infant crosses the Atlantic Ocean with a twenty-ton burden on its back." We would listen to what Prof Green would say, and he would write it out, and he'd say, "Do this; you'll impress them." You had all these things in the back of your head. One I still remember: "*La primera vez que te vi, te quise*"—"The first time I saw you, I loved you." It did impress them in a lot of cases, but sometimes you got slapped in the face!

We had fun with Prof: the unusual scholar.

I'll never forget, he would sit under a tree and hold court. He was sitting out there indoctrinating the students before they even got into the classroom. The day you got there, he'd see you: "Hello, what's your name? Oh, you're coming here?" He would tell you, on the first day: when you get that enrollment paper, and you're supposed to say your race: "put '*human* race.'" Most people would say, what difference does *that* make? But that was right during the beginning of the feelings that led into the civil rights movement. "You're black, but you're human; if you have any sense in your head, you'll put 'human race'"— and people said, "I'll do it, man!" The professors knew about it, but they didn't stop him.

Prof had these magic pencils for the multiple-choice tests. He had the custodians working for him: the custodians would come in your room and clean up, and if you left one of your exams on the bed, they would get it and give it to Prof Green. So he had these pencils that he'd fix up, where he had two little dots for the first question, four little dots for the third one—the right answers. He had it all marked off. You could buy one of his pencils, and look at the test: a dot here, dot here . . . and nobody ever caught him. Of course, if you got out of order, you'd get *all* the answers wrong. So it was just like playing the numbers—you might hit it lucky, or you might miss them all.

He had an interesting thing, too: some way the phone service would call in the horse races from Hialeah Racetrack. That's what the numbers were based on, the Hialeah Racetrack. So he had this thing going where he could get the numbers, maybe, thirty minutes before they hit the street—and he was making money off this broken-down phone in one of the houses they had for the GIs.

I wasn't always with Prof, but sometimes he would call me because he knew I knew music, and he would ask me about different things. One day I was with him. We went down to where the Howard Theater is, in a little restaurant there. We were eating and had just seen the stage show.

A guy came in. Looked like a nice fellow, dressed nicely. And he sat down and talked with us. He would say, "Oh, you all go to Howard? They've got some beautiful girls up there." They would always say that.

"Yeah, man."

He'd say, "Where you from?" and he'd order a round of beer.

He talked. He talked; he talked; he talked. We were sitting in there about an hour. And he said:

"You guys are nice." Said, "I wish I could go to Howard like you all are doing." And he said, "I've got something to tell you."

Man, he pulled his coat back—the biggest .45 was sitting under his hand!

He said, "Now. I'm not going to do what I was sent here to do. Because you guys are really nice. But *promise* me. That you won't *ever*. Play any *numbers*. Don't ever go near that phone again."

Prof rared back with his little, short self—he was going to say something—and I kicked him. I kicked him so hard under that table—

This guy looked at me. I hadn't told him my name. He said, "Now you say your name was John Jones, right? Your name is John Jones." He looked at Prof. "And *your* name is Thomas Henry, right?" He says, "That's what I'll remember you by." And he got up.

"*Don't forget what I told you.*"

I tell you, we got out of there so fast—I was shaking for two days. And I told Prof, "Don't you ever take me somewhere like that again!"

He said, "Oh, that guy was just trying to get some *note*."

But that was the kinds of thing that happened often in Washington.

Something I never will forget at Howard is the class structure. I found out, there was a separation of people at Howard University: not necessarily by race, but by wealth—you had some *wealthy* black people there. And at Howard you had a class system. You had those that were well off, and you had the other element that was just sort of middle-class, and then you had the poor working guys, like musicians. So you see a beautiful lady: she might ask you to play a number, and then you'd probably have some romantic inclinations . . . and then she would give you a *tip*. Just like, "Boy, here's a tip." That's the way it was there.

I was playing one night, and this *beautiful* girl comes up. I said,

"Wow." She said, "I just love your music." And gave me a tip. Five-dollar tip! That was a lot of money. But, see, at Howard there was this difference. It was just like somebody coming up to you at the Birmingham Country Club. Although we were both students, we were on different levels.

Before I came there, I thought my folks were pretty well off. You never realize how poor you are, really, and you never really know how rich you are, if you have a controlled situation.

One time in the freshman class: they would have you read a certain section of the assignment, and somebody else would read another section. I read something. And when you made a mistake at Howard, nobody would laugh. Nobody would say anything. They called it being cool. That was the thing: "Hey, man, be *cool*." They wouldn't put anybody down, they'd just put it in the back of their head that you mispronounced a word, and they'd go along.

But this was critical: I got in that class; I was reading. Instead of the word *fatigue,* I made a horrible mistake. I said, "fattigay." Nobody laughed, nobody did anything. I didn't know what had happened. And when I came out of the room, the most beautiful girl in the class says, "Hey. How are you doing?"

I say, "I'm doing fine."

"What's your name?"

Ask me what my name is? I say, "I'm Frank Adams."

"And where are you from?"

"I'm from Birmingham."

"I've got some *people* that live in Birmingham, Alabama!" Says, "I want to take you on a"—*what*—"a date. I want to take you out."

I say, "Take me out?"

"Yeah, we're going to lunch. That's tomorrow, we're going to lunch."

Man, I started *whistling.* I started whistling all the way to my dorm room. The prettiest girl in the class, man. And she's going to take me out on *her.*

We sit down there; we're just talking. She's talking about a lot of things, and I'm talking about a lot of things. I offered to pay—but, "No, I'm paying for it, I'm paying for it." I said, "Well, what we got to do: I'm taking *you* out, day after tomorrow." She said, "Okay, okay."

I said, *wow,* man. I said, I want to take her someplace a little better than average, you know. So I got my little pennies together, and we went to this restaurant. And I was talking, I was talking. And just before we got to go out, she says:

"You know what?" Says, "When you were reading in class, you said a word . . . I thought it was what *you* said: 'fattigay.' But I looked it up in my dictionary," and she said, "You know what that word was? That word is *fatigue*. I didn't know that! *Fatigue.*"

It didn't dawn on me what a horrible mistake I had made. I thought I had gotten a relationship with the most beautiful girl in the class! But what she did: she befriended me in a way that I had never been befriended before. It wasn't pity; it was just a good soul helping a good person. She thought I was a good person, so she let me down easy. We got to be good friends.

There was another young lady, we called her "Frizz"—because her hair was frizzily. She loved to keep up with the books in the band; she kept the music and kept up with everything the band did. And she was beautiful, too. She was a writer; she wrote all kinds of poetry. We'd go into the cafeteria and Frizz would be back there with everybody sitting around, and she would be reading her latest documents. She was heavy. And she would tell you about Omar Khayyam and then she'd talk about Rubén Darío, and she had one guy that said lightning was like "God scratching a match across the universe." All that kind of stuff.

I saw her sitting in the cafeteria once, and I walked up to her and said, "Frizz. You like music. I know, because I see you—every time the band plays, you're there."

"Yeah, Frank, you knock me out, man. I love what you're playing."

So I asked her: "Frizz, let me give you a call. I can call you up sometime . . ."

She said, "*François*"—they called me "François" then—"François, you don't need that."

I said *why* I don't need that.

"You just don't need to *call* me. You can see me anytime."

I said, "What?"

She said, "No . . . the reason I don't want you to call me . . . my line may be busy." She said, "I got to marry a *doctor*." See, I was such a little lowly creature—they didn't want you to get in the way of someone *else*. We were not lowly, exactly, but it was a class society: you had those that had money.

We had a couple of girls at Howard named Inez and Myrt. I think they came from Oklahoma—they came to Howard University together, and it wasn't long before people knew that they were brilliant: Inez and Myrt. They were inseparable. Now, Inez, I remember, was a real thin, nice-looking little girl; and of course Myrt was real *stout*-like, like she could beat you to *death*—but they were both brilliant. Evidently they were together through elementary and high school, and when you saw one, you saw the other.

Inez and Myrt were always recognized as being *heavy*. They knew everything. And if you wanted them to do bookwork for the band or help you with a report, they would always be there to do it. They *loved* music. They didn't have any romantic relationship with anybody in the band—nobody approached them sexually or anything—they were just always there, like somebody in the band. If they were late: "Where's Inez, where's Myrt?"

We had so many interesting people that I met. You can imagine a school where everybody is free to say what they think about. People like Frizz, who appreciate poetry—without the coercion to do it, they just find a groove in it. And what I want to tell you: they were *different*. Howard was *rich* in characters. The teachers were the best in the world. They would take a personal interest in you, and they had some compassion for you. They were human.

I had the great pleasure of being at the university when you had people like Alain Locke and John Hope Franklin, the great historian: I was in his class when he wrote *From Slavery to Freedom*. That was in about 1946, his first edition of *From Slavery to Freedom,* and that book is used universally, in all the colleges. He was inquisitive: when he learned I was from Alabama, he wanted to know about Selma, and all those rural towns; he wanted to know about Demopolis, Alabama, and all the intermarrying and miscegenation that went on there.

I went to Alain Locke's lectures. He was a great philosopher and was one of the primary movers for the Harlem Renaissance. When you got to the classroom, you'd sit in there, and you could hardly hear what he was saying; he would just be working his mouth. But he had proctors, and he had everything set up where he could fly to Boston University and do another lecture that day, and a test was given by what we call "associates," youngsters who were in graduate school. They'd give you this written test, and the test wouldn't be *anything* about what we *thought* Dr. Locke was talking about.

Dr. Locke was just aloof; he was there, and he wasn't there.

I took one class with Dr. Leo "Africanus" Hansberry, who knew all about African antiquities. He was the uncle of Lorraine Hansberry, who wrote *A Raisin in the Sun*. He had traveled through Europe and Asia, and had been through all the libraries in Britain. He had this thing that would go across the board, over here, from 10 B.C., all around here, with all these names. He would tell all the students, very first class: "Everybody who's in here is going to get a B, so don't worry. You won't get anything lower than a B, and you won't get an A." But you had to keep a notebook. His thing was: "Don't worry about the test, just copy all this information I've got on the board. This is the dynasty of Sultan Bello Socato, and this is the great university of Timbuktu," and he'd talk about the Egyptian times, and Pliny the Elder and Pliny the Younger. "Write that down, now, because you'll be able to tell your children about it."

Bam. That's it. No midterm, no nothing, man; just get your notebook. And I discovered that's when you really learn: you're free, then. Some would take advantage of it, but strangely enough, in Dr. Hansberry's class, I didn't see many people that did that. They got their notes.

When I was on initiation for the fraternity, I'd be sleepy; he'd say, "Wake up, Brother Adams, and write this down." I'd write it down. "You can go back to sleep now."

Then, of course, you had Thurgood Marshall: he was just a firebrand. He'd go down and stay in the bar, and he'd come back and do his lectures. Prof Green would talk about *him*: "Oh yeah, Thurgood's on a *rage*." He would be *raw* looking, and he probably had been out all night, with his shirttail hanging out—he would be like a barking dog coming down the hall—but he was still *Thurgood Marshall*, you know what I mean? He *knew* the law. And *you* knew: that's a person you need to respect.

The greatest experience I had at Howard was: we had a German Jewish professor who fled Germany during Hitler's time. And his credentials were: he was a lawyer; he was a doctor; he had degrees in all kinds of things. His name was Dr. Hamburger. Weird name, Hamburger, but that was it.

Dr. Hamburger lives *vividly* in my mind. That's the guy.

We had to go to this chapel for orientation and lectures, and I'd seen Dr. Hamburger lecture in the chapel. The very first time he got to Howard University, they say he was talking about one of the Greek tragedies or something, and he got so carried off that he started speaking German. It got back to the administration, and they didn't like that. They moved him out of the day school, and put him in the evening classes.

I enrolled in his class. He had a watch he'd put right on his desk; and he had this green bag that professors carried their books in. You could hardly understand him, really, unless you listened to him for a while. He would speak, he would speak, he would speak. Then there would be a break time, about ten or fifteen minutes. I noticed that I would get back on time, and he would start lecturing. The rest of the students were still out there getting Cokes, but he wouldn't say anything about it.

He would give these examinations every couple of weeks. My first paper came back—it looked like somebody had been shot in the war, there were red marks all over it. It was horrible. I couldn't understand how this guy could be so hard on me, and I was the only one getting back to his class on time—the other people in there weren't even respecting him.

I looked at him. I took that paper home.

The next day he said, "*You come here!*" He said, "*Haven't I seen you before?*"

I said, "Yes, sir, I was in your class over at the cathedral."

"*Well, why did you come in here?*"

I said, "I wanted to be in your class."

"*Why?*" he said. "*Tell me why!*"

I said, "Because I thought I could learn something." And I said, "I got this paper with all these red markings over it, Dr. Hamburger."

"*That's right.*" He said, "*You worry me.*" He said, "*I look at your paper. I go over it, over and over again. And I find the right answer in there— it's hidden in there. Why do you do that?*"

I said, "Well, Dr. Hamburger, when I went to school, I didn't learn all those things you're talking about: 'the conjugation of verbs,' 'colloquialism,' 'redundant structure.'" I said, "I'm *trying* to do this. I'm trying to write."

"*You're trying?*" He said, "*What does that have to do with it?*"

"Well, I'm taking freshman English—"

"You don't need that! To write!" He said, *"I never went to a class to write English!"* And this guy could speak all kinds of languages. He said, *"You do this: I'll give you a list of books. And you go, and you read these books. And you'll write!"*

He said, *"Read them all!"*

He gave me ten books. One was Shakespeare. One was—what?—*War and Peace*. *War and Peace!* *"You read these, and then you'll write correctly!"* So I studied; I did it, man. And I did improve, just by reading those books. I started writing, making up sentences, and I could even quote some things—Shakespeare and that kind of thing—in the writing.

At Howard they put up a list, and just before Christmas, you could go out there and see what your grade was. At the end of that semester, I went there—it was snow on the ground, man—and I got up to Douglass Hall, near his room. They had the grades posted up on that board.

I heard a noise . . . weeping. I said, "What in the world is this?" One of the students, she was pretty young, she said, "I can't stay in school! I should have never taken this course—I have to get all A's or B's; I'll lose my scholarship; I can't repeat a course . . ."

I said, "Oh, my God."

Dr. Hamburger couldn't be impressed. He had some pretty young ladies sitting up there in that class: they'd sit on that front row—they were as cute as a button—but Hamburger didn't care, man. He didn't even look at them. He would tell them, *"I thought you came in here to learn! Why would you want to pass this class before you've learned something?"*

I looked up there, at that list: I was the only one that had a B. That was the first B I had ever gotten. The highest grade in the class.

So, that went pretty well. Until one day, they had put him back in the day school. He was in a sort of historical English class: "exploring the great books." They were talking about *Othello*. And Desdemona.

He said, *"Why! Why are all black people jealous! He choked Desdemona to death! Is that just built into them—the blacks—and they'll do that to someone! Jealousy! Why did he have to choke her!"*

He was *raving*, man. And he had a diverse class in there. Some of the black students started looking around at each other. Nobody said anything. I took as much of it as I could stand.

I raised my hand. I said, "How could you say that, Dr. Hamburger?" I said, "I'm just disgusted with you. You came from *Nazi Germany*— and look what they did to the Jews. Look what they did to *you.*"

Pow, pow, man—and he's *firing* back, man, at me: "*You don't know what you're talking about!*" It went on for about ten, fifteen minutes. Back and forth with Hamburger. And here's what happened: he got up from his seat. I thought there was going to be an altercation. He started talking in *German* again. Just shouting. And he walks out there—guess what he did. *He grabbed me.* He says:

"*Now . . . you know . . . what to do! You are a* man *now.*" Man, he grabbed me and hugged me.

So that was a lesson. "*Now you know how to talk back. You know how to* tell *somebody something.*"

Boy, that was a great experience I had at Howard. And I found out that I could overcome a lot of things by simply applying myself. I learned that if you take school just like a job . . . because I was determined not to come home and be a failure, in music or whatever I was doing. So I said, now: every day, like I'm going to a job at the steel plant, I go to the library—whether I had any work to do, or not. I stay there— from twelve o'clock, if that's my last class—I stay there from twelve 'til about four thirty or five o'clock. My term papers, I'd get them all out of the way. And I would just *read,* all kinds of books. On astronomy and stuff—anything. Then I'd watch people. I was a *watcher.* I'd watch how people would come in and study. How they do things. What kind of *book* is that. I'd sit in the same seat; the librarians, if I was absent, would say, "I wonder what happened." I was on my *job.* It got to the point that I didn't have to do any work at home, because I had spent my five hours laying out things. Laying out things. Putting it all together. I could organize myself—didn't ever have to cram. And I started using this memory thing; I started memorizing stuff. Like Hamburger told me—like my grandmother and Mrs. Guy would teach you, and Mr. Handy—just memorize it, man.

I knew that if I put time on task, I could do anything. It was because I had a system: for those four or five hours, I would make an appointment to be in that seat. You get so intense—you get your mental faculties so close—I could be doing something, and you could call: "Frank! Frank!" I won't even hear you, because I'm actually in a hypnotic state.

Industrial High School debate team, ca. 1939. Oscar Adams Jr., second from left; J. L. Lowe, center; and cousin Victoria Foster, front right. Courtesy of Roberta Lowe.

Then, what I could do: I could go to the cafeteria at five o'clock, six o'clock, and stay there for a couple of hours, and laugh. . . . They'd say, "Man, that guy must be a genius. He doesn't ever study. He just comes over here, plays pool or whatever. He's making *A's*, man—this guy from *Birmingham*." And my name and everything got around— all from Dr. Hamburger.

When I was in the undergrad school, my brother, Oscar, was in the law school at Howard. Oscar was always a person who was very astute in his education. He started under Mr. Lowe, who taught at Industrial High School. Oscar was on his debating team; that's how he got his elocution and all. When he got to Howard, they were making these sensational lawyers. Thurgood Marshall was there, and all those heavyweights. A lot of people don't know that, during segregation, since you couldn't go to The University of Alabama, The University of Alabama would pay most of your tuition to go to another school. People don't understand that. But when my brother came up, a lot of the great lawyers applied to The University of Alabama, and they *knew* they would not be accepted. They knew that. But The University of Alabama paid their way through these other schools; they paid for those blacks who they denied admission. That kept a lawsuit away, for a while. My brother didn't pay a dime for his education, in law school. So you see how the world turns: one thing that looks like it's so awful benefited that whole group of lawyers. Judge U. W. Clemon and Oscar, Jim Baker, and all those that you hear about, got their education free—clothing allowances and all those things—because the university wanted to keep them away. And that thrust Oscar into people like Thurgood Marshall.

When I got to school, I could always depend on Oscar.

I remember one thing that really made me close with my brother. We were having concerts, and the Swingmasters practiced and practiced. They got things that Stan Kenton was playing, and a lot of elaborate stuff that nobody had in their books, like Tadd Dameron's arrangements and all. We were at Spalding Hall, right on the campus of Howard University, and we had prepared for months. I had this solo, "Mood to Be Wooed," I never will forget it—Duke Ellington's—and we were practicing. We had Bill Hughes, who went with Basie; we had Benny Golson; we were all in that band, man. We had Sir Charles Thompson—I think he was playing the piano that night on certain numbers. And it snowed—that night in Washington it snowed mightily—and nobody came to that concert.

We looked around: empty house. But all of a sudden, man, about the third number, here comes Oscar. His date was this woman in the law school, she got famous later—they've got stamps out with her on them, and she was in Carter's administration—Patricia Roberts. We looked up, and they were giving us a standing ovation. Just two people. What happened then—I wish you could have been there—boy, that band kicked in, and they played; they played, they played, they *played,* as if they had a *thousand* folks in that auditorium. The guys ripped into something that nearly tore the building down. We got such a satisfaction to know that we had those two people in there. And they stayed. You might say, "Nobody's here, man, let's go"—but they really enjoyed the music.

I said to myself, then: "I got a brother." He could have gone on some-where, anywhere, but he picked up to come over to that thing. And we never forgot about that: that made Oscar famous with the band, and it made me famous, too.

Another thing that happened that was a defining moment: Oscar and I met up one day, and we were both sick. I think we must have had the flu or some kind of virus. I had a little money in my pocket, and he had less; we met up in the restroom in Cook Hall, and we said, "What are we going to do?" Oscar could hardly talk; I was whooping and go-ing on. He said, "I got," maybe, "fifty cents," and I had a dollar. We put it together, and we did something we thought we would never do: he went over to the pharmacy and bought a bottle of Squibb's Castor Oil. That's the toughest stuff you could ever take. Grandma used to serve us this Squibb's, and she would pay us a dime to take it and heat it by the fire—I don't know whether that made its efficacy any better, but she would do that—and then she would put a little orange juice in it, and you'd hold your hand over your nose and swallow it down. Then you'd get that dime—but there weren't any dimes given out this time, and there wasn't any orange juice. We were so sick we had to drink it straight: we sat there in Cook Hall and we drank a whole bottle of that stuff, drank it down just like it was Scotch. We drank it. And we started getting better, right there in the bathroom.

We walked up the street. There was bad weather, and we were hun-gry, and we said, "Let's visit Mrs. Alstork's house." She was up on Keefer Place, about five blocks from the school. Mrs. Alstork was Bishop Al-stork's wife; they were from Birmingham, and they had come up to Washington. Oscar said, "Let's drop by there."

Mrs. Alstork came to the door; she was happy to see us. And then, man, we smelled some of the most *fantastic* food cooking. She said, "Are you boys hungry? Your mom would go crazy if I didn't fix you all something." I was about to lie, say, "We're okay"—you know how you try to be polite—but Oscar hit me in the side. "Well, we *could* stand something to eat, Mrs. Alstork." I said, "That smells good, what you're cooking; we'd love to have some of that."

She said, "No, that's just something I'm cooking for Pedro, the dog." Pedro the dog!

To smell that food—I said, "Mrs. Alstork, you sure that's for the *dog?*"

She said, "Yeah." But she fixed some ham and eggs—man, we had the best food we'd had in a long time.

After, I guess, my third year at Howard, I started staying at Mrs. Alstork's house. They had an extra room in the place, and she and my grandmother were great friends. I started thinking, maybe I could stay there—so I mentioned it to Mama and Mama mentioned it to Mrs. Alstork. She just insisted that I come and stay, and it was wonderful. They didn't charge me. I could live off campus; I could walk to campus and not be bothered with all that noise in the dorm. I was doing really well. I had gotten myself together.

Bishop Alstork was there, and he was just a fine fellow. He'd insist on the table being set, with the linens and all. He'd sit there, he'd say a blessing, he'd ask you to say a blessing. He was the kind of person that didn't talk very much. He was a strong preacher like Bishop Shaw, but he was more intellectual. We didn't talk much, but we got along super. Bishop Alstork had to travel a lot, around to his different churches. He'd go to North Carolina, South Carolina, all these different places. He'd be away from home maybe a month, or two or three weeks, at a time.

At that time I was doing a lot of playing—I was playing at the Howard Theatre with Tiny Bradshaw and all those bands that were coming in—but Mrs. Alstork would never say I was going to play a dance. If you would call and I wasn't there and you asked for me—I'd be somewhere with the Swingmasters, playing a job—she was so religious, she'd say, "He's not here right now. He's playing a concert." A *concert!*

One time, I had some of these little records made; we cut some celluloid records. And Bishop and Mrs. Alstork were out of town for a conference. Now, believe me, I didn't do anything wrong, but I invited some of my buddies to come by there—I didn't slip any girls in there, I didn't do anything like that. But we were listening to these records, and that was nice. We relaxed, because I knew that the Alstorks weren't coming home. I cleaned up everything—we didn't drink anything, I remember that—and I *know* everything was in order.

When Mrs. Alstork came back, she said, "Bishop, I believe we got some rats somewhere in the house." She thought something had been moving around—nibbling.

As I said, Bishop Alstork didn't talk much. He took his handkerchief, and he rubbed his mouth. He said, "No . . . it's just a little *mouse*"— and looked at me. So I stopped doing that: I would never bring anybody to their home after that.

I guess we all get that way at a certain age, but Bishop Alstork got to be a little iffy, so far as coherence was concerned. He was still delivering those masterful sermons, but he couldn't hear very well. He didn't use a hearing aid. He'd say, "*What'd you say, what'd you say, what'd you say?*" And then the terrible thing happened to him.

He was going to one of his churches to preach, and something happened down there. It was in North Carolina. He had a limousine, and it was in deep segregation times. The police stopped him for something—they didn't know he was a bishop. They were probably calling him "boy" and all that kind of thing. And he did what he would always do—I can imagine it—he said, "*What'd you say, what'd you say?*" They struck him with a billy club.

We got a call that there was a man walking in a field, preaching. He had some identification on him, and they called Mrs. Alstork. She got somebody to go and bring Bishop back. And he was really torn up. He wasn't the same.

He would walk around the house at night; he would say things and he'd be shaking, and then he would go back to bed.

She didn't want anybody to know, until it couldn't be avoided, that Bishop had been injured and was losing his mind. They'd have to replace him, and it had taken him so long to get to his position. So she spent a small fortune getting people from the hospital. They brought a machine out, one of these things that they'd put on your head and try to shock you back to your senses. But he never got over that. It was a desperate situation.

One day, he had been back for maybe a couple of weeks: he locked himself in the restroom, and Mrs. Alstork couldn't get him to come out. She wanted me to go over the transom to get him—but in there were razor blades and all kinds of things, and it scared me. I loved him dearly, but I didn't know whether I wanted to go over that transom: I thought maybe it was dangerous for me, that he might try to cut me to death or something.

He was preaching a sermon in there: "The devil get behind me" and all that type of thing. I kept pulling on that lock, on the door, before I went to that transom—and finally I got it open and got him out. And he immediately cooled down.

Mrs. Alstork finally announced to the world congregation that Bishop was ill, and they put him in a home. He lingered about a year and then passed away. Naturally, she loved him so much, they were so close, that it was about a year after that that she passed.

We were always great friends, Mrs. Alstork and I.

After a while, I had gotten to be really important with the Howard Swingmasters. I was doing so well, I got to the point that I figured, "Hey. I'm a free soul. I don't have to have anybody but me."

I overslept a job that we had at the Lincoln Colonnade. After I had learned to study, and I was living with the Alstorks, I had a habit of stopping by this little tavern on the way from school. You could get some beer for a dime, so you'd get a roll of dimes—for about a dollar, you'd be dead. I'd stop off about three or four o'clock, then I'd go home and go to bed.

This time they had the Sugar Ray Robinson fight on this black-and-white television. That was a terrific fight—they just killed each other, knocked the mouthpieces out and everything.

I sat there and watched the fight. I went home from the tavern and went to sleep—and I slept through the job. They made it through the gig, but they fired me; they let me go. They needed me, but they had so much integrity, they said, "We're just gonna have to do without him," and that was it. It took a long time before they called me back; and that taught me a lifelong lesson. You've got to be loyal to whatever you're doing. You've got to be dependable. I wasn't *un*dependable, but I slipped. That shows you how cautious they were, and the kind of spirit they had: they loved you, but you've got to cut it. You've got to cut the mustard.

In that band it was like we had our own culture—I think Prof Green must have started this, because of his influence on intellectual matters. He could—what was it?—he could prove how many angels could dance on the head of a needle; all that kind of thing. It affected us all: it was Prof's culture.

He was the one that gave out the nicknames. "François de Bullion" was the one he gave me. I don't know where he got that; I didn't even take time to look it up. But the guys—like Benny Golson and

Carrington Visor—when I'd be jamming and playing and I got in my groove, they'd say, "Look out, Wa!" Instead of saying François, they'd just say *Wa*. "Get it, Wa!"

They'd have somebody, his title would be "That Boy." If they didn't have a whole lot of respect for you, you're *That Boy*. You could be with the band for twenty years, and you're still That Boy—until they decided to give you a title.

In the jazz idiom, they always had some kind of nicknames for different players. I found out when I played with Ellington's band: when you get with it, you have to learn what those names are, because those guys have been calling them so long they don't even recognize their real names. Like Paul Gonsalves, one of my idols: they called him "Mex." He wasn't Mexican, but they called him "Mex." And Fats Navarro: Fats Navarro was as skinny as a pencil, but he's *Fats* Navarro.

We had a fellow, he came out of Birmingham, his name was Charles Sheffield, but they called him "Liquor" Sheffield. Paul Bascomb's brother: they called him "Dud." And I told you about George Woodruff, who played in Sonny's band: they called him "Jarhead," and that went to "Jarhee."

In New Orleans, they have these *excruciating* names: like Skinny Bolden, Bull Eye, and One Shot. They had a guy called "Few Clothes"—he was called "Few Clothes Jones," because he had very few clothes!

Of course, Billie Holiday: Lester Young called her "Lady Day." She's a sophisticated person. And he was called "Prez," which is an abbreviation for president—top of the line. Doc Cheatham, the white trumpet player: he wasn't a doctor, but he's got that "Doc." He's on a higher level. Or you look at Earl Hines—Earl wasn't an earl, that's an English title—and Count Basie was no count. But people put those names on them.

They used to call Louis Armstrong "King" Louis. That was something I always thought about: they wouldn't call him *Mr.* Louis, but they'd call him King Louis. For a long time, they didn't call Duke "Mr. Ellington"—but they *would* call him "Duke." In those days, they would say, for instance, "*Mr.* Guy Lombardo"—but they held back off these "Mr." titles for the blacks. In fact—who was this comedian?—he said he named his son "Mister," so you *had* to call him "Mister." "Mister Jones," or something like that. He said he named *all* of his boys "Mister."

What Duke would do: he would introduce the band: "Albert—*George*—Hibbler!" Instead of saying Al Hibbler, he would call the full name out. That would give the guy sort of an uplift. Or he might say "*The* Frank Adams!" That's grammatically incorrect, but "*The* Frank Adams"—that means of all the people, this is *the*. He's the *one*.

Of course, when I was just getting started, Mantan Moreland is the one who called me "Juniflip"—because I was the youngest one in the band. Another time I was called "Youngblood." When you're eighteen or nineteen, you're Youngblood; and you're with the *old*-bloods. You're in the learning stages; you might do crazy things. "Juniflip" is that you're just a little fellow: a little flip. You don't know what you're doing. You might flip over to greatness, or you might flip back into mediocrity.

You're a Juniflip.

So, they had several nicknames for me.

9

Bounce, Bebop, Blues, and Swing

LIKE I SAID: WHEN I GOT TO HOWARD, ONE OF THE first things Fess Whatley told me to do was transfer my union card. So as soon as I got there, I went to the union office. This man had a little room, and he was the executive of the black musicians union. He took my card and my information, and it wasn't too long before a lady, Alice Proctor, called me to play in her band at the Lincoln Colonnade. That's the big dance place in Washington, on U Street, right below the Howard Theatre. Alice Proctor had the house band.

It was a great experience, because they were doing basically the same thing as Professor Whatley's band: the same pieces of music, like "Tea for Two" and "In the Mood"; all those stocks and everything. Alice Proctor was known for her exactness, like Whatley. She had a disciplined band: they started on time, stopped on time, and just did what they were supposed to do—no ruffians in there. You wore dark suits, she had the numbers numbered, and it was a business for her. They had music for the clarinet, like "Woodchopper's Ball," and I was just a monster, man, playing the clarinet and the saxophone. I could play that music at sight, the very first night. That gave me a connection with the musicians in Washington.

There was a flourishing music situation on that avenue. There was a fellow named Buck Hill who had a minor orchestra—he was a saxophone player—and I got a lot of chances to play with bands like that. Most of the others in the Swingmasters didn't have their union cards, but if you had a card, then you'd get called to play, and you could get some money to help you in your schooling.

Bands would come to the Howard Theatre, and I would pick up a lot of substitution jobs when they needed somebody to fill in. If you were going to sub, you had to know the music. Because bands back then like Louis Jordan had all these dancing steps to them: "Caledonia, Caledonia, what makes your big head so hard"—*bop!*—and everybody would kick. You'd learn at least eighteen or twenty numbers, plus the dancing steps. They didn't want you to have any sheet music up there: when they call the number, you *play* it.

Lucky Millinder and those bands expected you to know their repertoire. Lucky Millinder was a showman. He'd do all the dancing, and he insisted on his band being perfectly dressed. On stage they had two or three sets of uniforms you had to keep up with. Lucky Millinder used to dance on top of some dominos, and he'd direct the band—and he didn't read music. He was another one that wouldn't know a note if it walked up with an overcoat on, but he could tell you when you didn't play that note just like he'd had somebody else playing it. You don't change those recorded solos: you play them exactly like it was.

Lucky Millinder tested me the first time I subbed with him. He said, "Can you play 'Sweet Slumber'?" Tab Smith did the introduction to "Sweet Slumber" on the record. If you played it like the record, you got the job. You don't have time to go back and listen to it—"I'll get with you next week"—you've got to know it right *now,* because we're going to play it tonight. Every time I played that intro, he said, "Don't add anything to it; don't take anything away from it. Don't add *your* notes to it." If you didn't play his music, you weren't the person that he wanted.

A couple of bands I played in specialized in what they called the "businessman's bounce." The businessman's bounce is like they get off at lunchtime: they don't want to do any frantic wheeling around. Not too fast, not too slow. What the businessmen want is a conversation; they don't want to be interrupted by the blare of horns. They could be poor dancers; they'd get out and turn the lady around one time and laugh about it and go bouncing across the floor. You had some bands— Fess Whatley's and others—who perfected that style. You could forget the band was there, but just listen to the rhythm.

In the meantime, right down the street from the Howard Theatre and the Lincoln Colonnade were the jammers, like Coltrane and Ben Webster, and the clubs where you could go and see those kinds of things—the wild jazz and bebop, where they were doing all the experiments.

I played in one of them, I think it was Cloe's Cocktail Lounge. I hadn't been in Washington a long time—we were just getting the Howard Swingmasters together—and I went down to one of the jam sessions. I stopped in there. They played a number—"Sunny Side of the Street," I never will forget it. I got up and played a beautiful solo on it, and I got applause. I was a little young fellow, so they appreciated me. And I knew when to quit, too, while I was ahead—because they were going into bop and all that. I knew not to go any farther.

I walked back to the bar—I probably ordered a Coke or something—and a guy walked up to me and said, "You know, it's been a long time since we've heard anybody come and play how you played that." He said, "You played that 'Sunny Side of the Street'; it was beautiful. You played it just like Johnny Hodges." Said, "That was magnificent.

"But the next time I hear you play, I want you to play like *you*."

Wham!

I said, wow, man. I'm in a different world now.

He said, "You got Hodges good. But next time, play *yourself*."

I had to think about that.

There was a fellow I met at Howard, I suppose it would have been my freshman year: Reese Knox. Reese Knox was a fellow that loved music. You see people like this: they've got their saxophone under their bed and they play it, but they know they can't play too much—when they meet a player they admire, right up the street, they're going to want him to come play so they can see how their horn really sounds. Reese was like that: he heard me play, and he wanted me to come down to his place, this little apartment right down from the campus. He would show me his Conn saxophone. I showed him something on it, and I made a friend out of him.

He was the custodian at the school, one of the janitors at Howard, and he would clean the offices—so he knew the genius, Prof Green. Professors would leave their tests on the table, and in the cleanup process he'd pick them up and give them to Prof. Prof, with his analytical mind, would evaluate it—"If this is what he gave last year, what is he going to ask this year?"—and most of the time Prof was right. He'd have a test printed up and circulated across the school.

Reese Knox knew a fellow, Eddie Hill, who had a little band with twelve or thirteen pieces. I got to practice with them on weekends, and if they had a little job, I could play. Now, Eddie Hill's band never would be on the Top Ten, but they had a *spirit*. They had rehearsals regularly, and when they went out to perform, they were dressed just like Duke Ellington's band. Of course, one thing that was so important in the forties and fifties, even in the territory bands, was the uniforms. You *had* to have a uniform on: your band had a jacket and a clean white shirt. You wouldn't go up there and one guy's in this and one guy's in that. No. Everybody had their hair processed, it looked clean, and that was the thing that sold the band: your clothes and the way you looked, and the way you acted and how precise you were. Duke Ellington had a wardrobe mistress that traveled with the band, and a whole bus with just his wardrobe on it, all his suits and uniforms. One time I had to meet Duke's band in Boston; most of the guys in the band would have their own transportation, but I rode all the way on that bus, alone with the clothes.

Reese Knox knew all the places around Washington, and he had a car when nobody had a car. It was an old yellow convertible Buick. I had no transportation, and I was trying to adjust myself to life at Howard, so I appreciated someone being able to take me off somewhere. We would drive all the way to Baltimore and the Propeller Club: that was where Charlie Parker and Miles Davis and Red Rodney, all those people, played. We rode down there one Sunday, and that's the first time I really got a chance to hear the real, real thing that was going on. All the fellows that came from Philly and New York to Howard had an idea about the modernization of jazz—particularly Benny Golson—they played the licks and things that were current. But when I heard Charlie Parker and *looked* at him, it was different than I imagined it would be. He was playing as if the world was coming to an end. Not one solo, but *two* solos, three solos, four solos, five solos, *six* solos, right after another: like a gun shooting off, and every one of them a new idea. Then, finally, he just stopped: left the club, and walked out. Bizarre behavior, at the least. Red Rodney would have to come up and play endlessly, until Charlie would come back.

The people in Washington and these places were worlds apart—for instance, everything was really nice with Alice Proctor's band. They weren't trying to do anything too creative: add just a little showmanship and people are satisfied. But in this *Bird* experience—they didn't care whether there were one or two persons in there, they're going to blast away. They're going to *bomb* the place—I mean, tear it down to shingles.

I remember sessions where they would play one number—I got involved on some of those sessions—the drummer would play so furious that you had to slide another drummer in there, to keep him from falling out; he'd gone on for twenty minutes, so here comes another guy to slide in to keep it going, keep it going. It's furious. It's a life-and-death situation.

I saw so much going on. I would go to hear Stan Kenton. They could play. They had on these *belts,* because they were playing these *screaming* things—the trumpet players were going above the sky in these solos, and they had to have a belt to keep their insides in, to keep their *body* together. And Buddy Childers, and Maynard Ferguson, man, the key high-note people: these guys would have their *lips* mutilated, playing those high notes.

I remember one fellow that nobody seems to know too much about. His name was George, and because he was from Georgetown, right outside of Washington, they'd say "George from Georgetown." He was a miraculous musician. Sometimes you'll find them like that: unknown, but to the musicians. They would send for him from Georgetown to come over. The musicians would pay a little bit for him to come. He had one of these *long* trumpets, like Professor Whatley had. And they'd say, "Play, George. Play like Roy Eldridge. Play like Dizzy Gillespie."

He was a fabulous guy, and he always had on a white shirt with a button broken off right here, his big stomach sticking out, and he'd hold his horn in one hand: *doo-doo-doo!* He was recognized by musicians like Miles Davis, Dizzy Gillespie—he was recognized by the musicians as the greatest trumpet player in the world, and he never got any kind of recognition.

That's the amazing thing I found out: I always try to go and hear somebody now if I'm in a new town. I want to hear what they're doing. Anyplace you play—whether it's Dothan, Alabama; Alabaster, Alabama; somewhere, anywhere—you're going to find a first-class musician that nobody ever knows about. That was my experience on the road. You're down in the subway—you see somebody down there that can outplay John Coltrane, selling some records. You see this guy that's out of luck on the street corner, but he can *play*. That's what life is all about. You can't find a town, no matter where in the country, where you can't find *one* excellent piano player. That's why, whenever you play somewhere, if it's a barn or it's Carnegie Hall, you have to do your best. Because there's somebody out there—you might not know it, but they know what you're doing. Like the guy that came up to me and said, "Next time, play yourself." Those are the kinds of lessons you learn out there. And you can't ever think you're the king of the hill, because there's somebody out there that's better—somebody nobody's heard ever of.

At every turn I was being enlightened.

All the big acts would come play the Howard Theatre. I remember Mr. Amos Gordon from Birmingham came up with Louis Armstrong's band. He came over to Cook Hall first, where we were playing, and he brought just about the whole orchestra with him. I looked up and there was Mr. Gordon and all these guys from Louis Armstrong's band, and they were applauding. That was an exciting night, and it just built my esteem. That night Mr. Gordon—I know it must have cost him money—gave me enough tickets to take everybody in the band to hear Louis Armstrong play. And as you say—*my note rose up*, man. You couldn't afford to go to the Howard Theatre, but I gave out all these free tickets, from Mr. Gordon.

We went, and Louis Armstrong was kicking—he was playing his heart out—and out came Mr. Amos Gordon with his clarinet, and I never will forget it: he played something on a New Orleans piece, called "Back of Town Blues." And we all went wild. We went wild. When I came back to school, I was like a king for knowing Professor Amos Gordon.

That's the kind of thing that went on with Birmingham musicians. In New York City, you could go and stand on the corner. If you were there about fifteen minutes, you would see somebody from Birmingham, a musician, come up, and they'd say, "Where are you staying, man?" and take you somewhere to stay.

Mr. Gordon was my mentor in a way, and my idol, too. I still think about Mr. Gordon. I had heard about him before I ever got to Professor Whatley's band, because he could write and arrange music. He was selling arrangements to Bill Nappi and other white groups in Birmingham, way before desegregation was ever thought about. He was Professor Whatley's lead saxophone player, and he wrote part of the book that we played out of when I got there. There were some things he had written for Whatley's band that it would challenge *Duke's* band to play—and that's saying a whole lot.

All this time I was at Howard, every year through my senior year, I would come home over the holidays, and I would always get some jobs to play in Birmingham. That's how I first heard Cleve Eaton. His sister, LaVergne Eaton, was a tremendous musician—one of the first black piano players to finish Juilliard. People don't know about that, but she was a fantastic piano player, and she was the one that taught Cleve. One time I came home at Christmas, and she called me to play with her, over at the Birmingham Country Club. Now, I came home from Washington armed and ready to play all the *way-out* stuff— "Things to Come" and "Perdido"; "How High the Moon" and "Lady Be Good"; *jamming*—all that kind of thing, because I'd been in that environment. When I walked in the country club, I saw LaVergne playing, and I saw this little bitty fellow with some khaki short-pants on, playing this bass.

I started the evening out, playing things like "The Waltz You Saved for Me" and little simple tunes that were popular. A few numbers that wouldn't call for anything but an elementary school knowledge of tunes, and not too much improvisation. I noticed Cleve was following along well.

I got tired of playing all this simple stuff, so at intermission I said, "I'm just going to *play* something." I was all wrapped up in this advanced music now: experimental music, and bebop. I knew LaVergne could keep up, because she had all this training. So I cut loose on something, and to my surprise, little old Cleve just kept going. He was very fast, and she could call out the chords and harmonies and he would pick right up on it. She'd say, "D minor! F7!" and he'd *"boom, boom, boom."* I said, "This guy is going to be okay."

I also had the opportunity, at that time, to play with some of the blues bands. Blues was what you had to know first. Some of the music you hear now by the great players: although they aren't blues, you still get the blues flavor. They flatten certain notes—the third and the fifth and the seventh—and make them like a voice: the voice from days of slavery. That's what they call a blues scale. Times got to where you had beautiful songs like "I Got Rhythm" by George Gershwin: some guys would play that, but you'd hear the flattened note somewhere in there, and you'd know they were *blues* players.

Some people say, "Blues? Oh, that's *slow*"—but blues can be fast; it can be slow; it can be *terrifically* fast and it can be very, *very* slow. Another misconception is, "My baby done left me and I'm all alone"— that the blues are always sad. But blues bands can be sad *and* happy. "Caledonia, Caledonia, what makes your big head so hard—*bop!*"— *that's* a blues. So not all blues are one way.

I was in Chicago in the forties, and I saw Howlin' Wolf at the 400 Club. I went in there one Saturday and I watched him rehearse his band. He didn't make any corrections; he didn't have any music written; but if he felt you weren't playing like he wanted you to play, he'd open your mouth and he'd pour some whiskey down in you. That was his rehearsal. That was Howlin' Wolf.

At the 400 Club, they had this long, long bar. Howlin' Wolf would be playing. You would be sitting at the bar with your friend, and he'd jump and slide all the way down that bar. You'd look up in his face, and he'd probably scare you to death—but that was one of the things he did, and that impressed me with Howlin' Wolf, because I hadn't seen that before.

After I got back to Birmingham, I got to play with Howlin' Wolf, I guess around 'fifty-two or 'fifty-three, at the Birmingham Country Club. You'd have some over-the-mountain people, young people over there, who would have a great curiosity to hear these so-called "primitive" guys, like Muddy Waters and B. B. King, Big Mama Thornton and Bo Diddley; the Greek fraternities would have their parties around those blues and boogie-woogie guys. I'd get to perform with some of them. In fact, I made a recording with this fellow in Birmingham— "Scratch My Back"—I think it was probably the cheapest record ever made. This fellow didn't even have a drum: instead of having a drum set, he just put some sand on the floor and worked his foot back and forth. That was his whole percussion section!

You see some interesting things, playing with these blues guys.

For some reason, it seems like I always had a penchant for being at the right place at the right time. In fact, I got a job with Duke Ellington's orchestra by going to the Howard Theatre. I met a fellow there named Jimmy Hamilton; he was a clarinetist with Duke's band. I talked to him and he invited me to play some duets with him on the clarinet.

The most peculiar thing I noticed about Jimmy: most of us will play our music from the music stand—he did, too, but he had his music on the ceiling of his room. That was weird. I said, "Jimmy, why do you do that?"

"Because if you practice lying down," he said, "it does something to your breathing; it increases your breath control." So we practiced, and there was nothing wrong with him—he was an absolute genius, and he could *play*. He was a scholar. He was studying all kinds of things. He would be outside in the hall playing a concerto for clarinet, while everybody else would be warming up on jazz licks.

Jimmy was what we call in a band the "straw boss." In other words, Duke is not there most of the time. So you've got a guy who is the unofficial leader: he calls everything, he makes sure the band is in tune. He rehearses the group. That was Jimmy's job. He was a college graduate of Boston University, and he had a lot of musical knowledge. Duke had a lot of them in there who had very little technical knowledge, but they created the music that Duke liked: the sounds that he wanted. And Jimmy was the one who could tell what Duke wanted.

I got a call one day when I happened to be in Chicago. There was a fellow that played in the Howard Swingmasters by the name of Morris Ellis, a trombone player. Morris Ellis was fronting the Swingmasters for a time, and then he and his brother went out to Chicago and put together a society band, like Whatley's. They would play all around Illinois, different towns, mostly on the weekends. He had been out of school a couple of years, and I went out there to see him—I guess it would have been New Year's. I ended up at the Princess Hotel. I didn't even know Duke was in town, but while I was there, somebody said: "Jimmy Hamilton came by to see you."

I said, "*Jimmy?* How did he know I'm in Chicago?" But Jimmy said to give him a call.

I called him up: "Duke wants you to come down to the Blue Note, down at the Loop."

"What for?"

He said, "Hilton Jefferson"—that was a player who had been with Duke for years—"Hilton fell down on the ice and broke his leg. He wants you to come play."

So, man, that was my opening to play with Duke as a sub for a long time. The experience there was one that every musician would have given his life to play. I was just fortunate enough to be there, and try to unravel what they were doing. When I came out of the Blue Note that first night, and I got in a yellow cab—and all of those sounds were in my head from Duke Ellington's Orchestra—it sounded like I had shifted into another orbit. They had some music on in that cab, and it all sounded so *simple*.

It would happen to anybody, if you immersed yourself into that environment—because environments consist of sound—and then you just heard some regular music on the radio, you'd say, "This is so simple!" Because you're used now to hearing *all* these kinds of sounds.

I was seated next to Jimmy Hamilton in the band and, I remember, they had one number, "Cotton Tail"; it had a saxophone chorus in it, where all the saxophones stood up. It was a *long* thing, and it was a terribly fast tempo. It was ferocious. So I asked Jimmy Hamilton one night, "Do you think I'll ever be able to play that fast, and get all those notes in?"

He looked at me with no surprise. He said, "Of course." He said, "If you had been playing this for thirty years, night after night, you would have to be an *idiot* if you couldn't play it." So that relieved my mind. You'd walk up and see some people doing this impossible stuff, but they had been doing it for so long. You can see the *time* that was put into that.

It was a learning situation, and it was an unusual environment. All through high school and college, we would say, "Here's the music." You'd have it numbered—"We're going to play number three, number five . . ."—you'd put your music up on the stand and it's organized, and you'd play. But it's another environment with Ellington. You didn't know *what* you were going to play. He would play something, and in all those flourishes you would hear a little tinkle of "The A Train" or a little tinkle of "In My Solitude"—and you'd have to be so attentive that when you got that last cue—*Bam!*—everybody would be there together.

You don't ask them, "What are we going to play tonight?" That's an insult. You sit there, and you listen.

A lot of times, a popular number would be, for instance, "In My Solitude," which was written back in the thirties. Now, there's the music for it—but which one of them does he want tonight? The one that we played in 1945? Or the one in 1938? We've got arrangements for all of those—which one of the "Solitudes" are we going to play? Because Duke, as one of the guys said, would always present *fresh flowers*. He would rearrange things.

I was amazed at how little playing, actual performance, Duke would do. He wouldn't be there to start off. He might be writing music somewhere, working on his arrangements. If the thing ended at two o'clock in the morning, he'd come in about one thirty. He'd see you sitting over there, watching the show, and he'd sit at your table, order a drink or so, then go to *this* table. Then he'd go up and play just about two or three numbers—a medley—and end up with his theme, "Take the A Train." Then you'd know it's time to go home.

At the end of a set, he'd say, "I love you madly." "Love you madly." Everybody, he loved them madly—especially women. He'd meet somebody, and he could *remember* them—all of them—in different states, they'd travel, and he had this thing of *remembering*.

He was always writing. Duke *had* to write: these things—these demons, he called them—would come into his head, and he'd have to write. On the bus, anywhere, he'd be writing.

That's the *drive*.

He would get one idea for a song—incomplete—so he'd file that away. Another idea for something, and he'd put that away. So if he wanted to find the middle of a song that didn't come to him, he'd go to his little notes—put a part of this one in that one, and then a part of *this* one in the other one—just putting pieces and pieces, like an erector set, putting these pieces together. He had them all lined up in his mind, all these pieces that he filed away until he needed something.

I got to observe all this. Duke walks into a rehearsal, or into the studio, with the music for an album. Then they tear it all apart. This piece here, they take it and put it somewhere else, maybe in another song. It's like you've got all these things in your icebox, and you're going to make something with them: if you don't want this here, you put it over there—save it for later. Then, when they get to know that *you* can do something, they start asking you things: "How would *you* do that? Hey, Frank, what would you do here?" And this is a whole new world. "What do *you* think, what do *you* think, what have *you* got? You've got something—come on, man, don't hold back from me."

Of course, Duke had this conglomerate of stars in his band. They weren't really stars at that time, but they welded themselves into these positions—the idea is that everybody was unique—and Duke blended them together. But I noticed some of them had this way of thinking: you could be a great performer, but you had to perform with a handicap. How much alcohol could you drink and still stand on your feet and play? That kind of thing was shocking to me. No matter how well you play, if you can't drink a quart of *liquor* and play, man, you're a punk. You're some kind of little freak if you can't do that. If you're a writer—you may be a magnificent writer, but that doesn't prove anything. Can you write *drunk?* How much whiskey can you drink and *still* write?

A good example is Paul Gonsalves: Paul Gonsalves was the greatest saxophone player I ever heard. But he could never accept the fact that he was a genius. He was a Puerto Rican fellow, and he just couldn't convince himself that he could play this black music—and play it better than anybody else. So he tried to *be* black. They said that in his soul he was black—but he just couldn't be black enough for himself. He couldn't convince himself that he was the real, real thing. And it actually led to his destruction. He started taking drugs, and messing himself up—but he didn't need to do that.

Something else I noticed, right away: they had been together so long in that band, they'd fuss. Sometimes this guy may not speak to another musician for a couple of months. I was just dumfounded, because they were all friendly, in a way, but you had a division between the musicians. You couldn't say that it was new school or old school, but you had these different groups: these cliques. They played together, but they didn't show a particular liking for each other.

If something happened to somebody in the band—if somebody got sick or something—they'd say, "Is there anything I can do? Where can I send flowers? Can I give him something toward the medicine?" You can be arch enemies all the time, but when your back was really up against it, they'll ask, "What can I do, man? Give him some money, but please don't tell him *I* did it—because I want to keep an enemy out of him! I don't want him to think I'm crazy enough to be his *friend.* Give him something, but let us keep fighting."

A person would come out to the microphone to play, and I would always sit back a little bit. If you're passing me, a courtesy is that I move my chair back and let you go by. One of the guys called me over and said, "Don't do that."

I said, "Why not? I was just trying to be courteous."

"Just don't do that. You don't *have* to be courteous." He said, "It's *his* solo, let him get out the best way he can. When you move like that, you disturb people."

That was their culture: it's an honor to have a solo, so he should get out there the best way he could. Every tub has to stand up on its own bottom. It's not tough love, it's just reality.

Little things like that were bothering me, so I asked Brit Woodman, the trombone player: "What's going on here?" He said, "The best was to describe it, it's like a Shakespearean play." He said, "You have a part to play, because of the way you sound. This guy with the growl trumpet—that's his part. This trombone player is real smooth; that's *his* part, he's a smooth trombone player. Whenever he leaves, Duke will have to get a new one."

He said, "You're here because Duke likes the way you sound—because you sound like somebody, probably, from twenty years ago, in his head. It's like a painting: he uses each sound to paint his music out."

We were playing in the Blue Note, and one night a fellow walked in. He said, "Have you guys played 'Sophisticated Lady'?" We had just gotten through playing it. I said, "Well, we did it in the last set. But I'll try to get word over to Duke to put it in another set."

He looked at me: "No, I don't want you to do that."

"Why not?"

He reached over and stuck a hundred-dollar bill in my pocket. He said, "I just wanted to know it had been played." Like it's his song, and he owns it in his heart—and he just wants to know that *somebody* had heard it and enjoyed it. "So you don't have to do it again. Thank you."

Bam.

I can't tell you how much I enjoyed that hundred-dollar bill.

I remember Paul Gonsalves said one night, "How old are you?" I told him I was twenty-something. He said, "Man, you can really read. You're a great reader for your age." I appreciated that. When they said "a great reader," it wasn't that they put so much credence on notation. They meant that if there was something to read, you not only read the notes and the rhythms: you interpreted it in a swing manner. You got the dynamics of it—the loudness, the softness. You don't just *read* the notes, like you do in a high school band or even in the symphony. You have to be able to play what's *not* written there. If you just play the notes, they say you're a mechanic. But if you can make a little crescendo that's not written down, they say, "He can really *read,* man."

I notice now, at concerts and festivals: some of the band directors who were not jazz-trained—who took jazz in college, where they learned all these techniques—they might get an A, but they don't really *swing.* They're missing that elusive thing. A guy could get up and play some notes or a young lady could get up and play some notes and you could say, "Well, that's great; that's technically right; but it doesn't swing." It doesn't have that little bounce in it. One thing is the interpretation of rhythm: whereas you usually would play a group of straight eighth notes, "ta-ta-ta-ta," the *swing* would be "*ta*-ta-*ta*-ta." Jazz musicians would do that automatically. Rather than a straight rhythm, it has this little skip that makes it swing. Somebody that's got a legitimate training would say, "Are you crazy, you don't see that on the paper!" But that's the swing. And I noticed you could play with a band for months on end and it would *never* really swing. Then, all of a sudden one night, it could be only a few people in the place, but the band could break loose and be on fire.

In Duke's band, of course, you had these absolute masters, and they really *knew* how to swing. In that band, it was just a different culture. And I was privileged to observe it. All this time, I was absorbing history.

Duke would play something and you'd say, "That was marvelous; that was magnificent." But he wouldn't be satisfied with it. It wasn't what he heard in his head.

He'd say, "That was fine. That was fine. But next year will be better." That was his thing.

"*Wait 'til next year.*"

10
Teacher

I came back to Birmingham in 1950. I didn't intend to be a schoolteacher. I had no idea that I wanted to teach—and it wasn't for any *altruistic* reasoning that I started. I didn't have any rosy ambitions. I started teaching at this school, Lincoln Elementary, and I taught there for twenty-seven years. I had no reason to ever think I would stay there; but the thing was, I'd go there at eight o'clock, and I'd sit at my desk—and the little ones would make so much *noise*. Of course, you can't develop a good band unless you put your time into it after school and everything, but I was thinking I wouldn't be there too long; I'll just sit here. And it got to be torture. It would be such a *bad* sound, I couldn't stand it; I couldn't last 'til three o'clock. So what I started to do: I started getting up from my seat, going out there, starting to teach them.

That's what I might call a profound experience: when you find within yourself and in spite of yourself that you need to do some good, for your own sanity. I got up selfishly and started teaching them—so they wouldn't *sound* so bad.

The first three or four months I was teaching, I was thinking about going back out there on the road. Unless you just have it in your heart to do this teaching, you're sitting there listening to people *struggling* to play an instrument, and you're still thinking about Duke Ellington or Tiny Bradshaw—you forget that you had to learn how to play *your* first note. I had intended to go back to Washington, DC, and probably do some more subbing with Duke's band; but Duke, at that time, had gone to England. Of course, all of his key players were on what they called subsistence money; they get a salary every week. If you're a sub, you don't *have* a salary, you're just waiting to be called. So I came home. They called on me to teach at Lincoln for a while, until they could find somebody permanent. I followed *my* teacher, William Wise Handy; he had been at Lincoln School since I'd left. He had been transferred to Ullman High School, and so they called on me.

I had my reservations about it, because when I left Howard, all the band people who lived there wanted me to stay. They said, "You can do well here, this is the best place in the world," but I thought about it: my daddy passed when I was in college, my second year, and my grandmother passed the year after that—but my friends were here, in Birmingham. We owned our own home, and my family ties were here. The guys in Washington, like Rick Henderson and Carrington Visor: that was *their* home. Their churches were there, their grand-folk were there. It's difficult to go in a town where you don't have any family roots. You can make your own friends, but it's not like being born there. You see somebody—"I remember his daddy, his grand-daddy"—and you know the ins and the outs of different places there. Well, in Washington I didn't know those things. And I felt that my best security would always be to come home if things were not moving along. So that's what I did.

One thing led to another, and I could have gone back on the road—in fact, I got a call to go with Basie's band, but by then I was hooked on the fact that, hey, these students can *learn*. Once I had gotten up out of my seat, I had seen that they could do something—but that was going to take more time on task.

I had no idea, coming out of the Ellington environment: how could you teach a little child—who was practically unable to make a complete sentence—how could you teach that child to be a marvelous musician? How could you *do* that? But I found out that it's not too difficult if you can get behind the mask: that's the mask of ignorance, and the mask of distrust. Once those students could achieve *one* thing—just one little thing—then the doors would open to other areas. The parents usually, you would think, would have a respect for their own children, but it's strange that, until they accomplish something, the bond between parents and their child is not as sticky, not as tight, as it should be. But when Johnny comes home playing "Mary Had a Little Lamb" and Dad's sitting there—he might not even be the real father—

but he's sitting there, and he's listening to this child *doing* something. So he says, "Well, I'll take this money I was going to spend on something else; I'll go down to the pawn shop and buy an instrument for the boy." That's the kind of thing that happens. When progress starts and they see it, you don't have to tell them about it: when Mary comes home twirling the baton with efficiency, they see something is happening. And when the child says, "I don't want to be late"—they might ignore it at first, but they find out that change is being made. When the teacher shows not just ordinary love and compassion for a student, but *extraordinary* care . . .

In teaching my first year I found out that you're not going to expect great progress unless you can get behind that iron mask. A lot of people would say, "Well, you're a teacher over there at the school and you're respected and you got a degree, and here I am, I'm not even employed, or I'm selling alcohol in my house. . . . You're all right, but I don't want to talk to you. I can't have a conversation with a professor." Then they see that "Professor" is doing something that they couldn't do at home, and they see a life being changed—because of a few *notes*—then they'll get word to you. Then they'll show up. Or I've had them send somebody, representing them, until they found the freedom that they can converse with you. You have to let them see that you're human, just like they are, and you really, sincerely want to do a good job with their children. You have to have something in you that they feel they can connect with. A lot of times, it takes a little doing.

That was a challenge to me—I knew it would be very difficult, because I had to get the support of the parents in the community. The parents were slow to come to PTA meetings. There was not any enthusiasm to do anything unusual. But when I started producing these bands, I started getting them to come. Some students that were not doing so well—I discovered that they had the ability to learn, and I worked with them. A lot of times, the parents had written the children off, and I thought that was so terribly wrong. So I spent a lot of my life trying to prove—really, to myself—that I could do it.

A parent will say: "Well, the child has been playing six months and I want him to play something in church. I don't care about the *scale*. Can he play 'Amazing Grace' at the funeral?"

So you teach him that. And then you've got a winner. You've got a winner because you've showed that there are some results. Like my dad told me: he said, "I bought these horns—the band is all right—but I bought these horns because *I* wanted to hear some music come out of them. *By you.* I don't care about all this marching—you've got a clarinet, you ought to be able to play something on it! Make some sense out of the doggone thing. Don't just sit there playing *toot, toot, toot.*" When you're teaching in an underprivileged school and a parent goes and buys a saxophone, he expects results. Not two years from now: if he bought this expensive trumpet in November, he's got to hear "Jingle Bells" before Christmas. Parents are like that. In certain cultures, I guess they can't afford to wait.

I found out that, even if it's not the best, you've got to get the children out there and let the folks see them—that, hey, they're *doing* something. You've got to come out and show what you've got. When I came on, most of the band directors, even in the high school, would have two concerts, one in Christmas and one in the spring, and you wouldn't see them anytime other than that. But I'd be out there every day, marching. Somebody would say, "What are you doing? What are you getting ready for?"

"We're just marching."

One day we were practicing, and it was snowing outside, and this deejay, the Playboy—he'd always talk on the radio about the bands, and who beat who at the football field—he said, "There's something *wrong* with those children down at Lincoln School! You know they're down there practicing, and school is out? In the *snow?* That man ought to get good sense!" He said that on the radio. But we were used to that.

I found out, too, that parents in some situations want to get together. They want to do something. They want to have all these little social events, selling tickets and raffles. If you could get a big donation—"Here's five thousand, don't raise any money"—they don't like that so much. They *want* to raise money. They want to get out there and sell hot dogs and have fish fries and all of those kinds of things. They want to run for president; they want to be the treasurer—and they get a delight in accusing each other of doing something wrong! But the demand comes that, hey: this is *our* band. We want to be the ones that buy the uniforms. Somebody wants to do this; somebody wants to do that. And that's when you get things going.

I remember when we were trying to get some money to buy majorette uniforms. We had just about enough, but we didn't have enough for the shakos: the hats. And one of the ladies that I never would have expected said, "Mr. Adams, I'll make them for you."

"What do you mean, make a shako?" I had seen Phillips High School, all those bands with those expensive hats that go on top. But she said, "If you can get me"—what?—"twelve oatmeal boxes . . ."

She took those oatmeal boxes and put some satin around there, and you had the darndest shakos in the whole world! And they'd *last*. This lady out in the street—her *idea*, you see—"Just get me some oatmeal boxes. Get me twelve of them."

We bought twelve boxes of oatmeal. And they ate the oatmeal and she made the hats, man.

That's what you call ingenuity.

Of course, for many years Lincoln School was the only grade school for blacks in Birmingham; we had all the students, from first grade up to eighth. Lincoln was a leaky old school with water on the floor— whenever it rained, the band room floor would be flooded—and with no facilities. It was designed, really, as a carbon copy of Industrial High School: it had the sewing, the woodworking, the tailor shop—all those domestic trades—and it had the printing shop and band. When I started teaching there, they were playing the same broken-down instruments we had with Mr. Handy, when I was a student, and some of those horns were just falling apart. The band room was in this old wooden building with a potbellied stove, and the students had to volunteer to come in the morning and get some coal and put it in the stove. They had fun getting there early and getting that coal. They had it all warmed up when I got there, and they'd be ready to play.

When I was in school, Mr. Handy had band practices early in the morning. So I went back to his tradition of early practices. I found out that you can make progress if you don't make it a punitive thing. If you make it where they *want* to do this, then you can accomplish something.

If you told somebody, "Hey: I come in here at seven o'clock. I want this room opened up and I want you to have the fire already built in this potbellied stove"—if you do that, you get negative results. But if you say, "John, you're a big fellow. Can you get here just a little early? This will be your duty. Have you got anybody that wants to do it with

Lincoln Elementary students outside band room, 1965. Courtesy of Frank Adams.

you?" Then you say to the class, "We've got one person that makes our practices possible: this is John. He gets here before seven o'clock, around six thirty"—and somebody might say, "He gets here earlier than that!" Then they're interested in doing it.

You might say, "Well, John, you've been doing this a long time, do you want somebody to help? Who wants to help? Anybody big enough to do that?"

"I'm big like he is, I'll go and help!" "I'm big enough!"

And you make them honored. You honor them.

Then somebody comes in there—I had a lot of cases where a student was just too big for their grade and would have behavioral problems, and the teacher doesn't want them in the classroom. So you talk with them. You say, "Now, you can't be tearing everything up. But could you learn to do this?"

They say, "Can I take that horn home with me?"

"I'll tell you what. If you come here for, perhaps, a couple of weeks and I see you get started, I might be able to let you take it." They're going to look forward to doing that. You find out who their friends are, and if their friends get in there and try to do something, too, you've got your group. You've got your group growing.

Next, I found out: here's this band, maybe over the mountain, like Smith Ridge School. They're getting all of these honors for their performers—and these youngsters of mine never even *go* to a concert like that. Then it was a challenge: how can you overcome this? How can you get competitive? So, you have to add more time to task. You have to practice regularly. If you practice five mornings a week, and then probably two afternoons a week, on your own time, you start getting results. You start closing the gap. And once you do it consistently, you end up superior. You end up *better* than Smith Ridge, or those schools that have all the equipment and everything; because music has become a *daily* part of your students' lives.

I would always tell them, "Now, what we do: in the morning we make a tape. Then we go home and eat lunch—dinner—and we come back and put the tape on. Listen to it just like you listen to the radio. If you can't stand it, then we're not ready."

What you do to a community: they see that Johnny can *play* something—he's made F's all this time—now here comes an A? "I don't go down to the school, because my child is flunking and they say he's handicapped and he can't learn anything . . . but here's this *crazy man* sending an A home; what is this?" They come out of inquisitiveness. And they see you working at it. If you're doing something different, they want to watch you do it. They want to see how you get that magic going with them—and the magic is just that you're yourself. You're sincere with them. That's all. When they're flunking, you make them feel like you're going overboard with them: that you're flunking, too. "Hey, if I can't get you to learn this, man, *I'm* the failure."

Then, it travels through the neighborhood: "If you want to learn music, go where that man, Frank Adams, is."

"Who is he?"

"Oh, he grew up in the neighborhood, right down the street!"

"Oh, he did?"

They start trusting you. And they start saying, "Well, I'll get my child over to you—you do what you can with him."

I remember the first time I organized a trip to Atlanta, to Six Flags. "Who's taking them? Oh, Mr. Adams? The one who has the band?

Okay, my child can go." Sometimes we'd be going to Montgomery or Mobile, and the normal time to leave would be, probably, about nine o'clock. But I would say, "We're going to leave at three o'clock in the morning!"

"Why?"

"I just want to be there when daybreak comes up." And they would be there. Somebody would say, "That fellow does unpractical things." But you find out, instead of ostracizing you for that, they enjoy it. They *like* to be up at three o'clock in the morning.

It got to the point where the schools started having free breakfast at seven o'clock. I knew all my kids were hungry, but I had to run them out of the band room. I said, "Go get your breakfast—"

"But we want to practice!"

"No, you got to *eat.*"

The parents said, "Well, they want to go to practice. Could you wait a little bit later to serve the breakfast?"

"Okay, we'll do that."

That's when you start building this confidence in you. That's when you get their overwhelming support. And it showed me: all you've got to do is do a few little things to be different.

Every Christmas, the school would have a Christmas party. And I had a Christmas party just for the band students. We would start a little earlier than the party for all the classes. I wouldn't charge them anything—the schoolwide party would take up a quarter—I said, "I'll buy these things, and I'll go out to the garden"—I was elaborate. I had oranges and apples, and a little peppermint stick they'd stick down in the orange; I'd have raisins in their little sacks, and they had some ice cream that was multicolored. I lived a couple of blocks from the school, so I'd have a group come to wrap everything. They'd sit in the front room, man, and wrap it all up. They took pride in that. Then they'd exchange gifts. Everybody had to give a present, and the gift couldn't cost over fifteen cents—anybody that bought something over fifteen cents was penalized!—so that gave everybody a chance to have something. And I used to always give a little prize for the best-wrapped fifteen-cent gift.

After that they would have the party they paid for; they paid a quarter or something for the closing-of-school Christmas party. The bell rang, it's time to go . . . they would still be sitting there. One of them would say, "We want to clean up the room, so we can get the ice cream that's left." And some of them just wanted to be there anyway. I said, "Okay."

I stayed out there twenty-seven years, and I had been doing this every Christmas. We'd have a little dancing, and a little party. I'd have my little jazz group get together: they'd do James Brown and that kind of thing. After everybody left, they'd always give you a little gift, too, a little ten-cent or fifteen-cent thing. One Christmas, this little boy came in, we used to call him "Nut Head"—we had nicknames for everybody—he came in and he had his gift wrapped up in a little red foil. He said, "Mr. Adams, don't open that 'til Christmas." So I put it under the tree, and I waited.

On Christmas day, I opened it up—my family was standing around—and it was the prettiest little *shot* glass! His mother sold bootleg whiskey, and he just picked up one of the shot glasses and wrapped it up.

When he came back to school, he said, "How did you like that?"

I said, "That's the best gift I had."

But that shows: when you get that kind of thing, you know they really care about what you're doing. And you get into the community, and the word gets around that something's going on. Then, all of a sudden, you go to one of these competitions and you get *Superior*.

"Superior?"

"Yeah, we got Superior." They start pushing their chests out, man. Then they'd *look* for success. "What are we going to do next time?" "The basketball team never got a Superior. But here's this *band* getting Superior."

After that, you get to the point where they value being uniformed and obeying orders. Everybody sits down at the same time, like Fess Whatley used to do. Everybody up at the same time—it's like the military.

One defining moment was the first time we went to a competition. We went to Smith Ridge School, and we were the first to integrate that competition. I had my students uniformed, and they went onstage, and they stood there—everybody else would walk on and get their instruments out and start relaxing and playing. The band directors would wear that little blazer, relaxed and cool with their collars open. I had my John Philip *Sousa* uniform—white, with the cap on, like Mr. Handy's—and walked up to the stage. When I made a motion, they all sat down together. When they left the stage, they left in a line. They didn't leave with everybody going this way and that way. The other band directors were talking to the judges; I didn't say anything to the judges. I just stood there.

They give you your grades, where if you pass, you go to state. A guy came up, and turned his back on me—he didn't want me to see him call us "Superior"—but he said, "*Y'all passed.*"

The kids knew then that they accomplished something.

The next year, all the seniors, the good players, had gone to high school. And I said, "Well, this will be an off year. We'll practice for parades and all, but we won't go to state." I thought I had reached closure on it. And here comes a committee of youngsters, man: "We want to go to district."

I said, "We're not able to go to district."

"Yes, we are. We can play better than those other folk!" Talking about the old students.

I said, "You can't go this time." They said, "Give us a chance."

"*Give you a chance?*"

Man, they went over there and blew Smith Ridge *out.*

They made up in their minds that once they got on the top, they could not stop going forward. The thing about it was: the community was so poor, but there was this *spirit* I've told you about. Like the little fellow who gave me the shot glass: that's what he had. And he wasn't ashamed to give it to me. He thought I could use it—which I could! And I found out that, no matter what the conditions are in a school . . . for instance, you may have some absolute, hard-to-teach youngsters in your class. Some who aren't interested at all. And then you've got some who you can see they're going to be successful. But your challenge is, and my challenge was, to *see* how rough it is—and the genius in you is when you can overcome it. Here's this guy, he's so mean, boy; you can see him looking at you, he's going to *spit* on you. How can you get to him? How can you get him to sit up straight, and how can you get him to be respectful? You can find a way, but you can't do it by just beating him. That's what he wants you to do. He wants you to add to the pity.

So you find a way for a little achievement at a time. You have to crack the nut. If you get just a little bitty crack in this guy that's got all this prejudice in him, and he's sitting there full of gall . . . when you finally open this up, it's full of jewels. Then the relief comes to them. They'll find that other people haven't noticed them, but *you* did. Your peers will say, "Well, why do they like him so much? Is he giving them candy or something?" No, no. He's just giving them some self-respect.

All this moaning and groaning, and "Somebody did this to me, somebody did that"—"That's why I cut somebody's head off, because my mama didn't give me my oatmeal on time," or "we didn't have anything in the house to eat"—that's the biggest lie. It's *nothing* that could prevent you from doing whatever you want to do. Particularly young people. How old are you now? You can tear the *world* up. Go around and do circles, and start over again twice. It's no excuse that would prevent you from being Super Person.

That's what we had going on in that old band room, with water all over the floor. It got into me where the game is not equal—this is not the way it's supposed to be—and it's a joy to overcome it. It's a joy for the worst student in your class to come in there; he's destined to make an F or a D; and somehow, in the time that you have with him, he comes up and he earns a B. When he gets that, he's going to go on and make some other marks.

When he straightens up and starts doing good things, it proves that he can *be* good things.

When I first got to the school, there was one person that really befriended me: his name was Joe Jones, and he was the printing teacher. Joe was the type of friend that would criticize you—jokingly criticize you—and spur you on to do great things. He would make jokes about the band, and our beaten-up, old instruments: say, "Every time that band marches, they have to have a man with a bucket at the end of the line, picking up the pieces that fall off the instruments." But Joe seemed to befriend me more than anybody else when I started teaching. He was much older than I was, and he just sort of mentored me.

Joe's father was the one I told you about, back in the fraternity days, who they had to get out of town for cutting the guy on the streetcar, and the Pythians dressed him up as a woman. That was Joe's daddy. He was a tailor, and he went up to Chicago for years and years. After I came back in 1950, I got a chance to meet him. He had been away from Alabama maybe twenty years, because they were looking for him. He was a well-educated gentleman, and all.

I may as well tell this one, too: when I first got to school, as I said, I had never, ever taught. And some of the students in those days would be as big as you are, or bigger: it wasn't anything out of the ordinary that a person, eighteen or nineteen years old, could still be in grade school.

It was cold that day. We were all sitting in the band room, eating lunch. I looked up, and this fellow was as big as a man, and *mean*-looking—and there he was with his hand draped over this girl, right on her breast. This was all out of focus: I didn't know how classrooms were supposed to be, but this was bad behavior, and right in my face. I had these drumsticks, and I just—*bam!*—hit him on his arm. He jumped up, and ran out.

There was a coalhouse right by the band room, maybe twenty feet away, where they got the coal to put in the stove. He started hurling this coal at the door and cursing, saying, "You must be shell-shocked, you son of a—! You better not touch me!"

Jerome was his name. I put my coat on—and I didn't intend to have it, but I had a knife in my coat pocket. I went out there, and I flipped that knife open. It was insane, maybe, but I said, "Drop that coal!"

He dropped that coal.

I said, "If I ever see you again, that's going to be the end of you, do you understand?"

He looked at me. He said, "You don't sound like a schoolteacher."

If somebody had looked out of the building, I'd have been fired.

I looked at him: "You don't look like a school *student,* either. Get out of my face."

The children, man, said, "Oh, my God." They were scared.

Listen.

He went to Mr. Jones, to the print shop, and he told Mr. Jones about it. Mr. Jones said, "Well, you go back and beg his pardon." Said, "He wouldn't have hurt you; you just went and rubbed him the wrong way. You should never do that. Just go back and tell him you're going to do right and help out. He's a fair fellow; he's not going to bother you."

Right after lunch, Jerome comes up to the door. I pick up a chair— *BAM!* I didn't hit him, but I hit *at* him, and he was so scared he messed all over himself.

I'd never been like this in my life. But it flashed in my mind: what kind of control would I have over these youngsters if I didn't confront him? I can't take him to the principal, because the principal would be afraid of him and send him back. If Jerome had been victorious, he wouldn't have stopped. It was a lesson, also, to those girls who were coming up: it meant that I wouldn't take any disrespect to them. I wouldn't tolerate that kind of promiscuity.

Finally, Jerome got to be one of the best students I ever had. He was about seventh grade, then. The next year, he started getting his lessons, and he just made a wonderful success.

A few years passed, and my wife Doris and I were at this club, the Mo-Mo Club, one block down from our home. All of a sudden, I get this extra drink. They said, "What would you like to have? A friend wants to send a drink to you."

Dot said, "Who is that?"

"I don't know."

It was Jerome.

He was so happy to see me. He said, "Listen. All my life I wanted to ask you this question." He said, "I was wrong, and I was sorry," he said, "but would you have hurt me that day?"

I said, "Jerome, do you want to know the truth?"

"I sure do."

"Well," I said: "If you'd hurt me, Jerome, you'd have been dead."

His looked at me for a second and didn't say a word—and then he threw his arms around me. Because I'd told him the truth, unadulterated. I didn't know what I was doing, but God must have intervened that day—because I didn't throw away my life, and I didn't throw away his.

We just stood there and embraced.

The supervisor of music when I came to Birmingham was a man named Reuben Martinson. He was the choir director of the First Baptist Church on the Southside for many, many years, and he was the supervisor of music for Birmingham schools for many years. His forte was singing. And he got to be one of my best, dear friends.

I remember, he would come to my room, and of course we had that potbellied stove in there. First of all, he said he couldn't come in there because he sang in the choir, and he said that coal wasn't good for his throat. He finally got over that. But he would stand outside of the room, and he would want to know how many people you've got in there.

When I first got to the school—this is going back to my early days of teaching—I ordered some pictures of instruments. The very first week, I bought some cards with music pictures on them. When you start teaching, you have something around the walls, this instrument or that instrument, so I had all these pictures from Kohn's Music Company. They sent the conventional instruments like the bass horn, the tuba, the trumpet, the cornet; and they sent a package of *stringed* instruments—the violin, the viola, the cello, and bass. I put them up in my room—this old, wooden shack—all along the wall.

Mr. Martinson came to my classroom. He didn't know me, and he looked at that and he said, "What are those up there for?"

"Well, those are violins."

"How'd you get those?"

I said, "They came in the pack with my instruments around the wall."

Now, here's the question: "*You don't intend to teach those, do you?*"

I said, "Well, not now, anyway. I don't have any violins."

He didn't want me to put that violin in that school.

What it was: as fair as he was, this was a threat. It was a threat because nobody in the black schools had ever touched a violin. There was nothing *looking* like a violin in the black schools. On the other side, they had all kinds of orchestras and fine equipment: a school like Woodlawn or Phillips had string orchestras, and their string programs were stronger than their band programs, because strings are always equated as being such educational instruments. So they had the strings and choral groups and what we call "color" instruments: flutes and oboes and piccolos. There was emphasis in the white schools on that: *fine* music.

He wanted to know if I was going to change anything about this.

I assured him that that wasn't it. It was just that I had to have those cards, so the children could at least see what those other instruments *looked* like.

He asked me, "Where did you go to school?"

I said, "Howard University."

That didn't satisfy him.

"Are you from here?"

I said, "Yes, I am."

"Where did you do your high school?"

"At Parker High School."

"Oh." He said, "Okay."

That gave him some relief, because he knew I hadn't had training in high school on strings. That took a threat away. Later on, I did start the strings, but it wasn't the time and place for it yet.

The thing about it was, for me, I could feel that nobody wanted to stretch the limits. Nobody wanted to do what hadn't been done before. *I* wasn't too interested in it, really, but it did touch a chord with me: why *can't* they do this?

In the Southern cities, you had certain instruments that people thought were in a class by themselves—a flute, or an oboe—those were instruments that had certain cultural connections to them. Other instruments were just common: an old, broken-down cornet, or broken-down saxophone. You might look in the garbage can in Louisiana and find a bent-up trombone in there; old musicians would pick these instruments out and play them. The banjo: it's not expensive. Somebody buys one, then they throw it away, and somebody comes and picks it up. That's where jazz came from. Somebody asked me, "Doc, why don't you ever hear jazz on a bassoon?" You could have jazz on a bassoon, but it wasn't what people were exposed to. You don't hear much about flutes in jazz either, because those were thought to be angelic instruments. Or the French horn: that's a delicate instrument. It just wasn't available. And it was the same way for us, in the schools.

After time went around, Mr. Martinson got to be one of my best friends. First, he started telling me, "Listen on Saturday, we're broadcasting from the Southside Baptist Church." He had a tremendous choir. He said, "I want to know what you think about it." And we got to be friends.

Mr. Martinson started bringing instruments to the school. He would say, "Mr. Adams, I've taken this around to everybody. Can you do anything with it? It's an E-flat clarinet, and the fellows say they don't want it because it's just an out-of-tune instrument. All the band directors say it's just *made* out of tune." Said, "Would you want your children to have it?"

I grabbed it. I said, "I *started* on one of those!" I guess I was magically playing mine in tune!

One day Mr. Martinson came to my band room. He still wouldn't come in—he didn't want to go in there and expose himself, get that soot or whatever on his lungs. And that was all right with me. He came one day, and we were *really* playing, boy. He was standing at the door. He said, "Play that": we'd play this thing, *bam-bam-bam,* and we jumped down to the little soft part, *da-da-da.* He said, "That's good, that's good. How'd you get them to play that way? That's good."

He'd get ready to leave, then he'd say, "Mr. Adams, would you play that last part again?" I'd say, "Sure."

"That's wonderful. Play that again. That's wonderful."

I started thinking: I wonder why in the world he would keep coming back in here. One time was enough, but two or three times, something's crazy going on.

Then I found out what it was. This little boy—he's famous now in New York City—Rudell Houston. I never will forget it—you remember the exceptional ones. He had a stutter. And he said, "W-W-When Mr. Martinson was here, my horn fell apart." Instead of bringing the piece up to me, he said: "I just hummed my part."

I went over to the office, and I called his mama. I said, "Don't worry about *him.* He's a musician, if I ever heard one." His horn's broken, and he's singing: *bum-bum-bum!* He's matching the pitch *perfectly.* Mr. Martinson kept hearing it—it was a weird sound, but he couldn't place what it was, because it was so correct—it was a human voice, and he's listening for the sound of a horn.

I said, "Don't worry about *him.*" From there, Rudell went on, and he's recording in New York City. Trumpet player. He was just one of those that could listen to it—and it didn't come automatically, but he listened to it enough to know exactly where he was supposed to be. You find some like that in your classroom: you can tell, in grade school, that they're going to be exceptional. No matter what their situation— if they want to do it, they can succeed.

Once I got things going, the band started going back to the parades again. It wasn't the Odd Fellows this time, but the Bethlehem Star Society. They had an annual parade that was three or four blocks long. Another one was for Epps Jewelry Company: they had these elaborate things on Easter. Mr. Taft Epstein was a Jewish fellow, and he promoted my band out at Fair Park; they would plant Easter eggs and the band would play. We did the Veterans Day parade and the tuberculosis parade.

At that time, TB was still rampant. They had this elaborate fundraiser, and this was the TB Game I told you about: a big football game at Fair Park, and the bands would compete for a little trophy. It was a great battle to see, especially in the grade schools, who had the best band. That went for, maybe, nine years straight. They'd get ready, as soon as school started, for the TB Games. They would scout out the other schools—it was like football—to see who your players are, what you're going to play. And we were fortunate at Lincoln to have the best band just about every year.

We had this fellow in my band, we called him "Hardhead." He came from Florida, and they say they had a tornado down there, when he was just a little fellow, and it blew him up in a tree. He fell out of that tree onto his head, and nothing happened—that's why they called him Hardhead. He was a fine little fellow, and he was my bass drummer: *little* fellow, and he carried that big bass drum.

We were having one of the parades, and we were in this church where you had to stay for three or four hours while the sermons would go on. We were sitting in that church for a long, long time—they preached, preached, preached—and Hardhead had his bass drum in front of him. Just before the dismissal, before they had the Doxology, he took that mallet and hit that drum: BAM! Everybody jumped in the church—they thought maybe a *bomb* had gone off.

The children said, "Mr. Adams is going to tear you *up* when you get back to the school."

We marched all the way back. The little fellow had tears in his eyes; and the children were looking back to see what I would do to him.

I said: "*Hardhead.* Why did you do that? Why did you hit that drum like that? And just *excite* everybody like that?"

He said, "I don't know. But I was just looking at it. And I wanted to *hit* it." He was crying. He said, "I *love* my drum. And so I hit it."

I said, "Listen. Don't you *ever* do that again, Hardhead. *Now get out of here!*" Those other children—they were looking—they said, "Why didn't you do something to him?"

I said, "You just go home to your families. Leave that boy alone."

I could see that he was so sincere. He loved that drum, and he wanted to hit it. Now, how could I punish him? He had a passion, and it left him no choice: he *had* to hit that drum. That was one of the things that I always remember about those days.

After my band had started getting all these Superior ratings, the principal came down one day. They had some teachers that were holding my students, because they wanted to keep them in their class and didn't want them to come and practice—you run into some that want to hold their students and keep you from doing what you're supposed to—but he told them in a teachers' meeting: "Don't *ever* keep those children out of Mr. Adams's class! This band and Mr. Adams, they just add a new dimension to this school. Some of you don't send those children to that band on time—you think it's an extracurricular activity, but I went down there, and they're speaking a different language"— things like *ritard* and *allegro, mezzo, sotto voce*—he said, "You're going to have to see *me* if you don't send those children on time for band practice."

That was Professor Traylor. He was very supportive, one of the ones that did the most for the band. He was a *fine* principal, but some of the teachers had told him that he didn't have any culture—that he was born over in the mining district, and he didn't know, for instance, anything about *Bach* or all those folks. "He's just uncouth," you know; they talked about him.

Something happened one day: we were having a concert, around Easter time, on a Sunday, and the choir sang and the band played and they had all these skits—and Mr. Traylor was just a realist. He got up and he said, "Miss Chambliss"—Miss Chambliss was the choral teacher—"can we go home?" He said, "We've been here all day," and said, "We're tired." He said, "The band has played all of its numbers, but we just keep going on."

She was very insulted by that, so she said that he was uncouth and ignorant and he didn't appreciate the music. That hurt him real badly. He called me into the office and said, "Mr. Adams, why would that lady do that to me?" He said, "I'm so proud of the band; I try to do everything I can"—he'd been in tears, it was just tearing him up.

So he started going to the symphony. Listening at the symphony. He saw this fellow with a double-reed oboe playing. He came back and said, "What's that man playing, with this little thing, where it looks like some little stick . . . ?"

I said, "That's an oboe."

"Have we got one of them?"

I said, "No! We're an elementary school, we can't afford that." They didn't even have an oboe in the high school. Nobody had one.

"I'm going to *get* one."

About a week later, here comes an oboe. So I started teaching oboe.

He called me in there, and he called his friend on the telephone—another principal, about twelve blocks away—and he said, "Listen at this thing!" I had to play a tune on the oboe on the phone. He said, "You don't have *that!*"

And he kept going.

He would come back. He would say, "What about that great *big* thing?" Talking about a bassoon. "That big wooden thing."

I said, "Man, that thing cost *thousands* of dollars— "

"I'm going to *get* one, I'm going to *get* one."

About a month later, here's this big bassoon. I'm teaching oboe and bassoon now. And all of a sudden he starts getting *all* these instruments.

"What's that thing that that man is sitting up there playing, it's a long black thing like this? It looks like a something, I don't know what it is, but he's sitting there playing it: *Boo-ooop!*"

I said, "You must be talking about a bass clarinet."

"We have one of those?"

We had a clarinet; he gets a *bass* clarinet. And this bass clarinet was expensive.

Mr. Traylor.

Every time he'd get a new instrument, he'd call me to his office, and he'd call the other principal. He'd say, "Boy, you don't have one of *these,*" and I'd have to play "Danny Boy": *Doo-doo, dooooo. . . .* But the band was building, and he took that as a challenge. He wanted it.

When that got around to the board of education, the music department, they found out Professor Traylor was buying all these instruments, and they start coming down, listening. About a month later, here come all these trumpets and flutes from the board—because they found out we were *doing* something with the instruments.

And that's how I started the string program, a million-dollar program.

I went up to the high school, up here on Eighth Avenue, and Mr. Martinson and I went down in the basement to get something. There was this broken violin. A dead rat was laying on top of that violin, man, and it was broken. I kicked that rat off of there. He said, "You don't want that!"

I said, "*Yes I do.*"

"What're you going to do with it?"

I said, "I'm going to teach with it."

"You can't—"

I said, "I know somebody who will fix it." I put it in a brown bag and I took it out to Pops—Pops Williams—and Pops put that thing together. That's how I started the string program in Birmingham. The first time somebody played something real well on it, that convinced the whole community that the violin is a good instrument to play. And that's how we got a million dollars for strings in Birmingham. Right now, youngsters are walking around with those violins.

Pops said: "All you people want to do down here, regardless of everything, is the marching; you all are still marching." All through the South, all through Alabama, we liked that kind of culture. He said, "In other places, like Boston, they have symphonies and everything. But way down South, we're just marching to the Civil War; just marching in the football game. Marching is in our blood."

Now, we knew, man, the great University of Alabama Million Dollar Band—five hundred folks playing their horns and marching—it's spectacular. It's wonderful. But where are the great orchestras?

Pops told me: he said, "Listen. You call yourself a musician?"

I said, "Yeah, I do, man. I make a living—"

He said, "You can't call yourself a musician unless you teach *stringed* instruments."

I said, "Pops. I had some elementary strings in college, but I don't know—"

"All you need to do is get you a book." He said, "A great teacher prescribes. Like a doctor—you prescribe this book. They're already on their way. They're motivated. Just keep a couple of pages ahead of them."

I said, "Okay, Pops."

And it worked. It worked! Because there was a hunger for it. People didn't realize that there was so much ability.

Then along came Mrs. Dathia Means. We were so fortunate to have Mrs. Means come in as a string specialist a while at Lincoln School.

She had been taught violin pedagogy—she went to college and mastered in that—and this was the first opportunity that we had to get a real professional to teach the violin. She got the string program going at Lincoln, and then she wanted to spread it to the high school. She went to Carver High School and she developed other teachers, because other schools wanted the program—and this is when the City Council voted to equip *all* the schools with stringed instruments. It was an idea of mine, and I did a lot to help it, but Mrs. Means deserves great credit for developing that program.

When the string program got started, you would go to Sunday school, where you always saw people with saxophones and clarinets—and you would see the kids standing around with *violin* cases. Changing culture. Because when they heard it could be done, they said, "Listen! My daughter not only plays the flute, but she plays the violin. And plays it in the *church*." And people would say, "Wow. We just haven't been doing that before."

So I found out that it's just how you size up the enemy. And I'm not talking about the person; the enemy is this thing in their *head*. You have to figure out how you can change that.

That's good, because that gives you a challenge.

I taught at Lincoln for twenty-seven years, and after that, you might call it a promotion, but I went to the board as a program specialist for another twenty years. That must have been in 1977. So when you put the eight years that I *attended* Lincoln in grade school, and the twenty-seven years I *taught* there—and that's not even talking about the supervisor years—I was just like one of the bricks in the wall.

I got a letter from Hugh Thomas. Hugh Thomas was a great musician at Birmingham-Southern College. He directed the choir and is really the grandfather of choral music in Birmingham. He would stop outside on Eighth Avenue and watch my band rehearse. When I got promoted to the board of education, I got this letter—I think I have it at home, now—he said, "I congratulate you on being made a supervisor. But," he said, "I regret the fact that you were doing a most important thing, that you were destined to do." He said, "They will miss you forever." And he signed it, Hugh Thomas.

Now, what he meant was that what I should be doing was to still be there with those children: *not* to take a promotion. And that's the way he felt, I guess, about his life at Birmingham-Southern. He spent his whole life down there teaching the choirs. I think about that, and I appreciate him for respecting and appreciating me. He would stop his car on the way to work, and sit out there and watch them: watch, watch, watch the children. And you do find out—you might not know it now—but you're in a situation where in years to come you'll look back and say, "What I was doing, it went by pretty fast, but there were so many things in there that I'm so proud of doing." That would be: making the thing that seemed impossible possible.

After I got to be a supervisor, after about four or five years, I visited Lincoln School and they were going through a band practice. I looked around and I said, "You're a Roberts, aren't you? Aren't you a Johnson?"

The next generation. The same heads, the same faces, but they're another generation in there.

I go to the grocery store now; I can't stop before somebody comes up and says, "Hey, Mr. Adams, how are you doing? Here's my grandson." Here's my *grandson!* I say, "My goodness, I must be Rip Van Winkle, man." They tell me what they're doing. I've got some working in the White House; I've got some in prison. They're everywhere. I remember, I was playing at the Redmont Hotel, this is some years ago; I was playing in a small group about three or four times a week in there. I noticed there were some young ladies that I taught, and they were standing on the street—they were prostitutes. I said, "No matter what you do, I'm still your teacher. I'm always your teacher. You don't have to be ashamed; just do better."

They're everywhere. I was up in Chicago some years ago on a little trip, and I went down there to the worst bowels of the city—*tough* neighborhood, man—and all of a sudden: "Hey, Mr. Adams! That's my teacher! Hey, Mr. Adams!" It's wonderful when you see them. Not all of them are going to be the top of the line, but they've still got that thing in them. You put it in them.

I was at Lincoln School when they were having all the marches, during the civil rights movement. A lot of children in my band class were jailed—but the thing about it was, they didn't want any special credit for going. You have other people who say, "I was in the movement! I won a medal for doing this; I was one of the Freedom Riders; I was one of those who marched; I was in jail, and all . . ." Well, that's good. But there were some people: they didn't want any recognition. I see people now, they walk up in the grocery store and say, "Doc, this is my child here. Do you remember when we walked, man?" I say, "Yeah." And you have some that come and say, "I know you know I was there, Doc, but that's over now." You have some cool ones—they did it, but so what? This is 2012. They don't want to go through that again. They'll just say, "I tell my child about it, and I work to educate my child so it won't happen again."

Then some will come up to you and say to their son: "I want you to meet Mr. Adams. He's a good man."

And that's enough.

11

Bandleader

I TAUGHT AT LINCOLN SCHOOL FOR TWENTY-SEVEN years. That's a long time. I would have these little dreams, sometimes, that I never *graduated* from Lincoln: I would just be recycled ad infinitum.

I knew every brick in that school. I remember when I went there as a youngster, and all the little things that went along with that—how I enjoyed the marching parades and the Odd Fellows—I think about those things all the time. But I found out very early that I wasn't content just to have a job and then on the weekends do like most teachers: they would go to each other's homes, have some ham and some drinks, and when the game would come, they would all go out to see Alabama A&M. They were in different clubs that met and socialized. But what was missing in my life was the fact that I wanted to *play*. I wanted to play some music.

When I got back to Birmingham, everybody around here was playing the old tunes. I'd been around groups like Louis Jordan that would do the kicks and movements while they played, and wear the little outfits and all. I thought, that's a great way to break in *here,* but who could play it?

I met some fellows that had been playing at a lot of little places— I guess you would call them "hillbilly" places—out on the highway. It was an old blues singer, Robert McCoy, and he had a drummer, Clarence Curry. They played at this honky-tonk, the Ironwood Inn. These fellows couldn't play any *jazz,* but Robert was one of the old barrelhouse piano players. He could play the old ragtime piano, and

Jimmy Chapell, Clarence Curry, Frank Adams, Martin Barnett, and Robert McCoy, 1950s. Courtesy of Patrick Cather.

I'd get in there some kind of way with the clarinet or the saxophone. There wasn't any leader; it was just three guys playing together, and it was enjoyable.

A man ran that place named Mr. Charles. He was a typical, mean fellow, but he liked the musicians, and Robert was liked by the clientele out there. They'd have a big Saturday night, and they'd dance and everything. We didn't even have a microphone, I don't think, but he'd sit there and he'd play that piano, and they'd tip us.

It got to the point that even though we just had a drum and a piano, it got to be pretty tight. Robert would play these things: "Red Sails in the Sunset," and the old barrelhouse pieces; "The Yellow Rose of Texas," "She'll Be Coming Round the Mountain," and that kind of stuff. There was not a song he couldn't sing—even though he didn't know the words to a lot of songs, he'd ad-lib them. And there were times when you could really feel the authenticity and *sincerity* of Robert's stuff. He composed songs, and he knew some things that you'd never heard before. He had those old beats going on, and he could play all those shouts and things. He'd drink a lot and say, "Come on, come on, Clarence!" But when people called for any *jazz* music, he and Clarence would know nothing about that. They'd find a key, and I would play the melody. They'd make all the wrong notes—nobody knew the melody but me—but we just went on and played it. There were little bands going around like that, then—it wasn't far removed from Banjo Bill—and there wasn't a lot of money involved, like a big job, but you worked so regularly, and you got tips. That really helped me out: the tips were just little bits of change, but you always knew that if you did "When the Saints Go Marching In," you could get about five or ten dollars, back in that day.

It just progressed from there. Finally I saw that I could probably do a little better, so I took Robert and Clarence along with me, and I added a trumpet player, and I started getting my band together. We went into a place on the Southside, a black club called 2728. It had a good clientele, and we had opportunities to play there on Sunday night. The 2728 Club wasn't a *classy* place, but people would come dressed up, and it was a different environment than Clarence and Robert had been used to. They started getting a little nervous.

The fellow that ran this club was a fellow named O. J. Grey. He was a guy with a great personality, and he drew people to this 2728. It got to be the most popular place in town. They had all kinds of shows coming in there—stuff from Detroit, and what they called "homosexual shows"—where they'd have male dancers dressed as women. They'd go in the restrooms with the ladies and all that kind of thing—and you had some guys complaining about it. This guy would say, "Listen, O. J., it's a disgrace. You're paying those folks up there—and that ain't no woman, that's a man!" He said, "When it gets out, people are going to boycott this place!"

O. J. said, "You're wrong." He was a very astute guy. He always knew exactly what was in his cash register, and he ran his business well and had some good white friends that would back him up. He wore good, nice-looking clothes, and he loved everybody. He was sort of like Duke: "Love you madly."

But this guy was complaining about the dancers. O. J. told me: "You see that guy over there? That guy don't want me to have these women in here that are not women. He's complaining about it."

I said, "Doesn't that worry you?"

"No. I just want you to watch," he said. "At one o'clock, I want you to look over there."

I looked over there at one o'clock: the guy was *kissing* one of them.

Frank Adams, saxophone, backing a female impersonator, left. 2728 Club, late 1950s. Courtesy of Frank Adams.

Those were the kind of things that happened there. In fact, the first time I saw Diana Ross was at O. J.'s club. She came down with a group from Detroit, and she was on the chorus line. She was the skinniest thing on there, and everybody said, "Whoa, what they got *her* on there for?" They had some female impersonators on the line, and this little teeny thin girl that you wanted to take to the hospital if you saw her—but she was out there dancing, and it was Diana Ross. We never knew she was going to be a famous singer.

Meanwhile, my band was developing. And what distinguished the group was we would stand up and play. Most of the bands in Birmingham were sitting down—and it was so dead to me, because I'd been used to stuff moving. You've got to move one number after another, and *you* have to be moving. The bands in Birmingham had their sheet music, and they all sat down. We were just a little bobtail band, we didn't have any music at all, and we stood up. We played one number after another, then another, and people started saying, "Wow."

Some of the musicians said, "Man, you're making things bad for us." In fact, I got a note from one fellow, said, "We want to sit *down* and play, why are you coming here with all that moving about like that?"

Ivory "Pops" Williams, Selena Mealings, Frank Adams, and Martin Barnett, 2728 Club, mid-1960s. Courtesy of Frank Adams.

But people started liking it: "Well, they sound good." "That band is *hot.*" Then, when I started buying some little coats and all—oh, man, that was just first class. People hadn't seen that around here. Little jackets that looked alike, and everybody moving alike—then we were able to build and build and *build,* and that job ended up in a lot of other jobs. Especially, I guess, in the white clubs: little places that people come in and drink a lot of beer and tip the band—nothing formal or anything—and you play. They get around and they start to know your name, and they say, "Well, that guy can play the saxophone, you ought to get him." And Robert: "That's a real, authentic blues player." He'd drink his bit of whiskey and fall out—people liked that kind of stuff. Word got around, so the next big job that came along, when my band was getting to where it was really being recognized, was at the Woodland Club.

That place you could write a book about. We were there fourteen years.

The Woodland Club was run by a man by the name of Mr. Red Hassler. And something had happened to Mr. Red: he had quite a sum of money, because he'd had an accident. Somebody had run over him with a tractor or something—it looked like his fingers were all mangled up—and he had a big settlement, so he didn't have to worry about anything, moneywise. He could run his club the way he wanted to.

He ran the club, and that was his life. It was an old wooden building, and he wouldn't do any kind of improvement on it. He didn't *have* to improve on it. He didn't care about whether you came there or not. People would say, "When are you going to get that toilet fixed?"

"When I get ready." There was no compunction on him to do anything. But when he finally did it, he would do it right.

Mr. Red would come out there inebriated, particularly after an Alabama game. He was a staunch Alabama football fan—he didn't attend *any* school, but he was an Alabama fan, and Bear Bryant was his god. When Alabama would have a game, he would be the last one to leave the stadium. They'd have to carry him to his club; he'd get there real late, and then he'd make the folks leave. He'd tell everybody there, "Y'all get out of here! I want to hear my band by *myself*."

"But we've been waiting to get in the club."

"I'm closed today! Go down the street to some other club."

He would get *mad* when the place was making money. I've never seen anybody like that. On a New Year's Eve, after the other clubs had closed down, before day in the morning, people would come out there—and he'd get mad at them. They would be drunk, and he would say, "What did you come out here for? You ain't got no business coming up here on a night like this. Where *you* been, over at the Mountain Brook Country Club?" And he'd charge them triple the price. "You already spent your money, and now you want to come here? You're going to *pay* to get in!"

We started playing at the Woodland Club, and the band developed a bit more than the little group that played at the Ironwood Inn. We added some pieces and we had gotten the steps and uniforms and everything. But this was strictly a hillbilly place, and it was racked with all kinds of folks in there. They would turn over the tables and make a lot of noise, all that kind of stuff—especially after an Alabama football game, it was horrible.

It was a place where there was diversity: not racially, but you had Jews, you had Italians, you had all kinds of folk. And you had a lot of *wealthy* youngsters—I still see some of them now—that lived over the mountain. They had the Birmingham Country Club and those places, but they'd rather come out there, especially the young ones: the young elite. They had privileges, but it seemed to me that they were just trying to go down into the hole—of course, they could always come back *out* of the hole, but they wanted to see how it was, roughnecking. Red didn't believe in advertisements, just word of mouth—but he'd have the biggest crowds in town. We had people that would come religiously— they liked to have fun, and they wanted to be out there in the raw. Handicaps were a challenge to them. When the sun was out, very few people would come to the Woodland Club. But if it would snow and the cars would get stuck in the mud, that's when you would have the biggest crowds. They had to go down a long dirt road, ditches everywhere, and they'd have to have their car pulled out Sunday morning— and they'd enjoy that kind of thing. That's a funny thing about human nature.

Of course, you had some people at the Woodland Club who would really fight. They had a fight every night. And you had these good college students—they would be in there, looking, and they would try to stir up a fight, too, but you could tell they weren't really for real.

I found out that if you're in a predominantly black club and they start fighting, you might hear pistol shots; but in a white situation, you'd have the tables turned over. You'd turn your tables over, and you'd break glasses, but you don't really hurt anybody. It's more of a "Wild West" thing; it's a matter of tearing up something, turning things over—"Let's make a big noise." Excitement. On New Year's Eve, instead of saying "Cheers," man, they'd *break* something. And the way I settled it, one night: this fight had broken out, so I stood up and played "The Star Spangled Banner"—and everyone came to attention. That's how I stopped the fight—in fact, I stopped a *few* fights that way at the Woodland Club.

The Woodland Club didn't have any pretense about it. In fact, once Mr. Hassler did have the bandstand decorated with elaborate curtains and all—it lasted about a week and people tore it down. So we went back to the old way.

What happened: Red knew a fellow who worked at Blach's downtown department store, and this guy put up the most beautiful bandstand. They had drapes here, and pictures, and a ball hanging down, like you're at the Waldorf Astoria. He got some things they used to decorate the windows at the store, and he had it all up and glittering.

We were sitting up there one night, and Red said, "How do you fellows feel about it?" Well, it didn't make any difference to us.

It lasted awhile. And then on New Year's Eve it started coming down. I had gotten married to my wife, Doris, then—I call her "Dot"—and she was singing with the band. Everybody was drinking and having fun, and at a table in front of the band, this couple was so much in love: they were hugging and going on, and Dot said, "Look at that. Aren't they just in love?"

As soon as we started playing "Auld Lang Syne," that lady pulled her shoe off—it was a high-heeled red shoe, I never will forget it— and she hit the poor guy in the head. "I don't want to be with you anymore"— *Bam!*

I looked at Dot: "How do you like *that?*"

All of a sudden, people started turning over tables—and this was the beginning of the destruction of the canopy. Somebody knocked one of the boards out of the bandstand—and Red was of the bent that he'd just leave it there, and folks would just be dancing all around it. When it was all over, they said, "We got things back to the way we want them, Red. We don't want to look at the crap—we can go to the Holiday *Inn* and look at that."

Red would curse them back out: "I don't see why you come out here anyway."

That was Red.

He had only one thing on the menu: a ham sandwich. Somebody would say, "Don't you have something to eat?"

"No, you go *home* to eat." He'd say, "If it's an emergency, you eat one of these ham sandwiches." And he would charge you more for it if you were hungry. If it's nine o'clock, you might get a decent price, but ten o'clock he'd go up a dollar and a half.

Another thing about Red's place: he would sell beer on Sundays. And he was sort of a clearinghouse: they would bring a lot of beer into Red's, and if you were in a dry county, you would come to Red's and he'd sell you that beer.

There's a whiskey that Mr. Red would serve—it was the worst thing in the world. I don't remember what it was called, but it had a little dog on the front of the bottle. I don't think they make it anymore. That was the *cheapest* liquor, and he would pull it out after everything else had been sold. Then he had these glasses with a false bottom. You've got a shot glass that's *supposed* to be a shot glass, but it's got a great big indention in the bottom of it—so you're paying for a shot, but you're actually getting half. Or he'd give you a false-bottomed beer; the bottom would be raised so you're getting half a beer. That caused a lot of fights. A guy would say, "Well, look-a-here, *I'm* not drunk," and he'd probably swing at the bartender: "What are you trying to pull?" But most of the time it worked.

Mr. Hassler had these bouncers, and they were fierce guys, big guys. This little fellow did something one night and the bouncers just *beat* him, bad, and they were going to throw him out. He said, "Look at me, they hit me in my mouth"—he was whimpering—but he said, "I'll be back. I'll be back."

Red said, "He ain't coming back here."

"Mr. Hassler," I said, "the bouncer really hurt that guy. That man will *be* back."

We finally finished that night. And we got home. The next night we went out to the club—out there near Irondale, you go down a dirt road—we turned down that road . . . *all the siding had been shot off that place*. That guy had a submachine gun, evidently, man. We were scared to go in there.

That kind of thing was serious.

We had another fellow who worked at the Woodland Club, who would take things. He was a waiter out there and he sang with us, and he would steal some ham sandwiches or throw a case of beer out the back of the place; he'd go out and get it and go home with it. We had a little station wagon, and one night we got home, my wife and I; we looked in the back of that station wagon, and this fellow had put two cases of beer in the back of our car. We turned right around and took that back to Mr. Hassler. And I think that was where the bond between us—my wife and Mr. Hassler and me—came together, as a real firm relationship.

Now, Mr. Hassler was strange, and he had a weird sense, I guess, of pride. He was suspicious of this fellow, so he said, "I'll get him." He didn't want to turn him into the police; he wanted to catch him at it himself. So he went to the extreme of buying a *bear* trap. He went and put a bear trap right outside the club, to catch this guy throwing the beer out there—but it never did happen. One night we were playing and we heard something—*Bam!*—everybody ran outside to look.

Red had caught a rabbit in that thing. He never did catch the guy.

There was a fellow who used to come to the Woodland Club, and he became a good friend. His name was Patrick Cather. He was a young, white guy, in high school, and he used to follow the band around. He was really into old blues records; that's how we met him.

He was just curious about the music. He started putting an ad in the paper buying old records. He was interested in rhythm and blues records, all the old Bessie Smith kind of stuff, and he'd pay you something for that: maybe two or three dollars for a record. His daddy had this publishing company, Cather Publishing, and it was a family thing. His daddy knew Professor Whatley because Whatley would assign some of his printing to Cather when the work was too complex for his students. And Mr. Cather would give Fess Whatley work; it was a mutual relationship. In the black community, you might not talk about it, but a lot of things happened like that: partnerships between black and white.

Patrick had a burning fire to find out all about those old players. That was his ambition: to relate to something that probably wouldn't pay big dividends but would give him a sense of self-worth, and a sense of involvement in this passion he had for music. He had been going around to Robert McCoy's home, which was right down from Bomb Hill. This is in the early 1960s. His folks were very supportive of him: his daddy or somebody would bring him, in spite of the fact that there was great turmoil out there. At that time it was odd, because he was a little white guy, and he would come around in the black neighborhoods and play, and just follow us around. He wrote a lot of good things about the music: he wrote for *DownBeat* and some magazines, even when he was just in high school. He learned to play pretty good piano—Robert coached him some. And something that impressed me so much about him: we made a recording with Robert's songs, and what he did, instead of taking all the royalties, which a lot of them would do back then, he gave us all a share in the recording—"McCoy, Adams, and Cather"—and he sent the record to Broadcast Music Incorporated, BMI. That was the first money I got for recording, and I get royalties now.

That was Patrick. They put him in the Hall of Fame, and we were proud to have him in there.

I mentioned that my wife, Dot, was playing with us. She lived in Homewood, Alabama, and she had five sisters and two brothers—and their father was very protective.

I'd been playing with a fellow named Vic Cunningham for about three or four years. He was playing piano, and Herbert had gotten in the band by then—Herbert Bryant, my little drummer friend from elementary school. He played excellent drums. They got together and said, "We want Frank to be with Doris." I didn't know anything about it, but they were going to put us together.

Vic lived in Homewood, and he talked about this family: that all the sisters were very attractive, and how nice they were; how her daddy worked at the plant and was protective of his daughters—he would run somebody away if they came to see them—all that type of thing.

One Sunday night we were playing the 2728, and O. J. said, "You know what? There's a young lady that comes out here, and she takes a table; she sits right back in that back corner, and there's nobody ever there with her, but," he said, "every time you play, she looks like she's *eating* up notes."

I said, "Eating notes?" I had never heard of anybody eating notes. I was skeptical of matchmakers, but when I found out that she was *eating* up notes—I said, "I'd better find out who that is."

It happened to be Doris. And I finally got to meet her.

I asked the guys in the band. They said, "Man, she comes to see you. You didn't know?"

I didn't know she was back there.

I spoke to her.

I said, "I want to see you." She said, "Okay," and gave me her telephone number—I still remember that number. I called over there, and of course I'd heard her daddy would jump out there with a shotgun, and run you out. He had a *terrible* reputation. The whole community knew that you just don't mess with those Williams girls. I got to meet him and I found out that he wasn't so strict; he was just protective of his daughters. It was just that you're not going to be fooling around: you've got to be up straight if you're going to be calling on *my* daughter. He had a lot of them, and he felt that he had to protect them. And

Doris Adams, 1953. Courtesy of Frank Adams.

Dot: right from the start of it, you would know from her conversation that you couldn't be successful flirting with her. You had your place. It wasn't like most young girls you'd meet at that time.

We started going around together. We'd hear a band somewhere: I'd get a cab and take her back home. It sort of grew from that. And it turned out to be the best thing that could have happened to me.

It came to a point where her father said she had gotten home a little late one time, and he told her, "I don't know about you going out with him." Said, "That's a musician, they always use drugs and everything." He was a country fellow, worked at the steel plant, and he said, "I'd rather you not see him anymore."

Now, I resented that, because I hadn't made any overtures to her for anything serious, and I had been strictly a gentleman. But he said all jazz musicians probably had needle marks on their arms or were alcoholics, all that kind of thing: he didn't know that I had a job, and that I came from a family. So I said, "I'm going to talk to him and tell him, man, that I'm just as respectable as he is." I had that little itch in me, it must have come from Prof Green: "Man, don't trounce me." What is he, going to tell me I'm some *crumb* or something? I'm teaching school, I've got credentials—and who does he think his *daughter* is? There's a lot of people I could connect with. So I said, "I'm going to have a talk with him."

I made a mistake. I told my friend Joe about it: Joe Jones. And Joe was the kind of guy who liked trouble. He said, "I'll take you out there, man"—he wanted a *war*. He had a double-barreled shotgun that he was going to *shoot* Mr. Williams with.

We drove out to Homewood, it was drizzling rain—I never will forget it. There was a little bridge that divided her house from a ditch. I stepped out of the car—I left Joe there, waiting—and I went across that bridge. Here comes Mr. Williams out of the house: "Hey, son, how are you doing?" He shook my hand. "Let's go inside!"

He had probably gotten some information on me by then, to find out that I was a teacher, and wasn't one of the regular ones that he'd run away. We went in and started talking. Doris was sick and I didn't get to see her, but I sat and talked to him. We talked about the union. The union was going on strike, and he was doing little odd jobs, painting people's homes out there; he didn't own a home but was renting this house. I told him how much I admired him for taking care of all of those girls and everything. What it was: we were talking on another level—talking like a man to a man—so when I got back to the car with Joe, he was just *disgusted* that we didn't have a fight. He wanted to fire off something. But Doris's dad and I got to be close friends. We struck it off and we kept that way, all through his life.

Of course, it happened that on the weekends I'd be playing in the band, so Doris would come to some of the performances—especially at the Woodland Club—and just sit there on the bandstand. She wasn't singing at that time, at all, but when you take a lady out, people always think she's a singer. They kept getting at Doris to sing. So I started some little things with her.

One night at the Woodland Club she was singing this song, "After Midnight." A blind man, Mr. Hightower, told Mr. Hassler, "You ought to hire her."

"You're crazy, you can't even *see* nobody."

"Well, I can't see, damn it, but I can hear!" Red listened and said, "Hightower's right. Bring Doris back next week. I'll put her on the payroll." So that's how we got started.

I wrote a piece of music for Dot called "Little Girl Blues" that we recorded—we had a hit with that. In fact, Mr. Hassler paid for the recording; he was the one that financed that thing. He wasn't really interested, but he saw we wanted to record something, so he found a studio out there somewhere and cut some records. It was the Christmas season, and we recorded "The Bells of St. Mary's," and a number called "Jambalaya"—"the coffee pot" and "me-oh, my-oh"—Red told you what he wanted you to play. And of course, "Little Girl Blues": it's a type of Billie Holiday thing, and it sold pretty well.

We had music tailored for Red's audience: a few hillbilly numbers, and we did whatever Elvis Presley was doing—we could do all that kind of stuff—then we'd do the real *jazz* pieces. We had a lot of variety. We played some Latin music, and for a while we had jam sessions. Red would say, "Now, I don't want any *runabout* music." That meant music that was too fast. He liked the boogie-woogie and barrelhouse stuff—but "don't play that runabout music."

Martin Barnett was playing with me then. He was one of the old guys out of Fess Whatley's school; one of Whatley's old band members. He wasn't such a heck of a trumpet player, but he could sing those things like "Stardust" and "The World Is Waiting for the Sunrise"—all of those old, good tunes—and he had a voice like Louis Armstrong, so he was a good selling point. He could harmonize all the time with his little cornet, so we had a good man there.

We had another male singer named Robert Kelley. He would do things like the blues—"Flip, Flop, and Fly," and all that—and people would dance. Kelley was a comedian, too, cracking a few jokes. And Herbert was the monster. He would play those long drum solos. The people would feel good and would want to hear "The Saints Go Marching In" or some of these fiery pieces, and he'd play this ten-minute solo. That would get them all excited.

We had Pops Williams in that band for a long time, and for several years we had Joe Guy, who had come back to Birmingham after his

Frank "Mr. Sax" Adams promotional card, 1960s. Courtesy of Frank Adams.

marriage to Billie Holiday. When Dot was singing, Barnett and Kelley would harmonize behind her, and Joe would play his muted trumpet—it was a heck of a combination. Joe was the *master* with that mute. He'd get up to the microphone: they'd sing something; he'd play, like he did for Billie Holiday, just little dibs and dabs in there, a little improvisation; and I'd come up and play. One was "Trouble in mind, I'm blue, but I won't be blue always"—and the people just saw the *spirit* in it.

We had a wonderful thing, and it was a thing that can't be repeated.

I had a lot of time to build my band and a relationship with Mr. Hassler. That was during the time that Martin Luther King and the civil rights movement was going on, and some people would call my school and say, "Tell them not to come out here, because the Klan's going to get hold of them boys out here." Red would call and tell me; I said, "Well, we're coming anyway." "You're doggone right, you're coming!" So we'd come out there, and sometimes you'd see somebody sitting there, and you know these are the ones that are going to cause a problem. Red would have somebody with him for protection. We'd play our program, and maybe about halfway through they'd get up—"They ain't doing nothing, let's go"—so they'd leave.

We had this one restroom for men, right by the bandstand, and one restroom for women. I went in the restroom one night and, I remember—Dr. King was in Birmingham, and he's on the rise—these two guys came in, talking about "that Martin Luther Coon." And, "Yeah, somebody needs to do something to him." I was in there, urinating; I turned around and said, "You'd better get out of here! Don't come around *me* with that kind of crap, man, I'm *crazy*"—and they ran out of that place. I never saw them again.

Another night we had some people out there, and my wife went into the restroom. A lady followed her in there and started to curse her out. This lady came out and was just *screaming*. She told Mr. Hassler she didn't think it was appropriate, Doris being in that restroom. Red *jumped* on that lady—he had her put out of the place—"Who do you think you are?" He said, "She has a *right* to go in there! What do you want her to do, go out in the woods somewhere? Now, *you* get out of here!"

We all listened to that. And that brought a bond between us and Mr. Hassler, because we found out that, despite everything else, he was a good person. He was a fair person. In fact, he got to know everybody in the band, and it got to be more or less like a family thing. During the last years Mr. Hassler thought so much of me and Dot that he wanted to actually *give* us the club. He just felt that way: said, "I'm probably going to leave this to you." In the end, the Woodland Club only closed because they moved the highway.

Mr. Hassler was a fellow that I wish you could have met. He was just rough and as crude in some ways as any of those people out there; but then, he had his own thing. He didn't want anybody to bother his band. And we never worried about getting paid. He'd always do that. We played when there was nobody there, but he paid; he paid.

The biggest thing I remember: I never will forget the night they had the bombing at the Sixteenth Street Church. We were playing at the Woodland Club. We would come home all the way from Lovick, out past Irondale, and to get our band members home we'd have to pass by the church, early in the morning, because we played all night. We'd finish up and we'd probably take a drink or something; then Mr. Hassler would come back and pay me, and I'd pay the band.

This night we finished playing and we were getting ready to go home. We waited and waited for Red to pay us, and finally I said, "We've got to *go*." He hadn't brought out the money for the weekend.

He said, "You don't need to go! Drink some more of this whiskey. Why don't you get a beer or something? Why are you all in such a big hurry?"

"We've worked hard, we want to go."

"No, I want y'all to stay here with me for a while."

He'd bring some of that whiskey out there—the worst whiskey in the world—and we sat there, we sat there, and he finally let us go. It was daybreak.

What Red did: he knew that something was going to go wrong. And we would have been right in the middle of it. He figured how long it took us to get back to Birmingham, and he kept us long enough to know that we wouldn't come into contact with what they were doing there. We never talked about it—but we all knew that Mr. Hassler saved our lives, because we would have been passing right there about the time they were setting that bomb to go off. By the time we got home, that's when we heard it. We were eating breakfast, and *boom*. That was it. If we had gotten there, maybe, two hours earlier, or an hour earlier, we would have run right into what they were doing, because we passed right by it.

I've always thought about that.

Red had all of the popular prejudices in his heart, but he never ceased to listen. And back in his head he had a sense of reality and a sense of justice. He knew something was going on downtown, and he said, "I'm not going to take a chance on it. I'm going to keep them here 'til daybreak." Now, he would never want you or anybody else to know that. But that came from deep down in Red Hassler. That's in the character of him. He had his idiosyncrasies. If he was in a group of segregationists, he would fit right in perfectly. But there was another side of him, too. Because there are those people, who, in their inner nature, know what's right. Some people you would expect to have hatred built into them—and they *wear* that hatred, on the outside, to blend in with the others. But beneath that surface there's something else.

So I would size Red Hassler up as a person with a rich heart, and a great sensitivity for us.

12

Friends and Mentors

WHEN I WAS FIRST GETTING MY BAND TOGETHER, I needed a bass player. There weren't too many bass players around, and I pushed Pops to play: Ivory "Pops" Williams.

We hit it off right away.

Pops was one of the most interesting characters I ever met. He was one of the very first jazz musicians in Birmingham—in fact, he was the one that brought Fess Whatley from Tuscaloosa, and he set up the first musicians union in Birmingham for blacks. Pops was an unusual fellow. And the thing about it was, he was a living history—because he was *there*. He took up the violin and he played in the early days of the silent movies; that was when they'd send the music to the theatre so you'd follow the music along with the movie. When they added the sound, Pops said he just lost his job—and he never went back to the movies. He held it against them. Even in the fifties, he never ventured back.

He was well trained in the violin, and he goes back to W. C. Handy and those early ones—Ma Rainey and Bessie Smith—he was back in their day, right after the First World War, and he played with all of them. He thought of them as just being like him, like they were youngsters together: "Yeah, I knew W. C. Handy—oh yeah, I knew that boy." Pops was in and out of the scene, and he took in more history than all of us put together. Another thing I found so impressive about Pops: he knew about all *kinds* of music. He was right there with Ma Rainey, but he could talk about symphonic music and everything, and he could play any instrument; he said we had nothing but trombones and trumpets down here, so we didn't know the real *sweetness* of music.

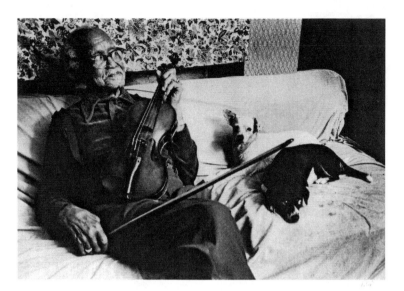

Ivory "Pops" Williams, 1970s. Courtesy of the Alabama Jazz Hall of Fame.

Pops's wife was Miss Ida. He loved Miss Ida, but when he was younger, they married one afternoon, and Pops took off on a road show—listen!—the *night* they got married, and he went all the way to California without his new bride. Pops said that *two years* he was away. One night he came back home, and he said he didn't know what had happened to Miss Ida, because it had been two years. He went up on his porch where he lived—he owned his home—and knocked on the door.

"Who is it?"

"It's Ivory."

The next thing he knew, a hand came out and grabbed him: "*Come on in here!*" His wife, Ida, was still there. He said he never went away again.

Pops opened my mind up to a lot of things. He said that they used to play out at Traction Park; and he said, when "Tuxedo Junction" came out: "That's Trigg's song!"

"*Trigg's* song?"

He said, "That boy took that song from Trigg! He used to play that at Traction Park." Pops told me, and I came to know, that you identified a person by something that he plays: all the older musicians had their own songs. So this fellow Trigg was a trumpet player. You'd hear that tune, and you'd know it was Trigg. "That's Trigg's song." He said, "I know it because he played it twenty years ago! That little lick that kicks off 'Tuxedo Junction'—that was his signature. Where did those boys get that?"

Pops said, "*Everybody* has a song. You got a song, I got a song." Every player would have their favorite little lick. Like Louis Armstrong: when he started playing a tune, he'd go *bup-bup-bup*, and you'd know that's Louis Armstrong. His signature. I had never thought about it, but I started listening: Cootie Williams had a song, all of them had one. I could hear Ben Webster on his saxophone and I could hear Paul Gonsalves, and they were both great players, but there were certain things that each one plays: not only a group of notes or figures that he would play, but his tonality. In fact, I was playing with Haywood Henry once, and he said, "I'm going to get out of here before Frank throws all those snakes on the floor." You'd probably warm up with something, and they know, after hearing you, what your songs are, what your patterns are: "He's got that bag of snakes. That's *him*. Frank and his bag of snakes."

Pops was the first one to really give me insight into that.

When I first met Pops, he was playing with Jimmy Chappell at the Madison Nite Spot. Pops was playing this upright bass, and he was playing well, but I noticed he was watching his music all the time. Now, Pops had been professionally trained; he played for silent movies and all that; but he had to have his music in front of him. I thought that was so peculiar. Pops told me that he could play with my band, but under one condition: he had to have the music for everything he played.

I said, "Pops, are you serious?"

"That's right. I don't play without music."

"Well, Pops, you *can*."

"No, I can't. I got to have my music, Hon"—he called me "Hon"—he said, "That's a jack-leg player that doesn't have any *music*." He was just from that school: "I'll do anything in the world for you, boy, but don't ask me to do that." He had been around a lot of musicians, and to read music was a status symbol.

I finally coaxed him into playing with me. I wrote down some music, but I begged him: "Don't look at that, Pops." It was a long time before he would do without the music, but finally he found out that he didn't need it. After that, whenever he was playing and we had no music up there, he'd just look over at me and smile.

The more I worked with him, the more we came to be fond of each other. Then Pops said, after he got to be in his nineties: "What I'm living for, Hon, is to see you on your feet." So, to accommodate, Pops bought a station wagon for me to travel in. And when we wore that one out, he bought another one. He was the type of fellow that would do anything to help you. And I found out, Pops could do everything. He was a jack of all trades. He was a musician; he was a brick mason, a barber, a painter; he was sort of a bootleg doctor, because he could prescribe something if you were sick. He was an embalmer—he just did all kinds of things—and then he was a full Blackfoot Indian! I didn't know that until Pops had a *teepee*—every year he'd have the tribe come, that Blackfoot tribe of Indians, and they'd set up a tent in his backyard. He would have these tribal meetings once a year, and that was the only time he would not play: when the Blackfoot tribe met.

Pops was a finished musician, and he traveled all over the world. And one of the things that struck me most was that he took us on a tour. We went to my drummer's home—Youngston, Ohio—and then we went to Detroit, and we did real well. We had a young lady named Selena Mealings with us, my first vocalist. Selena Mealings was a good little singer. She had a real jumpy personality, a real nice personality, and she would sing all those Joe Turner pieces.

We stayed at Selena's parents house in Detroit, and while we were there, Selena's family hit the jackpot. Her mother and her stepdaddy hit the numbers for over fifty thousand dollars. So when we left, Selena stayed. She didn't ever come back.

All this time, we were playing at Red's place—night after night, out on the old Leeds Highway. And one night we were coming home. Pops had his bass running through the back of the car, and we were sitting on the side of it. A guy ran across a light, and it was a terrible accident. It knocked Pops out. My wife Doris had glass all in her knees.

A fellow that knew us came and got our instruments, and we all went to the hospital, but Pops was the worst one off. He was in a coma for about four days. Then he came around, and we were talking to him.

"Pops, what happened?"

He said, "I was really dead."

"What do you mean?"

He said, "What happened is, it looked like I could never stop driving. Like you're driving a car: for eternity, you're driving." As if he could never reach his destination: "I just kept driving."

Pops nearly scared us to death with that—but that's what we got out of him.

When the civil rights movement was going on and there was all this hostility, Pops said: "What you do is don't panic." He just said, "Have you a good stick. And if somebody jumps on you, just holler, and start hitting them with that stick. You got to sound like *they're* hurting *you,* but you *pound* them with that stick." He said he'd carry his embalming knife with him, in case he was attacked by an assailant.

What we experienced was: you learn a lot about human beings when you're around people like Pops.

As I've said, we had one of the greatest trumpet players in my group, too, for a while: Joe Guy. He was married to Billie Holiday and he had been up there during the bebop movement. In the late thirties and forties, he was ranked as one of the greatest trumpet players in the world. And that greatness would still come out at times, even though he was supposed to have been a discard after so many drugs.

Joe was a famous trumpet player. But I think that Joe's influence, musically, was greater than what might have been said for him. People don't realize Joe's influence in bebop music. He was before Charlie Parker; he was experimenting before that. He was one of the ones that came from Birmingham with Reverend Becton—he didn't even get to Fess Whatley; he came right out of Lincoln School. Joe built on everything he'd learned in grade school from Mr. Handy and experienced out there with the religious show; he grew up and started playing with some groups in New York, and we heard that he had made a name for himself, playing with people like Lucky Millinder.

Joe was critical in the bebop movement, because he was doing it with Coleman Hawkins—Joe was on the original record of "Body and Soul," that Coleman Hawkins masterpiece. Joe is sitting there, doing a little harmony behind it, as Hawkins blew. They came out with pieces like that, which were the first indications of bop music. That was *Joe* doing that. Norman Granz, the great producer who had all the *Jazz at the Philharmonic* concerts—one of the very first ones that came out had Joe Guy playing on it, with Coleman Hawkins, Willie Smith, and all of them. Joe got to be part of the New York scene: he was at the experiment at Minton's, in the house band. Minton's Playhouse was run by Teddy Hill from Birmingham, one of Fess Whatley's students, and it was just the heart of everything.

Joe was very aloof, but he was one of the most intelligent people that you would want to meet: he was well read, and he could talk about everything. I first saw him when I was probably in high school. He came here with Lucky Millinder. Joe played a muted trumpet behind whoever would sing—he'd just kill you with that muted trumpet. I remember when he came to the Masonic Temple, he had on dark glasses—I hadn't seen dark glasses—and he had a camel's hair coat on, and everybody loved him because he was a *homeboy*: so every time he would play one of those obbligatos behind somebody, they would just cheer for Joe.

In the meantime, he was a young guy and he met Billie Holiday. His real role with her was as a procurer of dope. They would go into a town and he got up early and would go and get dope for her; and of course, he probably shared it. But it all came to a head when Joe was arrested with Billie Holiday for peddling and using narcotics. When the federal agents busted in on them, he was known to have flushed some of the narcotics down the toilet and was arrested with her. Now, there had been no deep feeling between them for quite a while, so in New York City at the trial he turned state's evidence to free himself from jail. Her connections were with everybody that was in the racket, the Mafia and everybody else, so he had to leave New York City. He was escaping for his life. And that's how I was fortunate enough to become a close friend of his—he came home to Birmingham, and he was playing with me.

Some people have written about Billie Holiday and say that Joe was responsible for her demise or for whatever happened to her. Billie was older than he was, and he was an up-and-coming trumpet player—she was probably the one that corrupted *Joe*. He didn't make an issue to talk about it. He had a way within himself that what happened happened, and the good outweighed the bad.

I had some of the best years of my life when Joe came back home, with all his experience and all these things he would tell me. We would be playing. And you know how people like to collect memorabilia, or they want to be related to some great artist or something. You run into

Joe Guy, trumpet, with Charles Clarke, Mary Alice Clarke Stollenwerk, and Jesse Evans, 1950s. Courtesy of the Birmingham Public Library, Department of Archives and Manuscripts, J. L. Lowe Collection.

these kinds of folk: they want to impress you that they've *been* there. This guy would come in the club and he would say, "Listen." Said, "Joe, I know Billie Holiday. And I know you had some problems. I'm so sorry that you and Lady Day had to break up." Said, "I'm going back to New York tomorrow, and I'm going to see her."

Joe's sitting there. "Oh yeah?"

"Yeah, I'm going. What do you want me to tell her?"

He thought a minute. We were listening.

"Just tell her . . . a little dog says: *bow-wow.*"

Joe worked for me for years and years at the Woodland Club, and he would often have to go to Lexington, Kentucky, for a cure. I remember one time, which was probably prophetic, he came to the home and we were sitting on the porch—he had just gotten back from Lexington—and I said, "Joe, we missed you." I said, "Look how wonderful you look," and I talked about what we were going to do together—he said, "Well, we can do some things, but it won't last."

"What do you mean, it won't last?"

He said, "It just won't last. I'll be back out there again."

I said, "No—look at you! You've picked up some weight, and you're thinking good, and your skin looks good—"

So he told me something I never will forget. He said: "Once a junkie, always a junkie."

He said, "You just can't cure it." And he said, "If I ever see *you* try it, I'm going to kill you."

I remember Art Pepper, the saxophone player, said that the first time he got high off of heroin, he knew that that was his life; he didn't want anything else. He just did it 'til he died. Joe was like that. And even though I was a mature man—he wasn't much older than I was— he was very protective of me. He was like a brother: "Don't you ever, ever try it. I'd come from anywhere and *kill* you—because you don't *have* to do that."

I remember that, and I always have a soft spot with Joe.

Something I often think about: you had these guys in the music business that had these wonderful minds, and you wonder—what could have happened to them if they hadn't gotten hooked on drugs?

I found out—one reason that musicians turn to narcotics—they hear this music in their head. *I* do. You probably do. You hear these things in your head, but you never, never can produce exactly what you hear. It's critical to musicians. You get a guy who hears these demons in his ears—you hear him playing and you say, "That was magnificent." But he says, "I didn't do what I *wanted* to, man." He hears something else. He could be sitting down, trying to work it out, and he can get *some* of it—but just when he gets that, before he finishes it, here comes something else. So he says, "Maybe if I can get a little taste of something, to make me relax, I can reproduce it"—but that drives him further away from it. He goes back again: "Maybe *this* time I can do it."

It's like searching for the Holy Grail. You can't find it. And a lot of musicians lose their sanity.

Some people, like Ellington and other great musicians, had sense enough to say: development comes in time. "Wait 'til next year." And Sun Ra: he made a decision that he would hear these things from outer space, but he would take his time in dealing with them. But the anxious say, "Hey, I hear it, I hear it; up here I *hear* it, man. So let me get something to make me cool down and *do it.*"

It's like Shakespeare said: some people can succeed, but they have that one damn spot. That one *damn* spot. That no matter what you do, that thing's going to come and get you. You step on the worm, but the worm's going to eat you in the end. That's the kind of thing some people have. We all have our frailties.

Some of the things that Joe Guy played were beautiful—most of them were—but there were nights that Joe would be *sickening*, because he'd hear these things in his head and he's got to go and get a fix to make it come out. He would try to get something that could make him climb to a level that wasn't natural for him to climb at that time.

My wife could never understand Joe, because she didn't know anything about narcotics. Late at night we would be coming through downtown Birmingham and Joe would say, "Let me out here." She would say, "No, we're taking you home. Why do you want to get out here?"

"I got to go."

The druggist.

She said, "Why can't you come back tomorrow?"

"No. Don't hold me here now. I got to go. He won't be here tomorrow." He never got violent, but he said, "He won't be here, he won't be here." And Pops, as old as he was, was smart. He said, "Hon, we'd better let him out."

I know it sounds strange, but Joe would get his narcotics from the druggist—it was a legitimate drugstore, but they'd sell this illegal stuff out of there, too. Joe would come late at night to pick up the drugs.

And truly, when he passed away, the *druggist* sent him the biggest floral design you could think of.

I noticed Joe's behavior could be bizarre.

He lived not too far from me, and we'd take him home. I remember one night, we got home real late—it was just before day in the morning—and Joe said, "Can I come in a minute?" I said, "Sure." I thought he needed to use the restroom.

My sweet mother was in there, asleep. Joe went back to Mom's refrigerator and started cracking all these eggs and swallowing them: just cracking eggs, cracking eggs, and swallowing them. Mom got up: "What in the world are you doing?" She had never seen anything like that. To the day she died, she would say, "What was wrong with that boy, eating up all my eggs?"

Joe had two trumpet mouthpieces. Both of them were old. He would take a mouthpiece, and he'd play something, like "Winter Wonderland by Night." If he missed a note, he'd take that mouthpiece and slap it—"You're no good!"—and put it back and get the other one. In about an hour, he'd slap *that* one: "You're no good, you rascal."

He would say—what was the word?—"Shuckaluckaduck." Shuckaluckaduck. He would say these things, and we didn't know what they meant, but we knew he was happy when he'd say that.

Shuckaluckaduck. Joe Guy.

Joe was another one who opened me up to a lot of things. We would play together, and he said, "Turn your back; your back to my back." We'd put our backs together and play—and we could really *hear* each other. I had never thought of that.

He'd say, "Anytime you pop your eye."

"What are you talking about?"

He said, "I've watched you, and when you pop your eye a little bit"—I didn't know I was doing it—he said, "then you're really *playing,* man!"

Joe's thing was, he wished I could be in "fast company." That I could have been another Charlie Parker if I had been around *fast company.* But he said sometimes I'd be playing and I'd pop my eye—and then the *real* Frank Adams would come out.

I remember, we'd be at the Woodland Club, and we'd have somebody come and sit in with the band. They'd come after hours, after we'd played our regular set, and they'd bring music for us to read. All the young arrangers—like Archie McRemer, he was a well-known white composer—they'd come with their little pieces: "Play this," and "Play this"; "Play this," and "Play this." Joe would sit there like a soldier, in this militaristic pose he always had. He'd have his horn in his lap, straight up, like a rifle—he wasn't going to play anything.

They'd say, "Let's have a jam session." You'd get ready to play, and Joe would hit you: "Don't play *nothing.* They'll steal everything you've got."

One thing about Joe: he had class. He had been around classy people, and he had class. He knew exactly what to do, and he knew exactly *how* to do things. He did not put down any music. You might hear another fellow say, "I don't play anything but bebop," or "Those guys over there are dumb." For example, the things that Louis Armstrong did back in 1920 were marvelous, but somebody would say, "Oh, that old crap—I don't want to hear that old slavery-time music" or whatever: "Man, get *hip*, get *modern*."

Joe never did that. He always found something good in music. And whatever he did wrong, he did to *himself*: it was his *self*-destruction.

But Joe revealed something that I was very disturbed to hear. I knew that he and his brother Jimmy had gone with Reverend Becton; their daddy was a minister, and he was so fervent and so enthused about what Reverend Becton was doing. It was like he said, "I love my son, but if you want him and you're doing all this, you can take him. His life will be better." But that wasn't true. Joe said that when he got to New York City, he found out that it wasn't all good with the reverend: that Reverend Becton wasn't beyond molesting some of them.

That was a shocking thing. It was so far back in his memory that he didn't want to talk about it, but he alluded to it: that Reverend Becton really wasn't what they thought he was. That in itself could lend a youngster to be confused—going to high school with all that going on. And the thing about it was, it would be impossible to explain that to somebody with a religious fervor like his father; he just trusted and believed that this man is so wonderful that "I'll give him my son— *both* of my sons." You can imagine how traumatic it would be to come home and say, "Well, no, Dad, this man is phony. This man has something wrong with him." It would be more than the wrath of God that would descend on you for something like that.

And so he just lived with it.

Once we were playing at the Woodland Club—these are things I remember so vividly—and Mr. Red was drinking heavily, as he would usually do. He had some of his cronies around the bar. I guess he wanted to show off. It was after one of those big University of Alabama games, and he was really inebriated.

At this time Joe was really himself: he hadn't had any drugs or anything, he was just *Joe Guy*. He was doing fine.

Red was the one drinking. He stopped Joe at the bar, and his friends were there with their beers. He said, "Joe, they tell me that one time, according to *DownBeat,* you were the third greatest trumpet player in all the world!"

As I like to say, Joe was like a soldier. He had been through all of these things, and he was at home, nowhere to go. He'd wear this old blue suit—a lot of musicians have these blue suits, where they've worn it out, and the stripes break loose, and they shine and all.

He said, "That's true, Mr. Hassler."

Everybody was listening. "*Now* look at you. Man, you're down here in my raggedy old place, playing out here with Frank Adams and all of them—you sure have fallen from grace. And they tell me you were the top of the line."

We're hearing this. Dot was getting angry. She said, "Why don't you *say* something, they're just insulting Joe like that?"

We knew Joe was a good guy. He's dressed up in those shiny clothes, with this old, beat-up trumpet—but when we got married, the first telegram we got was from Joe. He was supposed to be such a down-and-out, but he had this *class* about him. I wasn't getting disturbed, because I knew Joe could handle himself.

They were talking: "Yeah, Joe, you're such a has-been, and washed out," and all that kind of stuff. "What you got to say about it, Joe?"

Joe said, "Mr. Hassler, I'll tell you one thing." He said: "It's better to be a *has-been* than a *never-was*."

Boy, you could feel the climate in that club, and you could hear a pin fall.

He had this dignity about him. It's like he said: "A little dog says, *bow-wow*." When you reach the bottom, you're at the bottom. How far do you want to deflate me? I'm a dog: bow-wow. Nothing I can do.

But better a has-been than a never-was.

That had a profound effect on Mr. Hassler, and it had a profound effect on the ones that were standing around. After that day, they still didn't call him "Mr. Guy," but you could see this *respect* coming from them. Before long Mr. Hassler was telling people, "I got the best musicians here. That's *Joe Guy*." And Archie and all those who would come down to the Woodland Club, they didn't say it, but they *knew* that he was one of the greatest in the world.

That's why they would come out there: after they got through playing their thing, they wanted to hear the *real* thing.

13

Building a Family, Making Ends Meet

My wife, Dot: I call her my "tweety-bird."
Sammy Lowe—the great arranger, who helped write "Tuxedo Junction," and all those tunes for Erskine Hawkins—had come back to Birmingham to live. He came to me once and said, "Can you make your horn sound like a tweety-bird?" I said, "I can." He said, "I'll check you out."

He came back in about two weeks and said, "Show me the tweety-bird." I don't even know if a tweety-bird exists, but I blew some notes.

"That's it."

Two weeks later, he had written a magnificent arrangement that had me sounding like—what?—a *tweety-bird.*

So, my wife is my tweety-bird. We've been married more than fifty years; I've written songs for her, and all. You hear sometimes about "a marriage made in heaven," and I guess this would be one, or close to it. It's a romance, but in a way, it's more like your sister: you've been knowing her so long, she's just a part of whatever you do.

Dot's family was large. Her father and mother were here: Colbie Williams and Pearlie Mitchell Williams. There were six daughters—Doris, Carol, Patricia, Grace, Alma, and Annette—and there were two brothers, Edward—we called him "Buddy"—and Colbie Jr. With all these brothers and sisters, I found I had a different type of life than I was used to; I sort of took on another family. I had never had a big family, just Grandma and Mama and Daddy and Oscar—so that added a new dimension. There would be a family reunion, down in a little

Frank Adams, receiving award for work with the Boy Scouts, and Doris Adams, early 1970s. Courtesy of Frank Adams.

Georgia town nobody ever heard of, and they'd have an open pit barbecue and this big crowd. They were all very loving to me, and that became a part of the fabric of my life.

We were fortunate enough to move in with my mother in the old home-house, down from Parker High School. In the meantime, Oscar got married to Willa Ingersoll, who was a wonderful lady—we called her "Sparky"—and they lived with us, too. Those were some happy times. We had the old home-house on the corner, everybody respected us, but it had to be kept up: painting and all that kind of thing. Some of it went without being done, because I was in transition and Oscar was trying to get started.

Of course, he just launched off and did great things, and when he finally built his home, Dot and I stayed at the house to support my mom. While we were there, the city decided to tear down all the property and locate the football field for Parker High School there. So after all those years that my family had lived in that house—maybe fifty or more since Daddy's purchase of that place—we found ourselves having to move.

We found this house on Bush Boulevard, where we are now. We looked at a lot of places, but we were enamored with this one, because it had a downstairs and an upstairs, and it had two kitchens and two and a half toilets and two of everything, because we bought it from a fellow whose son-in-law and daughter lived in the downstairs. He was an Italian guy—a very, very fine man—and his family had lived there for quite a while. Mom got sick with palsy, so we brought her to Bush Boulevard with us to live—and I think I fell in love with Dot all over again because of the way she took care of my mom. I remember one day we were at Mr. Lowe's house—J. L. Lowe, the founder of the Jazz Hall of Fame—and his brother was there, Sammy. We were visiting, and when we got back home, my mother had fallen through the china cabinet and had cut her back and her head. She got over that, but then it was touch-and-go, and we had to have somebody stay with Mom during the day, because Dot and I were both working. Of course, Oscar was helping, too. Finally we had to put her in a nursing home.

When our son Eaton came along, it really affected me. It changed my life. Dot and I courted for five or six years before we were married in 1962, and Eaton was born in 1972. He was just adored by everybody, because after all those years he comes on the scene.

To tell the truth, at that time, marriage frightened me. When I got married, Dot was a teacher, but I said: what if one day she couldn't teach school? What's going to happen? I've got to be able to take care of her, like my daddy took care of us. I wouldn't want somebody who wouldn't be satisfied with me. So when I found out that Dot was expecting Eaton, I said, "Good God almighty, what am I going to do?" I would play a show and I'd get off the bandstand sometimes and get a drink and just sit there, worried. What it is, is: you're insecure. You're buying your first car and buying a house—and your wife might not want to live in the new house, because we lived at the home-house for years and years before they tore it down. So you're saying, *what if?* What if she wants this and that, and I can't provide it?

That was at a time when teachers received no salary during their pregnancy. Now you have maternity leave, but when my wife was ex-

Ella Eaton Adams, mother of Oscar and Frank, with Doris Adams, 1964.
Courtesy of Frank Adams.

pecting, you just had to stop working for three or four months, until
the baby is born. So where we'd had two paychecks, now we had one—
and here comes this baby. I figured, I've got to get some extra work.
The Woodland Club closed about that time. So I started playing music
with everybody I could.

I got a gig at the Tutwiler Hotel with some guys who couldn't play
so well. But I found out that, even a great player: his greatness comes
out when he plays with people who have a *lack* of ability. The ones who
can't play well depend on you; they need you more. For example, Louis
Armstrong: people knew that if he was playing with a great band—
with Jack Teagarden and people who really could play—you'd get very
little of his genius. But when he had people around him who *couldn't*
do very well, then he would really *sparkle*. To help the group. He's
like a football player, sort of like a defensive back: he comes in when
nobody else can make the tackle. If he gets a lot of geniuses around
him, then he doesn't have to. In fact, I was telling my students, this
morning: I found out in music, if you make all the right notes, and
you're precise, it's wonderful. But it's a truism, too, that if you make
all the *wrong* notes—and *everybody's* making wrong notes, which was
our case in those days—it's good, too. They're all wrong together, so

it sounds right. People like mistakes. They don't like you to be too perfect.

So we weren't perfect at all.

I was playing on the weekends with a rock band—Dee Clark's band—and they played *strictly* rock and roll. We played at a place down right outside of Tuscaloosa: it was a little barn, where the crowd came in at eight o'clock, and they would dance and sweat, perspiring all night long. I had been playing the clarinet and the alto saxophone, but this rock music demanded that I play tenor saxophone, so I had to develop myself on that; I didn't get to play the alto much then, because the tenor was the thing that was popular in the rock and roll bands—big, heavy sound. I could never get a sound like Paul Gonsalves, but I worked to get a real heavy sound.

I told you about the experience I had with the blues guys, where they would put some sand on the floor and rub it—well, this was just a little bit above that. It was an enjoyable experience to see the other side of town, and the liquor is flowing and all that kind of thing. Dee was a fellow who could really sing the blues, and we had a guitar player and a drummer. We only had one horn in the band, and that was me. We didn't have as many pieces as most of the rock bands had, but that was to make more money; we cut it down to about four or five pieces. And music *reading* was out of the picture, but they would come close to imitating whatever record was popular. If you could play "Shotgun" or James Brown, "I Feel Good"—they liked to hear that kind of thing, and you could play solos and solos and solos until they were about to fall out.

The audience wouldn't have much money. They waited for Saturday night to drink alcohol and have fun, and that audience would be packed. Of course, I appreciated knowing that I'd bring some money back home when I went down there—but in these places you had no possibility of getting a tip. That was out of the question; they could hardly get the money to come *in* the place and pay for the booze. They didn't have the money to say, "Here's something for doing a good job." They'd just holler and scream, to let you know they appreciated you.

As I said, I knew when Eaton was expected that I needed all the extra money I could get. And in the summer you could go off to Fort Jackson or one of the bases and receive some extra military training.

So I volunteered to go to Fort Jackson. That was just like going through basic training again.

That's where my army band career got started.

I was kind of familiar with army bands, because at Howard University, your first two years, regardless of what you were taking in undergrad school, you were obligated to be in the ROTC. That was compulsory, and you had to take something similar to basic training, right there on campus. It was rigorous. You had marksmanship at the rifle range, and you had swimming and the ropes, and certain classes where they showed you movies and talked about venereal diseases and all those things. Then you had your ceremonial drills. They had what they called an army band, and one of my jobs at Howard was as an assistant leader of the band.

Going through basic training *again* was a sacrifice at my age, but I did it because we really needed the money. Like I said about how I started teaching: it wasn't for some altruistic reasoning—and I'm very patriotic, I love my country—but it was the money that was so important. The little one had to have his milk, his rations, so I had to sacrifice myself.

When I got to Fort Jackson, they pulled me off this truck—I had a ring on, my dad's diamond ring—and the guy *snatched* my ring off and nearly broke my finger. Said, "You don't wear that around here!" I said, "That's not fair."

He said, "Where do you think you are? This is the army, we don't have to be fair!"

I said, "Oh, my God."

I went to the commissary. I had a twenty-dollar bill. I bought a toothbrush, a couple of little things; I was supposed to get about eighteen dollars back in change. The guy looked at me and said, "What are you waiting on?"

"I'm waiting on my change."

"This is the army! We *got* your money." I thought: no laws, no police, no nothing. You're in the military. So I had to work with a different set of values.

I was there with a bunch of young people half my age, and that was a challenge. One day I was going to the mess hall, and a young fellow stopped and saluted me. He said, "Are you the man the army sent here to show us that if *he* can do it, all of us can?" He really thought I was a plant—that they sent me to show them that if I could take it, at my age, then the rest of them *certainly* could.

Of course, if I had to do it all again, I would, because you get a chance to see a different side of life. You get the experience of being around people: people who were not so educated, and some that were educated, and some who had different outlooks on life. I found out that when you get people from all over the country—North, South, East, and West; different cultures, different beliefs and values—you learn a lot. That's a melting pot. It's like in World War One, when all these soldiers got together for the first time: all these Americans meeting together and fighting together. You talk about a revolution—that was a revolution. You get a chance to see that people—no matter where they come from, no matter what language they speak or what race they are in—they are more alike than they are different. And there *is* something, really, when you get to that age, about patriotism—that catches you when you see the soldiers and you know what they're going through.

One morning I was in the barracks and I started playing my horn. All the youngsters started coming around: "Wow, man, that guy can play!"—and here comes the drill sergeant. The brass, they don't want you to do that. "Put that thing up! You don't do that around here—we don't want them to hear stuff like that." In other words, you're giving the men some happiness they don't want them to have. No—they've got to go through torture. Don't play anything that reminds them of home or relaxation; that's a comfort, and we don't want them to be comfortable. We want them tense: they have to be *tense* when they go out to the firing line.

It's a process of dehumanizing you.

I witnessed some youngsters crying at night. And that wasn't *American*: you were supposed to never cry, you're a soldier! I had to console some of them. They wanted to go home; they didn't know it was going to be like this. We had one fellow I felt sorry for—well, they teach you not to feel sorry for anybody—but this guy had been in basic training, and they had a wreck. Their truck turned over; one guy was killed and the other was maimed. He stayed in the hospital a month. And instead of him going home, or even picking up where he'd left off in training, they recycled him: he had to go through the whole training program again. Another guy went home, I'll never forget him, and cut his fingers off on the leave. Did they get rid of him? No. He had to go right back there with those mangled fingers.

Meanwhile, I started playing with the 313th Army Band. The band was terrific: the 313th Army Band had crack musicians in there. And I was the one that integrated the band—I was the first black in there. The army band was a good experience, but it didn't start off that way. There were some that were against integration, and you would encounter a certain prejudice. When I started being featured in the jazz combo, we would play all over. I noticed that I'd play solos and get the applause of the audience. And my fellow soldiers—not all of them—would come and comment and say good things about the performance; but some would wait until I got into the restroom to tell me what they thought. I guess they didn't want the other guys to hear them give me a compliment.

When I got to be a first sergeant, we played a concert. It was raining, and this person handed me my new rank—and turned his back on me. He called me out there in the rain and handed me my first-class sergeant stripes, with his back turned, just like the judge at Smith Ridge School.

Those things you remember. But overall there was a great brotherhood. Some of the most satisfying experiences I had were with the army band. We built a camaraderie in there, and they could really play; in fact, the 313th was probably one of the best army bands in the country at that time. A lot of teachers were in that band. They traveled all over the South recruiting, and they promoted me quickly to a leadership position. I was the section leader, and—what really helped me out moneywise—I got to lead the jazz combo. The big band would be sent in its entirety to different places to play, different places they were recruiting, but the jazz combo would go places the big band couldn't. We'd have about six or seven pieces, and we'd go to Mississippi and all down in Georgia—everywhere. Sometimes we'd be doing special parties that the generals would want; they'd make all the dispatch papers and everything, and that would be an extra pay period for you. It amounted up, too, because they paid good money—you'd come home with five or six hundred dollars. Whereas a guy in the reserves had worked, maybe, two days a month, we'd play probably *ten* different jobs a month, all the way up to North Carolina. And if you played extra, you got extra pay.

The army band had strict ritualistic music, like "The Star Spangled Banner" had to be played a certain way. They played some popular music—they would play something like "The Man I Love" and have big band arrangements—but the jazz combo was where you were free: you were free to create something. It was the combo that did stuff like "A Train" and blues and all that type of thing. We had a guy that could sing the blues and could sing like Ray Charles, so that made that band a big hit. We would go to the officers' quarters everywhere; the army would pay for it and we always had good accommodations. We played in malls, in stores, at our own base; we would play auditoriums, play in schools; everywhere.

The army band recorded frequently, and they have a lot of recordings that I was featured on: all kinds of military songs and marches. On special occasions the combo would have a recording that they're going to issue to the top brass. We did "When the Saints Go Marching In," and some radio station out in California started using that as a wake-up thing, to get folks out of bed. A guy that I was in school with had moved out to California, and he called me; said he was sick of hearing me wake him up every morning. He called me on Christmas morning, before day, two Christmases ago. He said he thought he'd gotten rid of me after we had finished school—but "You come on every morning, about five o'clock, with this 'Saints Go Marching In.'" He said, "I thought you were dead by now."

I said, "I'm more alive than you are!" *Bam*—I hung up on him.

I was in that army band for a long time. And I was thinking about it: I taught school at the same place for twenty-seven years, and I don't know *how* long I was in the army band, maybe fourteen years. So sticking to something is very important. When I became a music supervisor, I stayed *there* twenty years. Some teachers call me and say, "Doc, what must I do? This principal is doing this to me" or "this to me," and I say, "What you do is just stay there." You learn that principals have a lifetime of three years. They have to get fired or get promoted; there's no in between. So you stay there; you stick to what you do. You don't want to fall out with principals.

You don't want to fall out with anybody, if you can help it.

Family portrait, 1975. Courtesy of Frank Adams.

Getting back to the family: When Eaton came around, he was a marvelous thing in our life. Being the only son, I guess all of your faith and love goes into that one—because that's all you've got.

I didn't drive a car when Eaton was born, so a lot of times I'd walk over to the hospital to see him. When he was born, they had all the babies in this little room: the girls had pink little ribbons, the boys had blue. I told Dot it didn't matter to me if it was a girl or a boy; whatever it was, if it had all its fingers and everything, I'd be happy. But I got over there and I got into another culture. Every time a boy was born and they brought another one in, they'd go to the phone: "It's a *boy!* It's a *boy,* it's a *boy,* it's a *boy!* Here's a cigar, here's a cigar. It's a *boy!*" I thought, what would happen if it's a girl? I guess they'd commit suicide.

One guy came up and looked at me. He saw I was looking at Eaton. "Oh, that's a healthy one, that's a healthy one." He said, "Are you the grandfather?"

I won't tell you what I told him.

When Eaton got to the grade school, quite naturally, I'd have him in music. So I had a clarinet: I said, "You take this down there"—there was a fellow at Wilson Grade School, Mr. Bernard Williams, and he took an interest in Eaton; and there was a teacher, Mrs. Nadine Sappho, who played piano off and on with my group. So I knew he would be in good hands.

I never would play a clarinet around him, because I had the idea that if you do something real well, like play a complicated scale or something, then the person listening would say, "Well, that's too hard, I don't want to do that." So I never did practice at home with the clarinet. That was *his* instrument. I listened to him occasionally and he was just average; then somehow or another he made up his mind that he was going to get the highest position for the band, first chair. They had this Christmas festival and I had to test people because I was supervisor of music—but I wouldn't test him, since he was my son. When the results came back, Mr. Williams said that Eaton had earned the first chair. I couldn't believe it. I thought there might have been some politics involved in it, somebody doing me a favor—but I don't want to *not* believe it if it's true.

We decided to put him in the Alabama School of Fine Arts. And I never will forget Mr. Les Filmer—he was the master musician and the artistic director of the instrumental department—Eaton auditioned for him, and they admitted him. Things seemed to be going okay: I would ask him, "How are you doing?" "I'm doing fine, Dad, I'm doing fine." He's majoring in music with clarinet as his instrument, and it seemed to me that he was making some progress. Then one day I was looking up in the closet and I pulled these books down—I found all these papers, and they were *all* red, from the top to the bottom. I called him aside. I said, "What are you doing? Don't you know you're going to flunk out of there, and that's going to be so embarrassing!"

I talked to Mr. Filmer about it, and he said, "He's going to be all right"—that's Les, a good friend—"just give the boy some time."

What happened was a miracle. He had suffered all through his freshman year, and Les stood behind him and helped him, and then Les said Eaton walked into his room one day—it was around the time, I think, when they got out for Christmas one year—and he said, "Mr. Filmer?"

Les said, "What do you want?"

He said, "I'm going to do this. I'm going to master it." He made up his own mind. Les said he didn't know what had happened to him. He asked me, what did I do? "I didn't do *anything* to him!" But all of a sudden, he started going blazes and blazes. He started kicking it and kicking it. He hooked up with a little fellow who was a fantastic piano player, and to sum it up, they put on one of the most beautiful concerts that the School of Fine Arts had ever had, and they were playing all these pieces above anybody's head. Les entered him in a competition that was held in Montgomery, and it was a scholarship to go to Interlochen, the music camp. They only pick one from the state, and they picked Eaton. His life changed then, because it was like going into a college or university, with all superior players in there. That really fired him up, and by his being there, the schools would offer scholarships to him—so he got a scholarship to go to Boston University. He got into it; he got fierce with it. He played with the Boston Symphony, and he was in a quartet that traveled to Romania and all over, and he stayed up in Boston and got his master's.

His mama wrote him a letter once when he was in undergrad school, and she said, "You're making good marks, but you need to take something like computer science or something like that: just something that you can fall back on."

He wrote a letter back. He said, "That's nice, Mom. But. I don't intend to *fall* back."

I said, "Oh, my God." That was Eaton.

I have to tell this one, too. One day Eaton was still an undergraduate, and he was home from Boston; he passed by my room, and I had a recording of Joshua Redman, a saxophone player that lived in Boston while Eaton was up there. And I said, "Listen at this!"

He took it to his room and listened to it. He said, "It's nice."

I said, "*Nice?*" I said, "You take that back to your room and you listen at it again." Because the guy was making two tones at once on the saxophone—that's very difficult to do—and he was *mastering* this stuff—new stuff.

He comes back again. I said, "How is that?"

"Dad, I *told* you it was nice."

I said, "Man, did you hear what he was doing?" And this is where the rubber hit the road.

"*Dad.* Did *you* hear what he was doing?" He said, "He's playing the same thing over and over again. The same thing, over and over."

I said, "Well, what do *you* do? At Boston University, with the symphony—you guys play the *same* thing, over and over: all that old moldy fig stuff, Bach and Beethoven, been dead for hundreds and hundreds of years, and you sit there and you play it *over* and *over* again! Some of them are good," I said, "but a lot of them are musty pieces in there, man, they've been playing for years and years—and you'll just be one of a number of people." I said, "It would take you ten years to be the first chair clarinet player in a Boston orchestra. Don't you want to do something *different*? Don't you want to *create* something? Don't you want to be a *creator*? You sit there every night with your tuxedo on, and this man waving his baton, and you'd better go exactly where he waves it." I said, "Don't you want to be your own musician?"

"No."

I started calling his mama. I said, "Listen! All this money, thirty thousand dollars a year, and you don't want to *do* something? I thought I'd have a son that wants to create something. Don't you want to—"

"*No*, Daddy." He said, "I like what I'm doing."

My God. "You *like* it?"

"Yes, I do."

I said, "Do you play any *jazz* at all?"

"I can play jazz."

I said, "I've never *heard* you play any jazz!"

"If I want to, I can play jazz." He said, "I *like* jazz. But this is what I do."

Man, I started thinking. I started thinking. I said, well, he just loves this symphonic music. He just loves it. He's in the quartet and all. He made good grades in Boston. I went up there, and I heard him. And I said: he doesn't have to do what I do. He doesn't have to be like me—I don't *want* him to be like me. As long as he's happy with it, that's it. So I embraced him. I said, "That's good. That's good."

He said, "Dad, I'll make you proud of me."

I told him, "I'm *already* proud of you."

That was what we call the great understanding.

14

The Movement

I WANT TO GO BACK AND SAY MORE HERE ABOUT the civil rights era, and about what I've witnessed—in terms of segregation and race relations—in Birmingham. I tell people: I was there during the civil rights movement; I was there *before* the civil rights movement; and now here I am—still here. I've seen all the changes, good and bad. So I say, if you want to know how things really were, just ask me.

One day I was going to the Temple Pharmacy, over on Fourth Avenue. This was in the 1960s, the early 1960s, when the demonstrations and all were going on here. We were supposed to play at the Woodland Club that night. I was at the drugstore, and this man walked up to me. He said, "You're Frank Adams, aren't you?"

It was Dr. King.

I said, "Yes, sir."

He held his hand out, and I shook it. He said, "You'll be at the meeting tonight, won't you, brother?"

I looked at him—*I was at that meeting.* I turned my gig down that night, man. It was something about *him.* I don't know whether it was all the talk about him, but I could look at him and tell there was something about him, for good or bad, that wasn't inherent in others that I had touched. Now, I don't put any religious connotations to it, but it was *different.* It was a different experience.

So was that movement: it was a different experience.

I could probably say that I saw the buildup of what was to come, but nobody expected that kind of change in his lifetime. It was always on my mind, going through elementary school and high school; there were ideas then of what it could be like—this *freedom* that blacks conceived of—but no one really had a great expectation of when it would come. It was like a pregnant lady, but the birth of the child was never expected in *your* lifetime.

I was born in 1928, and of course, when you're born at that time, you're in the midst of segregation. There was only one hospital for blacks, and it was a children's hospital. The only other place black women or men could go would be the basement of Hillman Hospital; and according to my mama, it was not sanitary down in there—it was filthy. That was just the order of the day.

In deep segregation, I remember Fess Whatley's band went to Cullman, Alabama; and they had a sign out there saying, NIGGER: READ AND RUN. IF YOU CAN'T READ, RUN ANYHOW. Right when you enter Cullman: DON'T COME IN HERE. We went to play there, and when we walked out to the car, Professor Whatley had a chauffeur's cap on. If somebody stopped him, he'd say, "I'm taking these boys to play for Mr. Such-and-Such." He would say that we were going to play for some white people—that he was the chauffer—and they'd let him go. That's how he played all of those places that were *very* segregated.

Along that time, when I was coming up, they still had the Klan going on. As a youngster, I'd have to stop over on Southside to let one of their parades go by. They were just like a Veterans Day parade, only they had their sheets on. They dressed in their robes, and they would go through the streets and they would blow their horns. They would hide their faces, but it wasn't so much that they hid their identities—because most of the maids that worked over the mountain could look in the closet and *see* where the robes were. So they knew that Mr. James was a Ku Klux—they could tell who the Grand *Cyclops* was, because he had a different kind of robe!

As I grew up, I would pass a place that sold keys on Fourth Avenue, and this man had a whole display, hung in his window, of lynchings—actual pictures of people being lynched, and crowds of faces gathered around them. I would look at that as a youngster, on my way to the music store. I'd look and I'd go on.

As I say, before the fifties and sixties there was a philosophy about freedom, but there was no concerted effort to *change* things. Instead, they would say: "Don't worry about that now. Just learn you a trade;

learn you a trade." This thinking about being free and having your civil rights was in the back of the minds of some people, but it was so far off. It wasn't until the movement came along that Dr. King and people like him would say, "You're *already* free. It's in the Constitution."

"Oh, am I? Okay, man! What do we do?"

"We march."

I remember, in days of deep segregation, people like my daddy would make speeches saying to develop yourself: that you couldn't be a slave if you could *think*. If you could be a George Washington Carver, you were free. It wasn't that those in my dad's generation had given up on what the Constitution said—they knew what freedom was—but the main thing they were looking for was not integration but an *independence*. They weren't saying, "I'm just going to *die* because I can't go to the Tutwiler Hotel"—they were promoting the hotels that *they* had. The ones on Fourth Avenue. The idea was not, "Maybe one day I can sit at the front of the bus," but "Maybe one day I'll own my own bus company." Those were the themes you'd hear about: independence. Do this for yourself; do this for yourself. And deep in my dad's speech was this fire, that you've got to stand up for yourself.

The strongest institution at that time, of course, was the black churches. They were the ones talking about socializing and equality, and they were the ones that had money, because they had joined together nationally—the African Methodist Episcopal Zion Church was all over the country—and they could make a dent in things. The other strong institution was the black fraternity organizations. They bound together, and they didn't directly attack segregation, but they would talk about "the freedom of man" and that type of thing. Those lodges were built so blacks could be together and combine their resources, and discuss things in a secret society.

Something else that was important when I was coming up was the newspapers. The black newspapers, the *Chicago Defender* and the *Pittsburgh Courier,* would report on atrocities, and my dad's paper did, too, until it folded. Then there was Emory O. Jackson, who wrote controversial articles in the *Birmingham World*. I used to deliver that paper. Emory Jackson talked about civil rights and everything. He spent his life doing that, and he sacrificed a lot—he didn't have all the fine luxuries of good clothes and all—he was one that suffered a lot to bring about a change. Nobody ever mentions him now. He had a sister who taught in one of the high schools, and she sued to get pay raises for blacks.

Meanwhile, you had the Great Migration to Chicago and particularly Detroit, because the Ford people afforded blacks the same wages as they did whites. Hourly wages were not even conceived of here. You just did a *job:* if you had to stay late in the evening harvesting the crops, you stayed. But here's the Ford Motor Company saying you work eight hours a day and you get top grade money, whether you're black, white, Haitian, or whatever: "Come on." And you go on.

People would come back from Detroit, and they would say, "You people are just stupid—you are so *handicapped.* You're still doing slave labor and we go up here—we're better than you—we're making union wages . . ." We heard that, but to me—in our community, and in my family—it wasn't relevant. The people that *I* saw didn't know they were in so much misery. Probably they weren't, until somebody came back and told them they were.

When the blacks migrated, some people, including my dad, would encourage people to *stay.* He influenced people not to be so quick to leave. Because historically what happened was, a group would come up from the South; they couldn't pay the rent, so you'd put three or four families in one apartment—and that's the cause of what we call the ghetto. Those were marvelous places in the early days; but when you put three or four families in there, they deteriorate quickly. I would go to Chicago, playing in bands, and would see a beautiful stained-glass window where some rich people used to live; I remember seeing chandeliers that used to be, and the beautiful winding staircases that had been broken because of all the little children crammed in there, running up and down the steps. I had the experience in Chicago of opening a closet door and there was a bed in the closet, with somebody sleeping. That's poverty. These families went away from the South because they thought their situation would be better. In some instances it was. But in most instances it was worse.

Now, it might seem that I put blinders on to a lot of things that happened here, which I knew were really cruel—the lynchings and all of those things. I *knew* the whites had the Ku Klux Klan. But I also knew that there were some whites that helped build Talladega College and helped build Miles College. Of course, I have to realize that I was privileged in a way, because if I got sick, I could call to the best white doctor in town—because of my father's influence. I had to ride the back of the bus, like everybody else—but we had an automobile at home that, if necessary, I could ride in. I read all the signs—IF YOU CAN'T READ, RUN ANYWAY—I witnessed that; but *after* that I could go home and have turkey for Thanksgiving—and rabbit—and Daddy loved *bear* meat! I remember sitting and eating these little pellets, where somebody had shot the bear. When air conditioning came out, one of his rich white friends gave him a machine that would circulate air all over the house. That's the thing that people that were born of another generation don't realize. All whites were not prejudiced or bigoted. And no organization could have achieved what the NAACP, the Knights of Pythias, the Masons—whatever the organization—did, unless they had some sincere white friends.

Another thing that was prevalent at that time: one little fellow lived about a block and a half from our house and was real fair-skinned. His name was Fred Ball. He left and went out to California and got in the movies. It was common that a lot of blacks with fair skin would leave and change their identity, and merge with the white race: whole families would go and pass for white. In Hollywood you had lots of them—another one was Harold Tillman. His daddy was the pastor of Metropolitan Church. Harold Tillman was a handsome guy—he had wavy hair, people just fell in love with him, and he died out there in Hollywood. We could see him and Fred Ball in the movies. One of them was a bronco cowboy in a cowboy picture, and Harold Tillman played a white slave master in one. You knew he was a black guy; you knew who they were, but if you went to California, you understood it was taboo to go see Fred Ball. "He's not the black Freddie I used to know. He's white Freddie now, so I'd better leave him be." You could write them or call them on the telephone, but you wouldn't visit them and expose them. You just say, "Well, they're gone. They passed."

In those years you knew nothing but segregation. And overall you were pretty secure and happy—you were enjoying your life, because you've got all these rich things going on. But you pass a place like Jeb's Seafood and you look in there and you see those black waiters—you could get an order, coming in the back door, but you would wonder, how would it be to *sit* in there? You're just curious. You brush it off; say, "Okay, so what?" But there was still this wonderment: how are these people, *really?* How does *their* barbecue taste? I wonder, does he wash his face just like I wash mine? I would wonder how they taught music at Woodland High School; or wonder how it would be to be free from sitting in the back of the bus, or how it would be to live someplace besides Birmingham. I used to wonder how a band like DeWitt Shaw—that was a white band that played at the white clubs—I'd wonder: how would *they* do this? I knew that DeWitt Shaw would buy arrangements from Professor Whatley, and I said, "I wonder how they play those numbers. I wonder what they sound like." Of course, I heard the great white bands like Paul Whiteman and I knew about Harry James; I could hear them on the radio, and I knew my teachers respected them. We knew that some of those players were terrific, but they weren't *here:* they weren't where I could touch them. So we had to listen to the radio and dream about how it was.

You had questions, because there were a lot of misconceptions. Then, you leave and go someplace like Howard University, and you discover that things are not always what you thought. All of my years at Howard, before segregation was even contested, there were people—Thurgood Marshall, Prof Green—who were already talking about what's coming; that we're a *human* race. They were different, because they felt a sense of urgency—to change things in this country, and not leave these feelings festering. To *do* something about it. That's why Prof was saying, "Put 'human race' on that slip."

That opened my eyes to a whole lot of things about the world.

When I got back from Howard, in the fifties, we were still going to the back of the bus; nothing had changed. I remember going to a board meeting after I started teaching. We had a superintendent of schools that came to Parker High School one day, and he couldn't find a place to park his car. He got there late, and he stood up—there must have been 250 black teachers in that segregated auditorium—and he said, "You teachers have got all these big cars out there. I don't like it. You people aren't supposed to have these large cars—your car is larger than *mine!*"

He said, "It costs me more to live than it costs you! That's why I make more money. I have to spend more money to *live* than you do." Insulting things like that. Well, that wouldn't fly; the teachers didn't say anything, but they looked at each other.

I remember, one day I was coming home from Lincoln School. I'm a young man, in my twenties, and I'm going up Eighth Avenue, past Philips High School, one of the white schools. The bus was getting kind of crowded; you had a board that blacks had to sit behind, and I'm sitting back there. One of the students at Philips gets on and *moves* the board—now, he's a student—he moves the board *back,* behind my seat, to let some other whites on the bus.

I got up.

I moved it back.

That was just the reaction in me. I'm a teacher now, and I've got students—and *he's* a student, and he's going to move that board? Now, it was just a thing that he did because he didn't know any better. His parents had probably taught him that, and it was just part of him. He sensed that the white section was filling up, so he automatically went back and moved the board; and I just, instinctively, moved it back.

There had been a lot of talk at that time about Rosa Parks sitting down on the bus and starting the boycott in Montgomery; it was in the newspapers, and it was everywhere. That was just the top of the iceberg—just the tip of what was going on—but it was publicized and even the youngsters would know about her not giving up that seat. There were some students from Lincoln School, not many, riding the bus that day, and they were watching. I put the board back, and this white fellow looked around—he didn't say anything. The person next to him didn't say anything. And the students behind me didn't say anything. But in my mind, there was a change being made. Nobody got up and called me a name or said, "Hey, put that back!" No; they just silently went on.

I remember another interesting thing: the Birmingham Symphony would have these segregated concerts, and the students could buy tickets, maybe a quarter a ticket. I wanted the children to see and hear the classical performance, and I remember walking, maybe fourteen blocks, from Lincoln School up to Boutwell Auditorium. I would insist that all my children have tickets. We would line up to go to this cultural thing: we didn't have any money for transportation, but we walked. We walked and walked. And one time in the late years, one of my students said: "Mr. Adams, why aren't you playing in the symphony?"

That's a kid: "Why aren't you playing?" See, youngsters have the freedom to say what they actually think. Of course, the symphony was entirely segregated; they didn't have a black person in there. I had to say, well, I'm sure that I *could,* but I had the teaching job. But I thought, "We'll see about that."

I applied to audition, and there was another fellow that I knew, a trumpet player, who applied, too. When we applied, they changed the whole system. They changed to a full-time symphony: whereas they had been practicing in the afternoons, they started practicing in the day—and that would prevent us or anybody like us from having a chance to play. You couldn't be a teacher and play in the symphony. Those were the kinds of things that subtly were done back at that time. Of course, they lost some great white players, too, because they weren't able to make the practices either. So it kept blacks out of the symphony, but it also hurt some of their white musicians.

I mention that story, because it shows that children are very, very perceptive. This was a grade-school kid; he had heard me, and he had heard them. So he said, "Why aren't you up there?" What happened is, he didn't see anybody up there that looked like *him.* That affects them. It affects them.

And that gave me the idea that youngsters were seeing something that adults were overlooking.

When Dr. King came along, there was this thinking about nonviolence. You had folks back there, before the civil rights movement—including my dad—who wouldn't have been able to *live* through that movement, because they would not have accepted nonviolence. If they had been pushed, they would fight back. Like my dad told the Klan: "Come and get me." My dad was armed to protect himself. He didn't welcome trouble, but if it came, he would be willing to die for a cause. I really think that, if it came down to it, the leaders of his generation would have been violent—and it would have been *unorganized* violence.

Dr. King knew that violence would not be to the advantage of anybody, that he could be more successful without it. In fact, violence, if it had been let loose, would have torn our country apart. And Dr. King, who was not without fault, understood that.

Some embraced that feeling. But there was a lot of fear—a lot of fear that it couldn't end up in anything good. Lives would be lost; people would lose their homes. So people were afraid of the change.

The blacks were not together: some people feared their survival. Some people knew it was not in their interests to have a conflict. But there were others who said, "We're just going to *have* to make a change."

Of course, there were blacks, like Duke Ellington and some of the rest of them, who didn't participate in the marching—but they contributed in the music. They wrote music about it, and they contributed money quietly to the movement. People in later years say, "Well, he didn't participate," or "She didn't participate"—they don't know *who* participated. You had some people in the schools who were afraid that their children might be hurt by the police, so they held them back. But their money and their hearts were in sympathy with the movement. There were a few that were afraid, and a few, probably, that for philosophical reasons felt that Dr. King was wrong. And there were those who were jealous of him, really.

A lot of blacks would be afraid for their jobs. If you were a white person and you were my employer—and you saw me out there demonstrating all day—if you didn't like what I was doing, you'd fire me. But not only would you fire me, you'd call everybody else and say, "Don't hire him. He's a bad nigra. Don't give him a job." If you saw me registering to vote, you might say, "You have a right to vote—but you don't have a right to work for *me* anymore." So it was easy to fear losing your job and not being able to feed your family; because some white person had your life in his hands and could tell other people in power, "Don't bother with him." In fact, that was one of the reasons they decided to put the children in the marches. Somebody might recognize *you* out there marching, and you could lose your job—but they wouldn't be able to connect you to your children. They wouldn't know *whose* children were marching.

Of course, it was against the law to dismiss the schoolchildren to go on those marches. That came from the supervision on both sides, black and white: "We'll take your job if you tell them they can go." But—"If they go and you can't do anything to *stop* them, then that's another thing." And there was a sort of understanding that "Those band children are going to go."

"Those band children *like* to march."

All that time when the marches were going on, they would give a signal down at this church, St. Joseph. They would drop a white flag; the children could see that from the classroom, and they'd leave. What

I would do: I would turn my back to write on the board—all of a sudden, you hear them moving, and you just keep your back turned—then, when you turn around, they're gone. They would be out, except for just a few who were still sitting there. I couldn't get onto them about not going, and I didn't wish I could—because that was their parents' prerogative, to let them go or not. I would take them to a safe place, to some other teacher; then I would follow the ones that went, on the other side of the street, to offer what little protection I could.

Lincoln School was four or five blocks closer to the park than Parker High School, so my children would get to the demonstrations before the high school students—which meant these little children would be put in jail first. But they didn't mind that. It was an excitement to them.

There are still a lot of unsolved cases from the civil rights movement. In years to come there may be an investigation of how many were killed anonymously, and nobody said anything about it. Some people disappeared. That was true in the Smithfield community, because you had Bomb Hill, where Attorney Shores's home was. Groups like the Klan would target those areas. Some of my friends, like Joe Jones, formed a vigilante group that confronted the Klan when they would visit the neighborhood. A Klansman might go into a black neighborhood and get shot. They buried him somewhere; he would disappear. And certain black people would disappear.

Sometimes someone, a white person, would warn you that the Klan was coming—"This caravan of Klansmen went through 18th Street," or whatever it was—so some blacks would be camouflaged at night; a guy would have a shotgun, waiting. They would have guns out there to protect people like Attorney Shores, and you could volunteer to be a protector.

The popular idea is that they were just defenseless blacks, but they weren't. I remember, there was a protest down by the police station; this lady came up there and she was inebriated, and she said, "All y'all are supposed to be nonviolent—but god-*dog*-it, I'm *violent!*" She's drunk, walking up the street and wielding, I guess, a razor, saying, "Now, come and get *me!*" Everybody, on both sides, just stood back and looked. She passed on, and they started back to activity again. There were people like that, who *wanted* to be violent.

There were things that I saw—when my children would get to the

park from school, some adults were already there. They did a thing—
it's frightening—where they would count, "One, two, three, *four*," and
all at the same time they would throw these rocks, these massive rocks
that they had brought from their communities. These things were like
birds in the sky—*thick*—all these rocks coming down, man, at the same
time; you had no escape. There was an incident where a group threw
a brick, and it knocked this man's jaw completely *off*. Those were the
kinds of things that you would see: a guy with a hole in his head, and
he didn't know who threw the brick. The police were armed with rifles
and everything, but what could they do? You had all those little children out there; could you shoot and massacre little children from the
schools?

It was a problem for Dr. King and a lot of them, until the movement got settled, to convince the violent ones: don't you go out there
and fight back or shoot back, because there are more of *them*, and they
have greater weapons. The odds were against you in a fight with all-
out ammunition.

But you did have those who would throw bricks, and the bricks
were like birds in the sky.

Of course, one person who opened my eyes to a lot of things—at that
time and from an early age—was my brother, Oscar. When he went
to Talladega College, I was still in high school, and he would bring
youngsters home from different parts of the country. Talladega was a
school that was way ahead of most black schools and probably most
white schools at that time. They had these debates about *rights,* about
freedom and the Constitution—and it was like heaven on earth down
there, as an incubator, for those who attended. I listened to Oscar prepare his debates, and he would make speeches. He was so scholarly in
his research, and the people he associated with were a different kind
of people. Some were aspiring to be lawyers, and they admired and
knew all about people like Thurgood Marshall. It was just another
world, and it was Oscar's influence on me to see things in a different
light. At the same time, I was able to tell *him* about things out there,
that *he* didn't know about—about the road, and the people I had met.
So it was an exchange of ideas.

Oscar was among that group that came from all over and happened
to enter Howard University when they were preparing the civil rights

fight in the law school. When he finished at Howard, everyone knew that he was brilliant, and there were people in Birmingham that said, "Come on in with us, and join our team." In particular, Dr. Gaston, the great entrepreneur, said, "Come join my business, and you'll be okay"—but, see, Oscar had some of Daddy in him; he didn't want to do that. He went on his own. And we weren't surprised by that. So the little inheritance we had, our dad's inheritance, we invested in his law books.

Oscar was really in the forefront of the civil rights battle. I don't think he did any marching, but he was one of the ones behind the scenes. Oscar was one of the first blacks in Alabama to take the Bar examination. He told me that when he took the Bar exam, it was three days long—this was in Montgomery—and they put him down in the damp basement room, because segregation was rampant. He said when he finished his exam, he took his pencil and slung it across the room—because he had been through hell, and he knew it—and it stuck in the wall.

When he was getting started, Oscar taught in the veterans' school in the afternoons. The veterans' school would meet around three o'clock to six; he'd work in his law office until then, and then he'd go teach the veterans. Most of them hadn't graduated from high school—a lot of them were working in the steel mills—and they just loved him. I remember he made some of his best friends by those old guys, and they were some of his first clients.

A fellow came to see him, and this turned out to be a pivotal case: a fellow who worked for the mines was dying of silicosis of the lungs. He lived in the company housing. This had been happening for years and years: you had a lot out there that were sick with silicosis, but they were afraid to file a suit, because they knew they would lose their jobs and have to move off the company property. This man came and said he wanted to sue the company, even though they'd put him off. He had made up his mind: blackballing didn't mean anything to him, because, he said, "I'm dying."

That was the first case that really got Oscar going and put him on his feet financially. He won a big settlement. And the next case that stands out in my mind was when Oscar integrated Elmwood Cemetery. They had a GI that brought a case, because they wouldn't bury blacks over there—now it's full of them, and it's due to my brother.

I remember, Oscar had a case down in South Alabama somewhere; this lady had a lot of property in her will and he was going to research it. He went into the courthouse and said to the clerk, "I'm searching for Mrs. Jones's file." The clerk didn't say anything to him. He said, "I'll say it again: I'm Attorney Adams; I'm a lawyer; I'm looking for Mrs. Jones's file." The fellow didn't even look at him. He repeated it again. He knew the guy could hear, because the telephone rang and he answered it; but he just sat there. Oscar kept repeating that he was a lawyer, looking for this file.

This guy finally just stood up and spit in his face.

Oscar was telling me this. I said, "My God, what did you do?"

"I just took my handkerchief out and wiped it off. And said, 'I'm still looking.'"

And he got that file.

Oscar told me once: "You just have to go with the flow until you get your chance." And he said, "When you get your chance, you be sure you do a *heck* of a good job." At his funeral they said that he wanted to be known not as being black or white but being fair. He said that if you could look at his cases and his judgments were all fair, that's the way it should be.

One of the reasons Oscar was so successful during the civil rights movement was that he could get things done with the Board of Education; he could work with the superintendent and those people in power, to avoid a violent eruption. That's why Dr. King and all of them preferred his services. He wasn't a radical. He believed in change. And he believed in change without violence.

Oscar's first wife, Willa, passed away in 1980. Sometime after that he married Anne-Marie Adams, a wonderful lady who grew up in the community. Oscar retired from the bench in 1993, but he still did work with one of the major law firms here. He passed in 1997. Of course, it's traditional to play a piece of music at the funeral; my son Eaton had finished Boston University by then, and people don't know, but he's a tremendous musician—so I figure I'd bring him in on the performance. We took two pieces of music, and in the end we got together as a duet on the "Battle Hymn of the Republic." It was an original composition, but it incorporated the "Battle Hymn of the Republic," because that's what they played when Grandma passed away: "Mine eyes have seen the coming of the glory of the Lord."

Justice Oscar Adams, portrait by Jerry Whitworth, 1993.
Courtesy of Jerry Whitworth.

I thought that was appropriate to Oscar, because he was a soldier. He fought the civil rights battle.

My brother always said that there was one superintendent, Dr. Cody, who was critical during that period: that if he didn't do what he did, behind the scenes, there would have been bedlam breaking loose. People would have killed each other. And it's true: a lot of terrible things could have happened if it wasn't for those unknown heroes. Usually you put your martyrs up, Reverend Shuttlesworth and those kinds of people, but you don't know who's behind the scenes, working to come to some kind of solution. My brother credited Dr. Cody as being one who kept there from being anarchy in the streets.

Dr. Cody was one of the silent warriors.

During the movement there was another fellow that came down here, a Jewish fellow from New York City; his name was Harvey Burg. He lived with my brother—and that was unheard of then. They had a swimming pool, and Harvey Burg loved to swim in my brother's pool. He was in his late twenties, and this guy was a genius. He was one of the ones that did all this legal work behind the movement. Nobody ever gave him much credit for it, but he was one like you find sometimes: nobody knows about him, but he changed everything. Harvey Burg.

Of course, the leaders during my dad's generation were fiery, but no one had worked out a *legal* framework to get their rights. They didn't have the weapons; they didn't have the know-how, the skills, to go through the law and get things resolved. That's why Thurgood Marshall and those were so important—Harvey Burg and my brother; all of them—because they had these great minds, and they were concentrated on the law.

After this was all over, Harvey Burg didn't come back to take any bows; he just went back up north and probably made a million dollars. So many things were not revealed about that period, because you had some people that just got the inner satisfaction that they were doing good. They did it for a purpose. But they don't have to tell you they were the ones that did it.

A lot of times, people glamorize and aggrandize themselves financially by talking about the civil rights movement; they pay that movement a lot of lip service. You have people who want to make a profit off of it. But they don't know anything about it unless they were *there,* in the air, to breathe it and smell the gunpowder. You should never rape the movement; you shouldn't exploit the movement for personal reward. No: that honor is in your soul; that honor is in your mind. And you will live with the memory that you did it. Like I told you about my children and the marches. They were there, but they're cool about it. They've *done* that. They marched. And they march on.

One by one, they just march away from that.

You find out that there were a lot of successes with integration, but there were failures. There was one disastrous thing, but it was inevitable: if you get a certain freedom and you're not prepared to make the most of it, then you've only got, really, a small amount of freedom. If I got the freedom to go to The University of Alabama to take advanced courses, what good is it if I haven't prepared myself to take those advanced courses? I'm free to go, but I can't do it because I'm not prepared to. It's like saying, "Frank, you have the right, now, to join the Alabama Symphony. The symphony plays, maybe, twelve pieces by Wagner and one by Mozart and two by Beethoven this season. Okay?" But this is all of a sudden—give me a year or so, so I can coach myself and prepare myself to play this particular literature; then I'll be able to do it. There's got to be a time of preparation.

The rules of the law had to be changed, and they were. But there were no plans for people after that. Freedom found a lot of people unprepared to take advantage of it. At the very beginning of the civil rights movement, there should have been some effort to train people: to *run* big business; to run a chain of big grocery stores; to lead a school system. There should have been some effort for self-sufficiency. It was "freedom, freedom," but freedom without any education or any training was just *freedom*. Freedom to do what?

One of the worst things about it is: now there's a generation of youngsters who don't understand what happened during and before the civil rights movement. This generation is very loosely connected to what happened back there. All they know is that they're supposed to have certain freedoms—but there's so many things they don't know, and they don't know what it was done for. They know it's Dr. King's birthday, and they enjoy being out of school for the holiday. They can recite Dr. King's great speech, but they don't *know*. They don't know how they got the rights, and they don't know how to use them. All they know is, "I'm free; I got my freedom; somebody named Dr. King did it—now, don't mess with me. You owe me something, because they tell me my folks were slaves." They think everybody is mistreating them, and they mistreat themselves. The thing that is so unfathomable is that they don't know where they came from, and they don't know what heroes were really there. They just know certain names, to get a grade in history. There's this gap. And unfortunately, those who don't know anything about the past have no hope for the future.

Integration has been successful to a certain degree, on the books. On the records, it might be successful. But it has to be a change in the hearts of people, and the way people think. Unfortunately, some people hold on to their old, antiquated ideas, and they hold on to the past. And to my dismay, it's on both sides—or on three or *four* different sides. But it's changing, and it has to change out of necessity. Historically, when things get to their lowest level, then change comes about.

What I mean is: we have always called ourselves the home of the free and the brave, and said, "Send us your masses." It's going to come where we really *have* to be that way, or we may self-destruct. Other countries that have never, ever felt that they were free—that have never *pretended* to be fair—look at us and say, "Well, those people are hypocrites!" That gives credence to those who really hate us—who really want to see us destroyed. The enemy sits over there and says, "Now, what did America say they were? The land of the free? The home of the brave? We *know* they're brave—they fight us. But this other thing about them being free, and them being fair. . . . They *pretend* to be fair, which put them above us around the world—but they're not. They don't want to see the Mexicans coming in; they don't want to see their schools really integrated. . . ."

The only way change will come about—I hate to say it—is from fear. I hope I'm wrong. But when you get a crisis—when government cannot act for itself, or when it gets so confused that it can't pass any constructive legislation—the enemy looks in and says: "It's time to strike." Then we all come back together. We've *got* to be together, because we're being destroyed. I might end up in your basement, or you might end up in mine. And say, "Send me a piece of bread down here, man, I'm dying in your basement. I'm your *friend*, man."

It took a lot of years of slavery and segregation before everyone in this country got what was promised in the Constitution. And I don't want to see our country taken back. When all these things are in your memory bank—what segregation was really like, and the marches, and all—you can't understand a political rally where they want to take someone's rights *away*. They don't want to tolerate homosexuals in the military—or we have the Mexican population increasing, increasing, increasing, and there are those who say, "Let's kick all these Mexicans out of here!" I'm quite sure that if we needed them—their numbers in the army, and their blood for transfusions—we could find some way to keep them around, couldn't we? So give them *something*.

The biggest thing is education. It doesn't make sense for people in America not to offer equal education for everybody. There should be a quality education—an *over-the-mountain* quality—right over here in the inner city. If you *don't* have that—if you don't do the right thing in education—then you create a great monster. You don't even have to abandon your old concepts—you could hold on to your hate if you wanted to—but when you don't provide the resources that are necessary to educate people, then you *create* the criminal. You create the one that will hush your beautiful life, or your wife's beautiful life; or your children could be shot and killed by some heathen that's on dope— why *shouldn't* you take some extra effort to educate him? Help him learn how to read and learn how to write; do something in your classroom to uplift him. If you don't, he's going to be your enemy: you can't get away from him as long as he's sucking air. But you could have stopped that. And we *can* stop that.

What we have to do is restore the spirit that we used to have in the school. And we have to get white and black students to come together. That high school on Eighth Avenue—which was once, really, the most successful thing in Birmingham—should be A. H. Parker *Academic and Industrial* High School. They should put half of the school to prepare youngsters to go to colleges and universities, and the other half should be for industrial skills like we had when Whatley was there. Doing things with your hands. Teaching music, not as a frill, but like it's going to be your profession. It could be like Industrial High School was, but it would be on another level: it might not be shoe repair, but it could be computer technology, or radio engineering. Then you'd have advanced academic courses for those who want a liberal arts education. You would have those who would want to get medical preparatory training, and you could have intense *teacher* training, right there in the high school. And it would be backed up by companies that could make donations or grants.

The big businesses—the Benz plant and the Hyundai plant, all those plants—would probably save the whole school system. You've got three or four automobile production companies here in Alabama, and they need trained workers; they could grant a million dollars for training, easily, because they're going to get a skilled work force from the school. They could pay the salaries of people who could teach those needed skills. That school would never, ever have to worry about enrollment. If we had an Academic and Industrial High School, all of the surrounding areas—white or black—would be coming in to take those courses. That would be a major development for the whole South, because you'd get another school like that, and another school. There's no telling what the outcome would be.

One of my professors in graduate school would always say that one thing that was so perplexing to him was that, in our Alabama constitution, there's a provision for "adequate education." Adequate education: in other words, just enough to get by. But adequate education is not going to enable you to do outstanding work.

If you want me to appreciate what we call excellent music, you have to let me *hear* excellent music. If you want me to appreciate good food, you've got to give me a steak sometime—you can't keep feeding me pizza. Growing up, a young person, I think, should *taste* caviar. I think a young person should ride in a *big* car sometime. When I was coming along, you had people that had those ideas: they wanted the best, they didn't want to compromise, and they didn't want someone to say it's all *right* to compromise.

You could have this outstanding high school right now in Mountain Brook or Hoover, and you could say, "Well, they've got community support." But what about this school over here? "Oh, that's adequate. They don't *have* to have trigonometry or calculus—just have a little arithmetic." It's like the superintendent who said, "It costs *me* more to live." I think about how Mr. Martinson asked me, "Why would you have those *stringed* instruments on the wall?" What he was saying is, "Hey, you're getting an adequate education here"—but at Philips High School, they had an orchestra! There was this disparity. And there's still this disparity.

So this "adequate education" is a lie. It's just not enough.

Dr. Locke, Alain Locke, wrote a book called *When Peoples Meet*. And his idea in that book was that when people get together—when a diversity of people meet, and they get to talk, and know each other—then you can start to see a change. Then things start happening.

When people meet.

I was asked to speak this year at Homewood High School for Black History Month, and they asked me to talk about music. I said, "I understand it's Black History Month, and that has a rightful place," but the first thing I said is, "You have to understand: it's not one person's music." In music, especially in *jazz* music, it's like a gumbo: it takes all races, all kinds of people—religiously and whatever—to make this jazz music up. When Gershwin walked by someplace in New Orleans, the story goes, and he heard this bluesy clarinet play something, he wanted to write down on paper what jazz felt like to *him*. It was on a rainy night, and that's how he started off and wrote his great "Rhapsody in Blue." I explained that to them: "George and Ira Gershwin were Jewish people—it was not only a black thing." There were a thousand people in that auditorium, a diverse group of students, and that feeling was appreciated. You could feel in their hearts that they understood and appreciated that.

This is one of the things that impressed me about Ellington's band: he had this diversity from the very beginning. He had Juan Tizol, the guy from Puerto Rico; he had Barney Bigard, the Creole from New Orleans; he had the trumpet player from Mobile; he had the conservatory guy on clarinet. He mixed all this stuff up together. That was his thing: the *mixture*. And he knew how to mix it.

This jazz thing went beyond segregation, to a certain extent. When I was playing music in different clubs, I'd look up and there were a lot of whites that would come out to play. In jazz, you're always welcome. We learn something from you, and you learn something from us. Then the reputation goes around that, "Hey. That guy is good. I want to play with him." So late at night, regardless of segregation, they would come and play. At the Woodland Club, and different clubs, they would play.

In other words, it's a thing that: "Hey, man, we play for different clubs and things, but when it comes to jamming and playing this music, this soul music, we get together on it; and we're brothers in this. We go our separate ways—but at *night,* when you're asleep, then we get together and work on this *jazz* music. We respect each other. We can't show this kind of love out in the open, because we've got so many that feel that this is crossing the line, that it shouldn't be that way. But the musicians: we're brothers. We don't show it, but we're just like each other. Look at Jack Teagarden; look at Benny Goodman; look at all these guys, man!"

So in jazz, you always had this other little secret society. The white players would come out to Red's place. Sometimes they'd sneak you in to where they were playing. Or you'd meet up in the store and talk about music, about where you're playing and what you're doing. "Have you all played this number?" "Frank, have you heard this player?"

That was a thing that existed in Birmingham. It was what I call a quiet brotherhood.

Sadly enough, we didn't include *everybody*. We had these reservations. Whites had reservations against other whites. Jazz musicians had reservations about Muddy Waters and those kind of blues folk: "That's *country* stuff." But that's against each other.

Even now, there's this great divide between different kinds of music —whether it's the blues brothers, or the jazz people, or the Cuban music—it's something that you can't translate over to. How many musicians do you know that are this way: "Man, they're not playing anything; *doo-doo-doo,* that's all they *do.*" There's this *divide.* The symphony musicians—they don't necessarily frown down on jazz, but most of them can't *play* jazz; and a lot of jazz musicians don't have enough interest to try to play *their* music.

But you take the musicians coming along now that are schooled musicians, like Wynton Marsalis: they go across all lines. And that's how it has got to be now. It's not one way—all of it has its place.

What we have to do is train youngsters to be able to do all of it.

15

Keeping the Spirit

ONE OF THE GREAT THINGS IN MY LIFE HAS BEEN the Alabama Jazz Hall of Fame. More needs to be said about the person who founded this place: Mr. J. L. Lowe. He's the reason that the museum is here. He lived a block up from my home in Smithfield, when I was coming up, and he was an outstanding teacher at Industrial High School. When we got to high school we heard about him as being a great musician and an intellectual fellow. Everybody talked about how he went to Alabama State when he was just a teenager, maybe fourteen or fifteen years old, because he would get these double promotions, like my brother did. Mr. Lowe probably graduated from college when he was seventeen years old—he was just that smart. He played an important part in my brother's life at the high school, too, because he organized the oratorical contests. These were big things in those days. The Elks and the lodges would sponsor these citywide oratorical contests and speech-writing contests, and they would find some very talented youngsters to compete.

Mr. Lowe was really fired up for education. He was one of the first ones that we ever heard of to go off and get a master's degree from Columbia, and all kinds of degrees. They called him "Professor" Lowe. And he came from the same cut as Fess Whatley. He played the saxophone, for years, in Fess Whatley's Vibraphone Cathedral Orchestra, and I heard about him ever since, I guess, the day I was born. My brother and I knew all about Mr. Lowe, because we watched him walk by our home, going to the high school. One day—and this was one of those defining moments for me—my daddy pointed him out; said, "That young man there: you boys ought to aspire to be like him."

One of the things that was very important to my life, growing up, was the fact that you had some professionals in your community. There was a dentist in your neighborhood and a number of teachers. You had people come out of there like Rayfield, the great architect. You probably had a professional person living within two or three blocks, who you could look out your window and see drive off in a car—or the way he dressed made you idolize that person. Your parents would always say, "That's a fine man. He's this," and "she's that," and you could aspire to be something like that. When a person like Mr. J. L. Lowe would walk down the street, the children would know that he was something special. You got that in your system; got that in your blood. His brother Sammy's writing all this music in New York City . . . why *not?* He's from *here.*

The thing about it was: you had people who were role models, who lived next door to you, or in your vicinity. The children could see their idols, because they lived in the community; they lived in close proximity to you. They *couldn't* move over the mountain, and they couldn't move to exclusive communities, so they had to live right there, amongst the people they served. Their concerns were the concerns of the neighborhood. So that's how this thing came about that I always talk about: the spirit in the high school, and the spirit in that community.

You had people like this lady I never will forget, Mrs. Scott: her husband worked in the rubber plant where they made rubber bands. He'd come home with all this debris on him, but she wouldn't allow him to sit on the front porch until he cleaned himself up. He had to take all his work clothes off, put his shirt on—*then* he could sit on the porch. Up front. *Pride.* He looked just like a professor. Or Mr. Rouse, who ran the pool hall: he was illiterate, but he would sit in his new home on the porch, looking at the newspaper. He lived right across the street from us. My daddy had to tell him to turn the paper right side up— "Turn that paper up, Rouse, everybody knows you can't read!" They laughed about that. It wasn't insulting; they were friends.

You had all of these people in the community, side by side.

You don't have that now. My son lives in Hoover. He has a nice place there, a fabulous home. The dentist I go to, a black dentist: he lives in Mountain Brook. They're gone. You don't have somebody to look out the door to. Right now if you were to go to Enon Ridge, or you go to Ensley, and you say, "How many black lawyers are here?"—you won't find but, maybe, one. "How many doctors are here?" None. "Where are they?" They live in Trussville; they live in Mountain Brook now. They live in Hoover. They went there because they were able to go there. They're at places now where they feel safe. And they know that their children will get a better education.

Integration brought in a lot of opportunities and a lot of good, but it broke communities. With freedom, people felt free—so they moved all *over* Birmingham. All the role models left. They can still be good examples, but they're not examples for the people who need them the most, here in the inner city. And one of the tragic things that I witnessed was that the spirit in the schools gradually, with integration, broke down. It took a long time for Fess Whatley's spirit to pass out of those schools. Mr. Lowe carried it on for a long time, and several others carried it on. But little by little, you saw it disappear.

As I say, when I was coming up, I knew all about Mr. Lowe, and Mr. Lowe knew about me, too—I grew up a block from his house, and he would hear me practice. I guess he knew more about me than I did about myself. In fact, he called me to Professor Whatley's attention: that "this little fellow at Lincoln School, who lives a block from me, he might be able to take a place of somebody in that band, if you work with him." I never knew the ins and outs of it, but I understand that he was very influential in getting me connected with Professor Whatley.

Mr. Lowe just idolized Fess Whatley because, when he was coming up, times were hard—and Fess went and bought him his first tuxedo, so he could play in the band. He never forgot that. Professor Whatley found out that that the Lowes were a wonderful family—they're still that way today—and Fess had a penchant for teaching entire families. He wouldn't discriminate, but he would look for a family that had some kind of support; some kind of a background. Fess didn't just pick anybody: you didn't have to be rich, or you didn't have to be poor, or you didn't have to be anywhere in between—but he had to see something in you that was backed up by your parents. You don't hear all that now—that "This boy came from a good family," and "An apple can't fall too far"—but that was his way of thinking. It wasn't like Sun Ra, whose background was such a mystery: Fess would want to know where his players came from.

I remember Mr. Lowe's passion after Fess had passed along. Mr. Lowe worked tirelessly to let people know about our Birmingham musicians, to promote their legacy. He always admired his brother Sammy, and he always kept the fire going for Erskine Hawkins's band. Mr. Lowe was at Alabama State when Erskine Hawkins was starting his band there; he followed the band and was really a part of the whole thing. He'd keep all the records for Erskine Hawkins—he had everything written down, the tour schedules and all. And he wanted to expose *us* to it—to show what we've got, here in Birmingham. So he organized the Birmingham Heritage Band, to honor and continue that tradition, and he founded this Hall of Fame.

A lady was asking me the other day, "When did you meet Erskine Hawkins?" I don't know when I met Erskine Hawkins. He was just a part of the community, as far back as I can remember—I told you about how they would come back and give these free concerts and just *inspire* everybody. Because when they came to Birmingham and to Parker High School, they were home. Each member of that band was worshipped, in a way. We knew everything about Erskine Hawkins. Over my lifetime I've played his numbers, and I've recorded "Tuxedo Junction" over, I guess, ten times—and other numbers, like "Tippin' In," I've done with the Alabama Symphony.

I remember one time Erskine Hawkins came to Parker and he had to get a player to sit in—he got a student named John Armstead. John was an excellent player; we were both in Fess Whatley's band at the time. Erskine came to town, and the place was just packed with folks. He needed a tenor player; I was playing alto, so he picked John. I just wished that *I* had been the one, but I played the wrong instrument. I remember, it was amazing that John was able to play everything in Erskine Hawkins's book. After that, whenever Erskine Hawkins would come, I always knew "Tippin' In" and "I Got a Right to Cry"—I knew *all* those solos. And I thought I brought a little touch of Erskine Hawkins with me when I went to Howard.

In about 1990, in his declining years, Erskine Hawkins decided to have a reunion tour. All the alumni of Industrial High School remember the days of Erskine Hawkins, and those out in California said, "We want to see him. We want to see Erskine Hawkins before he dies—we want to see what's left of Tuxedo Junction." And they sent for him.

Erskine came to Birmingham. He had been playing in the Catskills up in New York, making a good living playing with a small combo—as Fess would say, a "bobtail band," but they were very good. He came back and put together what he called his Reunion Orchestra. He picked up some who were left, and I got a chance to go. Mr. Lowe did all the booking and arranged for the transportation. We had Erskine Hawkins's music to play, the original arrangements, and so we were successful.

We went to Sacramento. We were shocked to see how many folk from Birmingham and other places would come to Erskine Hawkins's reunion. We stayed there a whole week, and the next year we had another one. It was a great time. There were alumni in Sacramento, and then the ones who were in L.A. would come. All the California people would come, and even those who lived in New York—some of them would fly out there for this reunion. In those tours, the auditorium would be filled with our classmates. So it was a reunion for the band, but it was like a reunion for the alumni out there, too. They *crowded* in there to see Erskine Hawkins.

In 1977, Mr. Lowe organized the Birmingham Heritage Band, which I've been a member of for years. Originally it was for the bicentennial celebration that they had here in Birmingham. And that started bringing all those people back to town; the Birmingham Heritage Band consisted of people who had played with the big bands and who had come back home. It was built on the same principles that Fess Whatley had—the same music, and the same discipline—and it was just like another Erskine Hawkins band. In fact, we still play from those original Erskine Hawkins arrangements. Mr. Lowe had the vision of putting young people in the band, letting them play side by side with the older musicians; that idea was a big part of the Heritage Band.

I know that if it wasn't for Mr. Lowe and his ideas, the Jazz Hall of Fame wouldn't be here. This place came about because it was always in Mr. Lowe's head and in his heart to honor Fess Whatley and all those who contributed to the music. Mr. Lowe felt that Birmingham had more musicians—not just leaders, but sidemen—than any other place, even New Orleans. He wanted this place to be here so that those

Saxophone section, Birmingham Heritage Band: Amos Gordon, Frank Adams, and J. L. Lowe, ca. 1979. Courtesy of the Birmingham Public Library, Department of Archives and Manuscripts, J. L. Lowe Collection.

people from Birmingham would be honored. He got together with Mayor Vann, who was mayor of Birmingham at that time, and Richard Arrington, who succeeded him as mayor—they got together in 1978 and had the first induction ceremony. The surprising thing was that, along with all those musicians, the very first ones inducted—Erskine Hawkins, Sammy Lowe, Haywood Henry, Amos Gordon, and Fess Whatley—he picked me to go in there. I'll always be grateful to him. You had others who had more experience here, but he picked me out.

He had a little place—nothing like the Hall of Fame is now—a little room somewhere on the corner, where he had some pictures and a few horns, and Mr. Gordon taught music in one of the rooms. Then they

Alabama Jazz Hall of Fame inaugural induction ceremony, 1978: inductee Frank Adams with two of Birmingham's future mayors, Richard Arrington, left, and Bernard Kinkaid, right. Courtesy of Frank Adams.

decided they're going to build the civil rights museum, so you fast-forward quite a bit. Mr. Lowe was well respected across Birmingham, to a great extent, and he connected with people of influence—white and black, they knew Mr. Lowe. He was one of those that crossed lines, like my dad. And he was this self-sacrificial soul who would do anything for music, and anything to represent the people of Birmingham. He brought up the idea: we ought to have a Hall of Fame for Erskine Hawkins and Sammy Lowe, Fess Whatley, and all.

They looked at him and said, "Well, what about that old Carver Theatre building down there?"

All the pieces fell together. They said, "We can have a jazz museum and the civil rights museum, and the city will take care of both of them financially." It was supposed to be like a little brother to the civil rights museum—in fact, the people on the board of that museum were on the board for the jazz museum. Same people. So they got together. They brought in some of the artifacts that Mr. Lowe had, and that's how it all got started.

When he passed away, it sort of flowed that, since I was doing well in teaching and all and had gotten to be a supervisor—and Mr. Lowe felt real close to me—I was the preferred person to be the director here. It was, to me, an opportunity to work and create music programs. Years passed and we developed things like the jazz festival every year, and we started the free instrumental music programs on Saturdays. Now I'm the director of education, emeritus. That means I've done my thing, really, but I'm still here. And anything I can do for the Hall of Fame, I do.

My main thing now is to try to get young people of all races college scholarships. This year, I had six students get full scholarships, and one won the Ellis Marsalis Scholarship down at the University of New Orleans. This fellow, Jeronne Ansari—that entitles him to go to school there, a full scholarship, room and board. Others got scholarships to Alabama State and Stillman and all those places. So my main focus now is spotting them in the eleventh grade and start working, working, *working,* getting all the offers from everybody. Having people come up and test them, and then letting them get those scholarships. Usually, when I send them, they're prepared: they always get something. Sometimes they get the full scholarship, sometimes they get half scholarships, but there's a place for all of them.

I often ask them the question—a profound question—and say, "How many people in your family have a college degree?" I tell some of them, "If you do this music the way I'm teaching you, you can perform it, you can teach it, you can write it; you can get a scholarship; and maybe you'll be the first one in your family to ever finish college." And this is really profound, because when they go home and ask mama or daddy, mama or daddy may say, "Well, no. I went one year at Miles, and I had to work," or "I got drafted," or something. So, "Hey: you don't have to tell Doc Adams, but *you will be the first.* I'm going to see *to* it that you'll be the first."

That gives them a hunger. That gives them something to work for.

Another thing I started at the Hall of Fame was the annual Student Jazz Band Festival. It's statewide, and I set it up to include all the schools that have a jazz band, whether it's a middle school or a high school or a college. We bring in the middle schools on one night, usually a Thursday, and the high schools on Friday, and the colleges and universities on Saturday. And the thing is, I set it up to where you don't pay to go; you don't pay at all. We have sponsors so that everybody will get a trophy, and that recognizes that you played in the festival. All of the trophies are the same. There's no "Superior" or whatever.

Most of the time, when you have a state festival or a district festival, there's always this competition: your band gets Superior, and one gets Good, and one gets Fair. Fair's the lowest thing you can get; that's terrible. Something I witnessed a long time ago when I went out to a district competition: all the kids that got Superior would holler, "We're Superior, we're Superior!" And the others would feel discouraged. I didn't like that.

So I set this thing up with some kind of controversy: people said, "You've got to have the *best!*" Like a prize fight. I said, "No, we want this to be a free-flowing thing. They don't pay to come; all we want them to do is to be here and to do their best." We have adjudicators, of course; what the adjudicators do is write down comments of what you need to improve on. We have the same adjudicators every year, so they can see how the bands progress from one year to the next. You still have some people say, "Doc, you've got to have somebody *win* the jazz band festival." I say, "*Win* the jazz band festival?" How could somebody win a jazz festival, when jazz is subjective? It's what you think; what you feel. My argument is that jazz is an individualistic thing. It's *you*. What *you* do. You have to be careful if you're going to give a graded score—you can't do that realistically. You can only give your interpretation.

But our culture is about having the *top*. This thing of who's the best goes deep into some people, and I think that's the cause of a lot of problems. I told my wife: "Having a son is one thing. But if you had a daughter, and she was in a beauty contest, and then she came in last—of all the people in there, she was the *least beautiful*"—I said, "I don't think I could live with that." I would think my daughter is as beautiful as anybody else in there. So if I had a daughter, I would forbid her going out and being in a beauty contest—because who can tell who is beautiful and not beautiful?

That all goes back to Duke Ellington. I think about it often: the most hoarse singer in the world would probably be Al Hibbler, the blind singer with Duke's band. But Duke *heard* something in that roughness that, when he put it with his orchestrations, was beautiful. And Ray Charles comes along with "America the Beautiful"—in ordinary circumstances, you'd put him in *jail* with that rough voice—and sometimes he says, "God Bless America," but it sounds like he's saying, "God *Dog* America!" But people love that.

The point is, people perceive things differently.

So whenever we have this festival, *everyone* is honored.

16

"Doc"

As I've said, my son Eaton was born in 1972. And when I got to the supervisory position at the Board of Education, I started thinking about a challenge: I said, "Before he finishes grade school, I'll earn a doctorate degree." I had done some study already at the University of Chicago—for theory, and writing music and harmony—and I had done some studies at Birmingham-Southern College and at Samford University, where I got my master's. I did a lot of study, in fact, after I got out of Howard University. In my department at the Board of Education, we were encouraged to get these advanced degrees, so I said, "Let's see what I can do." I went to work on my doctorate at The University of Alabama, and that took some time.

There was a series of secretaries that came up while I was working on it, and one of them just started calling me "Doc." Then, when I got to the Hall of Fame in 1997, everybody was so formal: "Dr. Adams this, Dr. Adams that." I said, "Let's stop that. Just call me *Doc*." And it stuck.

The Jazz Hall of Fame, really, defines a lot of things about me. I was the youngest one in that original group of inductees, and a whole panel in the museum is dedicated to those charter inductees. I tell people when they go through the museum: all of those people, hopefully, are playing in Heaven, because they've all passed away. And I'm the last soul left to tell their story. Sometimes I feel like they're calling for me—but I don't want to go with them just yet.

I've still got more to do.

"Doc" Adams, Alabama Jazz Hall of Fame, 2011.
Courtesy of Garrison Lee.

One day I was playing in an auditorium somewhere, and a little girl
walked up to me afterward—I thought she was going to compliment
me—but she said, "Mister, how did you get to be so *old?*"

It's interesting to me. I hope you'll get that way one day: I can go
into a grocery store and look around . . . and I don't see anybody as
old as I am! I can come talk to a class, and nobody in the school is
as old as I am. So I can say, like the Indians say: "You haven't seen as
many moons as I have."

I told this little girl: "If you live long enough, you'll get old, too."

When I was a little fellow, I used to look at people who were eighty-two or eighty-three years old, as old as I am now. I would see these people who would move so *slow,* and they would have to have these thick glasses on. Of course, in the church there were those gentlemen I admired who were aged, and they were known as wise men. They wore their clothes real particular and would be so neat and clean, and a lot of them were retired railroad porters—they had a class of their own—so I had someone to mimic. I noticed these qualities in older people, and I guess I aspired to be like that.

You find out: a lot of things that you didn't think would happen to you do happen. For instance, today I have to get a crown put on my tooth, and tomorrow it'll be something else: these aching pains that you get used to having in your back, and your wife has to tell you, "Stand up *straight,* you're bending over." The main thing is energy: you don't have as much energy, even though you still commit yourself to doing things. So far as work is concerned, I just don't have the know-how to say no. People call on me to do things and they expect me to do it. When I retired from teaching, I thought retirement meant that you could take some time to slow down—but then you find that you always want to be at the top of your game. In playing music, you don't ever want to be called old and fogey, and people say that you can't keep new ideas. Then—if you've been, like I have, around amateurs and professionals, and those who are even geniuses—you can't compromise. That's the thing that fires you, even if you are ninety or one hundred and ten. Like Duke Ellington said, "I'll never stop, until I just can't do it anymore: then the bus will bring everybody back home. But until then I'm out here."

Most musicians are like that. It's a force in music that is really in teaching, too: you're supposed to keep going until you can't go any longer. You're supposed to be productive. And I don't equate myself with a great person, but I think about all the great people I have seen, like Dr. Alain Locke: he would come to Howard University, and then he would catch a plane to Yale or Harvard to do these lectures, and he would stand up there and whisper his lectures—just *whisper, whisper, whisper*—so you couldn't even *hear* him. But everyone had so much respect for him, and he had so much respect for *himself* as a philosopher, that if you asked him, "Why don't you stop?" he'd say, "Why *should* I stop?" He had to keep doing what his driving force was.

So I still have that driving force, but I pick my time now to do some things like I'm doing here: to record some of the experiences that may help somebody, or may entertain them.

I've got a few other projects I'm working on right now. One is the barbecue sauce. When I came along in high school, the most famous barbecue place for blacks—I guess for whites, too, because they traveled miles to get it—was Palmer's Barbecue. Palmer's was on Eighth Avenue, right across the street from the high school. Mr. Palmer went to our church, and sometimes he would give my daddy some barbecue to bring home. It was *magical* barbecue. And I always wondered how they did it. I have been spending a lot of time finding the formula of how they made that sauce.

Last week I unraveled the formula. It took me three years. I went to a lady who lived in the projects, right across from where the place used to be. Palmer's Barbecue has been torn down now, and she's passed on, but before she died I asked her: "How did you all do that?"

"What are you talking about?"

"That sauce. I know that you worked over there."

She said, "I can't tell you much, but I can *make* you some."

"Okay, I'll pay for that." Then she saw I was sincere.

She said, "It's funny how people, when they work around something, don't feel about it like you do." She knew that particular sauce had made a fortune—they had people from California buying that barbecue—but she had worked there with it, so she said, "I don't know why you want to fool with that old sauce."

I got it all together and I tried a long time to do it. I couldn't get it right. But a friend of mine, Mr. Cottrell—we got together and he fixed it. So we're working on a project together. I tried out a whole lot of different sauces, and now I'm marketing it. I'm sending out samples so you can test it. I've got a picture of my wife, Doris, that I'm going to have put on the front of the bottle; it's going to be called Black Creola's Sauce, and it's going to rip the world open. The formula really came from slavery days, and if you taste it, it's habitual: you'll buy more and more. It works on hamburgers, it works on anything you put it on.

My next project is: I remember a little girl, she's a famous writer now. Sonia Sanchez, the poet.

She was born here, and her father, Wilson Driver, is in the Jazz Hall of Fame; he was one of the early members of Fess Whatley's band—the drummer. I remember, there were two little sisters that would be running through the church, and they used to sit on the parsonage steps. We used to talk about how Mr. Driver dressed them so nicely—later he took them away to New York City—but in those days she was just a little girl, running around in that church, and now she's a famous writer.

What I'm doing is getting some of her poems together. I have somebody who's going to recite those poems, and I'm going to play a musical background to them. I hope to take a lot of her poems and put music behind them.

I started this because one day I got a chance to go to the civil rights museum and they had pictures around the wall. I would look at a picture and create a song for *this* picture, *that* picture—so all through the museum I made up different songs. I'm going to try to expand on that with these poems.

Meanwhile, I'm trying to help my students get those scholarships. So if you look at it realistically, you'll find that instead of slowing down, I'm picking up. I'm doing more now than I would be doing out at Red's place; and I'm fortunate enough to be doing something exciting, just about every day.

Duke Ellington said: "If you're in this band for money, you'll never be satisfied. But if you're in here to create something, you'll be happy."

All those bandleaders I played with—even Sax Carey and some of the forgotten ones—they *lived* for their bands. And if you have the privilege of looking at some, like Duke Ellington and Sun Ra: you might not ever get to be on their level, but you can admire the fact that *here's a person that knows what his purpose in life is.* If you ask your students, "What do you want to do?" the popular thing is to say, "I'm trying to find my place. I'm searching. I'm going to college to find out where I should fit; what life is all about." That's the story you hear all the time: in a liberal arts college, you go to discover whether you want to be a lawyer or whether you want to be a doctor or whether you want to be a teacher. But inside of you—if you have that creativity and that *demand* for what your inner voice is *telling* you—you can know whether you want to be a musician when you're twelve years old. You can know whether you want to be a teacher. Some kind of way, something communicates yourself to you. A lot of people get messed up because they say, "Well, that's not going to pay me enough to have a club membership or be well known; this is a nice thing to do, but I can't support my family off this." Sometimes you go through life *fighting* that. "My brother's a doctor; well, maybe I should have been a doctor, too." Or, "He's a millionaire, why shouldn't I have done what he did?"

You know—*I* know, *most* people know, instinctively—what they should be, or what they were ordained to be; but they spend a lifetime denying it for certain reasons. Some people go all their life refusing to hear that inner voice. But I've observed that when a youngster really learns music—whether it's one song or two songs or three songs— and he can play it, or she can play it, and it's acceptable to someone who hears it: then something happens. When you get to the point that you know people enjoy and appreciate your music, then there's a dedication that builds. If you find out, in teaching, that people are benefiting from it—*one* child is inspired by what you're teaching— it's hard to break away from. When you are a great teacher, or when you have a skill that's not only valuable to you but to somebody else: it's like you *have* to do that. You can do something for your own self-aggrandizement or gratification—like Sun Ra said, "Joe Guy only plays for himself"—but when it helps somebody else, or when it vibrates with somebody else, then it becomes a *mission*. That's a thing that you just can't stop.

For instance, when I was in the military and they got at me about playing my horn because it would offend the soldiers they were in-doctrinating—I didn't want to offend anybody, but I *had* to pick it up. I had to blow something. I felt that, although I was only practicing, they would enjoy it—and they did, because they still had some con-nection with life as they knew it. They couldn't completely abandon what made them human.

We had the Function at the Junction the other day, our annual fes-tival out at Tuxedo Junction Park. The Heritage Band played, and it was *hot* outside. You see people out there dancing: this lady's up in front of the bandstand, and she wants people to see her enjoying her-self. No matter *how* hot it was—and I was about to fall out; I dropped my glasses three times from perspiration, and I didn't feel like getting up on that stage. But when you see them dancing, it fires you up—

your energy—and you can't say, "Well, I'm not going to give it all I've got," or "I don't feel like doing it." When you see them out there, you *have* to do it.

Now, a lot of young people don't understand that you can't just blow a horn and buy a Cadillac. You've got to do some other things. You've got to write music; you've got to play nights; you've got to teach it; you've got to do everything with it, to make it fulfilling. You can't just go out and say, "Hey, I've got a gig!" because those gigs might be far between. I remember somebody said, "Just buy you a tuxedo, and no matter how bad you play, you'll get a job on New Year's Eve. Everybody gets a musician on that night." But you can't sit around and wait on New Year's Eve.

When Eaton was coming along, I wanted to buy him a Volkswagen: a little bitty car. I always wanted one because I thought they were the height of engineering. So I told him, "Now, it's time for you to get a car." He was in high school. I said, "Why don't you go and watch this fellow up the street? He works on Beetles. Watch what he's doing, and you might be able to get you a Beetle like that."

He looked at me and said, "Dad, I don't want a *Beetle*. I want a Mercedes-Benz."

A Mercedes-Benz? I said, "You need to study something else, because music won't get you that! Don't you see these musicians, and they always have the violin and the bass and all, *crammed* in that little Beetle?"

He said, "Dad, *you* seem to be doing all right." I had a Cadillac at that time. He said, "Mom's got a fur coat—"

"But that cost me a lung! I had to blow a whole *lung* out to get a fur coat. I have to play, I have to teach—I have to do everything but sing in the choir to make ends meet. Don't you see how *worried* I look?"

"Okay, Dad, okay."

We had a fellow speaking at the Hall of Fame for our band festival this year, T. Monk—this guy is the son of Thelonious Monk—and I was impressed by what he was saying about individuality in music. He was talking about the value of practicing, and how you've really got to have your own concept. He was talking about how if you don't find your own individuality or go your own way to a certain extent, what you contribute is pretty useless—if it's a copy of somebody else's thing, somebody else's style. We always know that in doing anything you have to have some models, but then you have to break away from those models. Particularly in music or art.

I tell my youngsters, "You don't want to play like me!" I say, "You *can't* play like me." It sounds arrogant at first, but it's not. "You can't play like anybody but you, because there's a thing about how you are made. You're going to sound like *you* if you're turned upside down!"

I try to teach my children to really *hear* what they're playing. I say, "If I'm a B note, and I call you up and say *boop!* you ought to be able to tell me who I am. Your grandmother calls you from California— you haven't seen her in twenty years, but you know that's Grandma on the phone. So how come you can't tell Mr. A and Mr. B, and Mr. C and Mr. D, when you hear *them?*"

They say, "Doc, you're crazy."

I say, "No, no. That's the way Ellington did it. That's the way Louis Armstrong did it. That's how all the boogie-woogie guys did it. They didn't have any *books* up there in front of them."

You tell them that, and that brings out their latent talents. That brings out all that's in them. When they play with the book, they're not original creators. They copy Charlie Parker; they copy Louis Armstrong. But you can't copy *anybody*, because of morphology. My *mouth* is not like Charlie Parker's; my head is not like his. Sound comes from all of those places. It's according to your makeup and according to *you*. I tell students, "You can be great if you realize your importance."

I try to teach them, imitation is not the thing. Originality is the thing. Like the fellow told me at Cloe's Cocktail Lounge: "Next time, play yourself." We have youngsters now, and all they do is imitate somebody. It's not just in music. They join a gang—not for freedom, but to be locked into *imitating* somebody.

You might go to five or six different nightclubs now, and every saxophone player is using his technique or her technique to sound like Charlie Parker. You just get the homogenized thing. And when you get instructed in a discipline, you get the professor's sound. I'm not dismissing formal training—it's a blessing. I hold it up a whole lot. But the creative process—in music, or writing, or anything—has to come from within *you*, according to your experiences. That's the biggest lesson: it's not so much what you learn or what you can repeat, it's whether you learn to *do* something with it. If you teach a Shakespearean play, you want your students to make good on their test, but the main thing is: how much of this have they really—*really*—got into their fabric? How much have they got in there?

All the great players—Johnny Hodges and the rest of them—had their own thing. They listened to recordings and they built on some of what they heard, but they were free of the academic processes. They didn't know so much about theory or counterpoint. They were creating an art form. As Ellington said, all the theory of music makes no difference. "If it sounds good, it is good." And Sun Ra said, "If it's in you, it's going to come out." Then I think, going even farther: if it's in you and it comes out, it will be appreciated. It will find an audience. No matter how crude it will sound to somebody. It will vibrate with someone.

I was on an educational program where they had some questions and answers, and I was asked by one of the youngsters: "Why don't older people like you appreciate our music?" "*Our* music." My reply was that there *is* no "our" music. When I was coming along, music was universal. I've learned, and I try to teach the youngsters, that music and art have no restrictions when they're used for good. But life has taught me—through music, through art, through day-to-day experiences—that if I play a song that degrades anybody, it is unworthy and will not last. Nothing in art or music has any lasting qualities of magnificence if it stoops to degrade anybody. It's self-defeating.

For instance, I can't stand some of the things I hear in rap music. My criticism is not that it doesn't qualify to certain musical standards; the thing I criticize is the vulgarity in some of the lyrics. I try to warn my students that gimmickry in something like that won't work.

When I get a chance to talk to youngsters, I ask them, "How could a person like Michelangelo look at a stone and see the beauty in it? Some people who are in tune to that can understand, and can *see,* what can be in that stone." But I say, "When they *don't* have that vision, and they're limited to vulgarity and to gimmickry, they can't conceive of it." I tell them: I can see all the same colors as Picasso, but they don't form in my mind like they do in his. It's a matter of how discerning you can be.

In my life, I was fortunate enough to be around a whole slew of people who had different perspectives—who could see things differently. And I learned that if you have a *passion* to do something, you'll search out the things that others don't see.

If I had to say anything about education, and I've been doing it for, I guess, seventy years or more, it's that the environment—who they're around, what they hear, what their aspirations are—is the most critical factor for children.

My brother was in China, and he was learning to use chopsticks. He told me this guy was serving him all these dishes, and Oscar said, "How am I doing?"

"You're just fine, just fine."

He was there for three or four days, and he was improving. But he told the guy, "You say I'm doing fine, but I can't do it just like you."

The guy looked at him. He said, "Well . . . *you're* not Chinese."

So if you play jazz music, you need to be around people who play jazz music. It's a vocabulary. If you want to swing, you've got to be around people that swing. Like Joe Guy said, "You got to be around fast company." What he meant by "fast company" is not dope addicts or anything—but you've got to be around people who are *doing* something. Always be around somebody who can do it better than you.

My grandson is two years old. The other day I was talking to him on the phone. I said, "How old are you?"

He said, "I'm thoo."

"*Thoo?*" I said, "You can't be thoo, you haven't even started yet! Thoo with what?"

I call him up sometimes and I play an instrument, and he says, "Flute!" He can recognize the sound of a flute. They learn what they are around. The environment.

I often think: why did my daddy buy all those Harvard Classics? He was a good provider, but they must have cost him. Why would he buy all the collection of Lincoln's life? Twenty-two volumes on Abraham Lincoln!

It's a matter of having them there.

When I was at Howard, John Hope Franklin told me: *everybody's* got to have a library. Even if it's just four books, you have your library.

It's your environment.

So, what happened to me: the church and the neighborhood, and what was going on around me—the adventures on the road, and the characters I encountered at Howard—you put all those things together, and you see what comes out. The other thing was, I was always curious. I happen to be inquisitive: I wanted to find out what it *was* out there on the road. So all of these things just happened to happen to me— Sammy Green, and Mantan Moreland—they all just sort of flashed up on the screen for me. And the more I think about it, I think that life for me could not have been any better, because of the people I've met. I've learned so many things from Prof Green and from Frizz and all those people I've mentioned—so many that never, ever got the recognition that they should have gotten. I think of so many musicians that were never known. Some, like Sun Ra, got recognition, but there were so many others who passed along this way: Jesse Blackmon and George from Georgetown, Professor Wilson and Godpa Taylor. Great trumpeters, like Shelton Hemphill and Nelson Williams, Joe Guy and Tommy Stewart. It's good to remember those people.

A lot of things I learned in life didn't hit home until after the experiences came together. So with my students, I tell them: "I want you to pay attention, but this will really be valid later on." I think it was Dr. Hansberry who said, "Write these notes down—because you're going to be needing this after I'm gone, to tell your children this history. So *wake up*, Brother Adams, and write this down."

Youngsters need to know that they're going to have these defining experiences. I want my students to expect *shocking* things in their lives. And I want them to know: what they think is it isn't always it.

I learned that some of the magic—the things you conjure up in your mind—aren't always what they seem, when you get close up. I remember, I saw Nat King Cole. He was the ugliest thing I ever saw! He had eczema or some kind of something—looked like pieces of cotton on his face. But he went into the auditorium there, and he sat at that piano. The first thing he did was—what's this thing?—"Mona Lisa," and everybody, they just screamed. Instead of him being this *thing* I saw outside, he changed right there onstage into Prince Charming. I mean, his whole *face* changed when he started singing "Mona Lisa." I was sitting there witnessing it.

When you get out there and see these things, it's fascinating. I think about the little boy in Davenport, Iowa, who had never seen a black person; it's interesting how you might conceive of what people are going to look like, or what they are going to be. It's like Plato's allegory of the cave: this guy's tied there and he sees the shadows passing by; when they release him and he goes out into the sunlight, it's shocking, because he had only seen the shadows. People, a lot of times, make up their minds by what somebody tells them, or by what they *think* they see. As you grow older, with more experience, you have to evaluate and knock down some of these beliefs that you thought you had. You learn that you can't carry around a load of biases. You live in a world that is not always as it seems. And you have to get to know people.

I keep thinking back to the days when they had the steel mills and places like Sloss Furnace, where they had blacks and whites, Jews and Italians, working separately. You and I, at that time, could be working in the steel mill together. We could retire together, and you get a pen and I get a pen; you saw me at the job, and you saw me every day; and you saw me finish with you. But we never socialized together. You never went to my church, and I never went to your church. We never went to the same golf course. I didn't hate you and you didn't hate me—but there was this divide. After working together thirty or forty years, we might both wind up with silicosis or some ailment, and meet at the hospital for the first time.

My father-in-law retired from TCI, one of the plants; he had worked there for thirty-five or forty years, and his foreman was retiring at the same time. They got the same little award when they retired, a watch or something. I talked to my father-in-law, and he brought out the fact that, although he had worked with this man all of his life, side by side, they never got a chance to meet each other. His foreman would make an assessment: Mr. Jones is bad, or Mr. Jones is good. How could you make an assessment like that? Whether they liked or disliked each other, they didn't *know* each other. Just to sit down and talk: "What's your wife's name?" "Is your boy in school?" "What do you do after you leave here?" "How is it going to a black club?" "How is it going to a Jewish dance?"

One of the things my dad said before he died: he said, "I just wish I'd had time to go and know all my neighbors." He knew all of those around him, but he wanted to go out, ten or fifteen blocks away, into some of the slums and places. And "know my neighbors."

Something else he said:

"Why would I die and go to Heaven, when there's so many heavenly things already here on earth?"

I often think: in the opportunities that I had, if I hadn't had the background I did—a home and a family, and the environment I was in—I could have walked into a situation like Ellington's, or Count Basie's or somebody, and said, "Man, this is *it.*" I could drink, I could smoke, I could do all kinds of things and get a chance to be out there in the world—and that's where I would leave it. But sometimes it comes in your background, from your parents or something, that, hey: I'm going to have some fun and do this, and I'm going to master my craft, but I want to leave *something* behind, other than the good times I had.

One question I pondered again the other night: why did I come back to Birmingham? When I was in Washington, DC, I was doing real well playing. I had done pretty well in school, and I made some friends—and when graduation came around, it was, "Hey. You could stay here with us, and make a living. Why go back to Birmingham?"

But I started thinking. I said, "Well . . . Birmingham is my home." This is where my grandma was and my dad was. I remember when my dad got that threatening letter, that he had to get out of town—by sundown, I guess—and he wrote in his newspaper that he didn't have anywhere else to go; that they would bury him out in the cemetery at Grace Hill. So to come and get him.

I thought about that. I said, now, why should I leave *my* home, when people knew me here? I thought about Tanglefoot Carson, the little Italian fellow who lived in the neighborhood grocery store. I thought about my grandma, Mrs. Linette Eaton, and about how I went to Mrs. Guy's Bible class, with the oatmeal cookies and cow milk—see, all that's my home. And I thought about little Prof Green, who had everything going for him—and he wanted to be *heavy,* and everybody *thought* about him that way—but he couldn't go back to Boston, because something happened back there with his family. I said, here's a guy *longing* for home. I *got* a home. So that was the reason that I felt that decision—that defining decision—that, no, *I go home.*

I remember another defining experience I had: I had been teaching at Lincoln School for a while, and one day I was walking home from there. I heard this man working on somebody's house. And I said, "Mister, you're really doing a great job on those steps."

He said: "Is that little Frank?"

I hadn't been called that in a long time.

Guess who it was: Derricot. Henry Derricot, the carpenter—totally blind! "How you doing, boy?"

"Mr. Derricot, is that you?"

"That's what's *left* of me!"

I said, "Oh, man." So I talked to him and talked to him.

And that's how it unravels. I try to put all of these people into context. As I say, they all have their significance.

Like my brother, Oscar: I think about him every day. And the thing I thought about this morning was, in the very end, when he had retired from the Supreme Court and he had this cancer thing, and he knew that he was dying, I would go by there every day. Every day I would go by there and bring him something. And he would say, "Don't do that." He said, "Brother, you don't need to come here. I know you love me; I love *you.*" If you'd ask him how he felt—"I'm wonderful!" That takes a lot for you to say that: you're dying, but you say, "I'm *wonderful,* man." That kind of thing gets to the heart of the person. And he said, "You don't have to come here." He said, "Wherever you are, I'm there."

Then I think, sometimes, about Finktum, who was *entirely* his own person. He was a roustabout and he did what he wanted to do; he didn't have to prove anything. They all said that he would die a pauper and that he was just *bad.* He didn't jump off the bed and say, "Hey, I got some money coming"; he wanted them to learn a lesson. The people from Ringling Brothers were true, too—they could have said, "No, we'll just keep this money," or "We'll mail it to him." This was in *deep* times of segregation. He wasn't the boss of Ringling Brothers, by any means. But they took a trip off from their duties with the circus to bring that check down here for Arthur Prowell. They made a presentation. And so Finktum got the message over—when that money came, he shamed them *all.* He shamed everybody here—but they took the money! And now, every time they think about that church, they think about *Arthur Prowell.*

They had always called him "Finktum." But now they call him by his real name.

Somebody asked me, "Doc, what is it that you want to be remembered for?" A lot of people say, "I want to be remembered as a great teacher"; "I want to be a great performer." My brother said he wanted to be remembered as a fair, honest judge. I thought about it, and I really thought. I talked to my wife about it last night, and I said, "I want to be remembered as a person who didn't quit." She said, "Of all things, why would you say that?"

I said, "Look around. Everybody in our neighborhood: their husband quit them, or they quit their husband. Maybe they quit their job." But the job I started at Lincoln School, I stayed there twenty-seven years, 'til somebody had to move me to another job. I didn't quit.

I came up as a supervisor—I stayed *there* twenty years. I didn't quit.

I've been married fifty years. I didn't quit.

And I'm *still* here.

I didn't quit.

So it makes sense: "He wanted to be remembered as a person who didn't quit."

Got it?

Index

Page numbers in italics refer to photographs.

Adams, Doris (Dot) (wife), 84, 162, *203, 205, 211,* 249, 260; courtship, 183–86; marriage and family life, 202–5, 211, 213, 244; performing at the Woodland Club, 180, 181, 186–88, 193, 198, 201

Adams, Ella Eaton (mother), 2, 5, 6, 9, 17, 37, 43, 50–51, 66–67, 89, 131, 198–99, 202–04, *205;* education, 1; family history, 8

Adams, Frank Eaton, Jr. (son), 84, 204, 206, *211,* 246, 252; and music, 211–14, 227

Adams, Oscar W., Jr. (brother), *4, 128,* 203, *228,* 255; biography and historical significance, xxv–xxvi; childhood, 1–3, 19–20, 25, 38, 236; and civil rights, 225–29; at Howard University, 128–30; death of, 227, 259; impact on Frank Adams, xxvii, xxviii, 225; legal career, 7, 227, 259–60; marriage, 203, 227; and music, 1–3, 51, 75, 78

Adams, Oscar W., Sr. (father), xxviii, 1–20, *4,* 31, 32, 33, 35, 63, 67, 151, 202, 204, 219, 226, 237, 242, 255, 257, 258; biography and historical significance, xxiv–xxv; as community leader, 1, 7, 10–14, 19, 218, 222; education, 1, 8–9; as public speaker 29, 36, 217; and music, 1–3, 9–10, 152–53

Alabama A&M College, 1, 2, 7, 8, 26, 173

Alabama Jazz Hall of Fame, xxix n, 96; and Fess Whatley, xx, 58; and Frank Adams, xvi–xvii, 236, 240–41, 243, 246; inductees, 49, 83, 183, 241, 249; and J. L. Lowe, 236, 239–43; Student Jazz Band Festival, xvi, 243–45, 252

Alabama State Teachers College (Alabama State University), xxii, 40, 44, 52, 236, 239, 243

Alexander, "Big" Joe, 70, 78

Allen, Henry "Red," 71

Alstork, Bishop and Mrs. Frank, 130–33

A. M. E. Zion Church (national organization), 23, 217; and Oscar Adams, Sr., xxiv, 7, 11, 19. *See also* Metropolitan A. M. E. Zion Church

Anderson, Marion, 32

Ansari, Jeronne, 243

Armstead, John, 239

Armstrong, Louis, 80, 134, 186, 192, 199, 205; and Amos Gordon, 49, 141

Arrington, Richard, 241, *242*

Baker, Jim, xxvi, 129

Baker, Montrose, 92

Ball, Fred, 219

Banjo Bill, 88–90, 175

Barnett, Martin, *174, 177,* 186–87

Bascomb, Dud, xxii, 134

Bascomb, Paul, xxii, 134

Basie, Count, 85, 97, 102, 116, 129, 134; Adams turns down job with, xvi, 151, 258

Bebop, 96, 138–40, 142, 194

Becton, Rev. George Wilson, xxvii, 28–29, 58, 194, 200

Bell, John L., 97

Bethune, Mary MacLeod, 56

Big Maybelle, 109

Birmingham Black Barons, 1, 7, 26

Birmingham black middle class, xxiii–xxvi, xxix–xxxn7

Birmingham Civil Rights Institute, 242–43

Birmingham Heritage Band, The, 239, 240, *241*, 251

Birmingham jazz community, 95–98; and schools, xix–xx; and segregation, xxiii, 234–35; Birmingham musicians in New York City, 28–29, 56, 58, 96, 97, 141, 165, 194, 195, 237, 250; bond between Birmingham musicians, 141; foundations of community, xix–xx; role models in, xxii–xxiii, 57–58, 239. *See also* Birmingham venues

Birmingham News, The, xxiv, 7

Birmingham Reporter, The, xxiv, 1, 7, 32, 217

Birmingham-Southern College, 170–71, 246

Birmingham venues: Bob's Savoy, 92; Elks Rest, 61–62, 91–92; Carver Theatre, xvi, 242; Famous Theatre, 95; Frolic Theatre, 99; Grand Terrace, 94–95, 97; Ironwood Inn, 173, 178; Lyric Theatre, 32; Madison Nite Spot, 92–94, 192; Mo-Mo Club, 162; Tutwiler Hotel, 63, 90, 205, 217; 2728 Club, 175–76, *176, 177,* 183. *See also* Masonic Temple; Woodland Club

Blackmon, Jesse, 92, 97, 256

Blakely, Art, 109

Blount, Herman "Sonny" (Sun Ra), 67, 68–85, 100, 239, 250, 251, 254; Birmingham band mates, 70, 72, 78–79, 97, 134; early musical style, 70, 72–73; lessons to Frank Adams, xv–xvi, xviii, 76–77, 79–80, 82–83; letter to Howard University, 114; and outer space, 68–70, 79–81, 197; rehearsal style, 68, 71, 77–80; return to Birmingham, 83–85; and segregation, 69, 81; on significance of jazz bands to black youth, xxii–xxiii; teaching style, 75, 82–83

Blues, 89–90, 94, 100, 108, 109, 142–143, 177, 186, 206, 235

Bradshaw, Tiny, xvi, 110, 111, 131, 150

Brown, Lawrence, 113

Bryant, Herbert, 86, 183, 186

Burg, Harvey, xxvi, 229

Callins, Jothan, xxixn4

Calloway, Cab, 7, 53

Carey, Sax, 108–09, 250

Carolina Cotton Pickers, 82

Carter, Benny, 65, 91

Caswell, Melvin, 63

Cather, Patrick, 182–83

Chambliss, Grace, 74

Champion, Jesse, 112

Chan, Charlie, 34, 101,

Chappell, Jimmy, 92, *174,* 192

Charles, Ray, 93–94, 245

Chicago, Illinois, xix, 34, 37, 58, 94, 143–144, 160, 171, 218, 246

Childers, Buddy, 140

Civil rights movement, 187–189, 194; children's march, 171–72, 223–25, 229; legacies of the movement, 229–33; nonviolent philosophy, 222–25; precursors to, 119, 215–20, 225–26; "silent warriors," 228–29. *See also* Adams, Oscar W., Jr.; King, Martin Luther, Jr.; segregation; Sixteenth Street Baptist Church

Clark, Dee, 206

Clarke, Charles (Chuck), 96, 97, *196*

Clarke family (musicians), 96, *196*

Clemon, U. W., xxvi, 129

Colb, Vera, 23

Cody, Wilmer, 228

Cole, Nat King, 256

Coltrane, John, 138, 141

Connor, Eugene "Bull," 92

Cox, Charlie, 95

Cunningham, Vic, 183

Curry, Clarence, 173, *174,* 175

Dameron, Tadd, 78, 129

Daniels, Lucius, 26

Davis, Miles, 139, 140

Demopolis, Alabama, 8, 15,

Derricot, Henry, xxvii, 28, 259

DownBeat, 182, 200

Drinkard, Carlton, 115, 116

Driver, Wilson, *54,* 249–250

DuBois, W. E. B., 55, 81

Eaton, Charles Browning, 8

Eaton, Cleve, 142

Eaton, LaVergne, 142

Eaton, Linette (grandmother), xxvii,

3, 4, *4,* 5, 11, 16, 17, 19, 21, *22,* 30, 61, 108, 127, 130, 131, 151, 202, 227, 258

Eckstein, Billy, 109, 118

Ellington, Duke, 53, 65–66, 71, 79, 82, 84, 85, 100, 102, 111, 116, 129, 139, 142, 175, 197, 244–45, 248, 250, 254; Adams performs with, xvi, 34–35, 48, 134–135, 143–51; Adams's first encounters with, 32–34, 112–13; arrangement technique, 146; and civil rights movement, 223; diversity of band, 234

Ellis, Morris, 144

Epstein, Taft, 165

Ferguson, Maynard, 140

Filmer, Les, 212–213

Foster, Alice, 21

Foster, Lemeriah, 21

Foster, Victoria, 21, *128*

Fourth Avenue (Birmingham), xix, 13, 21, 33, 40, 69, 92, 215, 216, 217. *See also* Masonic Temple

Franklin, John Hope, 123, 255

Fraternal organizations, 10, 219, 236; fraternal parades, 45–47, 59, 165–66, 173; significance to black community, xix, xxv, xxix–xxxn7, 35–37, 217. *See also* Birmingham venues, Elks Rest; Masonic Temple; Knights of Pythias

"George from Georgetown," xxvii, 140, 256

Gershwin, George, 143, 234

Gillespie, Dizzy, 96, 109, 140

Golson, Benny, xvii, 115, 116, 117, 129, 133–34, 139

Gonsalves, Paul, 134, 147, 148, 206

Goodman, Benny, 53, 71, 80, 90, 116, 234

Gordon, Amos, *xvii,* 48–49, 50, 75, 76, 141–42, *241*

Gospel Harmonettes, The, 23

Guy, Jimmy, 200

Guy, Joe, xxvii–xxviii, 29, 79, 85, 91–92, 97–98, 186–87, 194–201, 251, 256

Green, "Prof," xxvii, 117–20, 124, 133, 138–39, 185, 220, 256, 258

Green, Sammy ("Sammy Green from New Orleans"), 99–101, 256

Greer, Sonny, 33–34

Grey, O. J., 175, 176, 183

Grimes, "Baby," 96

Grimes, Johnny, 96

Hamilton, Jimmy, xvi, 144, 145

Hampton, Lionel, 90, 97

Handy, W. C., 2, 9–10, 43, 56, 57, 190

Handy, William Wise, 43–45, *48,* 58, 76, 151, 154, 194; compared to Fess Whatley, 58–59; teaching style, 47–49, 127

Hansberry, Leo, 124, 256

Hassler, Red, 177–82, 186–89, 200–201

Hawkins, Coleman, 115, 194

Hawkins, Erskine, *xvii,* 42, 50, 90, 202, 241; reunion orchestra, 239–40; as role model to Birmingham musicians, xxii, 57–58, 239. *See also* "Tuxedo Junction"

Hemphill, Shelton, 91–92, 256

Henderson, Rick, 116, 151

Henry, Haywood, *xvii,* xxii, 58, 192, 241

Herman, Woody, 78

Hibbler, Al, 135, 244–45

Hill, Buck, 136

Hill, Eddie, 139

Hill, Teddy, 195

Hodges, Johnny, 106, 113, 138, 254

Holiday, Billie, 79, 85, 115, 134, 186, 187, 194, 195, 196

Houston, Rudell, 165

Howard Swingmasters, xvi, xvii, 115–18, 120–23, 129, 131, 133, 136, 138, 144, 239

Howard Theatre, 119–20, 131, 136, 137, 141, 143

Howard University, xvi, 5, 7, 18, 64, 75, 92, 97, 98, 136, 138, 142, 151, 207; attitude towards jazz, 114; class structure, 120–23; and civil rights, 119, 225–26; as eye-opening environment, 115–116, 121, 123, 127, 220; law school, 128–29; professors, 123–28, 248, 255

Howlin' Wolf, 88, 143

Hudson, George, 53

Hughes, Billy, 116, 129

Industrial High School (Parker High School), xxix–xxxn7, 42, 58, 204, 220, 236; Adams proposes changes for the future, 232–33; assembly programs, 54–66; debate team, *128;* and disease, 60–61; and Erskine Hawkins Orchestra, 57–58, 239; and industrial education, xx, 54–56, 154; and music, xx, 52–55, 57, 59; as source of community pride, xx, xxiv; school uniforms, 59–60; variety shows, 45. *See also* Whatley, John T. "Fess"

Iron Jaw. *See* Wilson, Iron Jaw

Italians in Birmingham, 37–39, 204

Jackson, Emory O., 217–18

Jacquet, Illinois, 117

Jazz at the Philharmonic, 194
Jazz Demons, The, 54
Jefferson, Hilton, 144
Jones, Bobby, 56
Jones, Eddie, 116
Jones, Jo, 83
Jones, Joe, 37, 160, 161, 185, 224
Jordan, Louis, xvi, 65, 92, 93, 95, 137, 173

Kelley, Robert, 186, 187
Kennedy, Monroe, 91
Kenton, Stan, 129, 140
King, B. B., 72, 94, 96, 143
King, Martin Luther, Jr., 69, 187, 188, 215, 217; and the church, 23; and nonviolence, 222–23, 225; and Oscar Adams Jr., xxvi, 227
Knights of Pythias, 10, 35, 160; and Oscar Adams Sr., xxiv, xxv, 7, 36
Knox, Elliott ("Blue Jesus"), 47
Knox, Reese, 138–139
Ku Klux Klan, 13, 187, 216, 218, 222, 224; and Oscar Adams Sr., xxv

Lincoln School, 28, 42, 58–59, 61, 194, 220; Frank Adams as band director, 150–72, 173; participate in civil rights demonstrations, 171–72, 224, 229; principals, 42–43, 167–68; student variety shows, 45, 90. *See also* Handy, William Wise
Locke, Alain, 118, 123–124, 233, 248
Lombardo, Guy, 134
Louis, Joe, 10
Lowe, James L. (J. L.), xxixn4, 96, *128,* 204, *241;* as educator and role model, 128, 236–38; as promoter of Birmingham jazz, xvi, 236, 239–43
Lowe, Leatha, 96

Lowe, Sammy, *xvii,* xxii, xxixn4, 96, 202, 204, 237, 239, 241, 242
Lowery, P. G., xxviii
Lunceford, Jimmy, 71, 111
Lyle, Thomas E., 40, 52

Marshall, Thurgood, 124, 128, 129, 220, 225
Martinson, Reuben, 162–165, 168
Masonic Temple, 32–35, 62, 65, 70, 71, 76–79, 90–91, 195
Mayo, Sammy, 90
McCoy, Robert, 90, 173–175, *174,* 177, 182
McRemer, Archie, 199, 201
Mealing, Selena, *177,* 193
Means, Dathia, 169–70
Means, Delmas, 95
Metropolitan A. M. E. Zion Church, 2, 11, 17, 18–26, 28, 219; Missionary Society, 16, 21, *22,* 61, 67, 108
Micheal, Dan, 78–79
Military bands, 50, 96; 313th Army Band, 207, 209–10
Miller, Glenn, 72
Miller, Walter, 70, 78
Millinder, Lucky, xvi, 85, 109, 137, 194, 195
Mills, Irving, 32
Minton's Playhouse, 195
Monk, T., 252–253
Monk, Thelonious, 97, 117, 252
Moreland, Mantan, xxvii, 88, 101–107, 111, 135, 256
Musicians union, 94, 99, 105–6, 136; significance in Birmingham, xxi–xxii, 64–65
Myatt, Fletcher, 78

NAACP, xxiv, xxvi, 37, 219
Nappi, Bill, 141

Navarro, Fats, 134
Norman, G. S., 24

Paige, Satchel, 1, 7, 9
Parham, Warren, 78
Parker, Charlie, 83, 106, 139–40, 194, 253
Parker High School. *See* Industrial High School
Parks, Rosa, 221
Parrish, Avery, xxii, 78, 90
Pepper, Art, 197
Proctor, Alice, 136, 140
Prowell, Arthur "Finktum," xxvii, 15–17, 31, 61, 86, 259
Pullman porters, 12, 22, 248

Quartet singing, 23, 26

Ra, Sun. *See* Blount, Herman "Sonny" (Sun Ra)
Ramsay, Erskine, 42
Rayfield, Wallace A., xxvii, 27–28, 44
Redman, Joshua, 213
Reese, Hampton St. Paul III (Hamp), 96
Roach, Max, 109
Robinson, Wilton, 52–53
Rodney, Red, 139
Roosevelt, Eleanor, 56–57
Ross, Diana, 176
Rouse, Charlie, 117
Rowe, Mattie B., xxiv, xxv, 36
Roberts, Patricia, 129
Rosser, Tolton, xviii

Samford University, xvi, 246
Sanchez, Sonia, 249–50
Sappho, Nadine, 212
Segregation, 64, 69, 81, 163, 189, 216, 219–22, 226; African-

American response to, xix, xxiv; and jazz, 141–42, 220, 234–35, 259; positive side effects for black community, 55–56, 237–38
Shaw, Artie, 116
Shaw, Bishop Benjamin Garland, xxvii, 16, 17, 29–31, 131
Shaw, DeWitt, 220
Sheffield, Charles "Liquor," 134
Shores, Arthur, xxv, 224
Simpson, Charles "Bull," 97
Sixteenth Street Baptist Church, 20, 26–28; bombing, 188–89
Smith, Bessie, 182
Smith, Tab, 137
Smith, "Teddy" Roosevelt (Velt), 72, 78, 81
Smithfield, xxiii, 15, 38–39, 224, 236
Stewart, Tommy, xviii, 256
Stovall, Don, 71
Summerville, Cat, 96
Sweetie Walker and Snake, xxvii, 99–100
Swing, definition, 148–149

Talladega College, 1, 84, 218, 225
Taylor, "Godpa," xxvii, 9, 256
TB Games, 61, 166
Teagarden, Jack, 205, 234
Territory bands, 109–11, 139, 144
Thomas, Hugh, 170–71
Thompson, Sir Charles, 117, 129
Tillman, Harold, 219
Threatt, Frank, 8
Titusville, 38
Tuskegee Institute, 27, 44, 51, 66, 112
"Tuxedo Junction," xxii, 57–58, 87, 191–192, 202, 239, 240, 251

University of Alabama, The, 169, 178; Adams earns doctorate

from, xvi, 246; and segregation, 128–29

Vann, David, 241
Venues and clubs: Cloe's Cocktail Lounge, 138, 253; 81 Theatre, 100, 110; 400 Club, 143; Lincoln Colonnade, 133, 136, 138; Propeller Club, 139. *See also* Birmingham venues; Howard Theatre
Visor, Carrington, 116, 134, 151

Warfield (tenor sax player), 78
War of the Worlds, The, 10–11
Washington, Booker T., xx, 9, 55, 81
Washington, DC, music scene, 34, 65, 104, 136–42, 150–151, 258. *See also* Howard Theatre; venues and clubs
Whatley, John T. "Fess," 54, 75, 85, 96, 100, 116, 140, 141, 142, 144, 158, 182, 186, 190, 194, 220, 236, 238, 249; and Alabama Jazz Hall of Fame, xx, 241, 242; and "bobtail bands," 65, 93, 240; and Cadillacs, 51, 52; compared to Sun Ra, xv, xxi, 70, 72–74, 83; compared to William Wise Handy, 49, 58–59; as disciplinarian, 51–53; and Frank

Adams, xxi, 50–51, 61, 63–67; as "maker of musicians," xx–xxii, 50, 58; and musicians union, xxi–xxii, 64–65, 99, 136; and music reading, 53–57; orchestra performances, 61–64, 87, 92, 137; overview of significance, xx–xxi; and school uniforms, 59–60; sets example for Birmingham musicians, 96–97
Webster, Ben, 138
Williams, Bernard, 212
Williams, Colbie (father-in-law), 183–185, 202, 257
Williams, Cootie, 82
Williams, Ivory "Pops," 177, 190–194, 191, 198; and civil rights movement, 194; emphasis on stringed instruments, 95, 169; in Frank Adams's band, 186, 192–193; influence on Birmingham jazz, xxi–xxii, xxviii, 64, 190–91
Williams, Nelson, 91–92, 256
Wilson, Professor James H., 26, 256
Wilson, Iron Jaw, xxvii, 102–103, 111
Woodland Club, 98, 177–82, 186–89, 193, 196, 199, 200–202, 205, 215, 234
Woodman, Brit, 148
Woodruff, George "Jarhead," 78, 134